THE NORTH AMERICAN TRAJECTORY

SOCIAL INSTITUTIONS AND SOCIAL CHANGE
An Aldine de Gruyter Series of Texts and Monographs

EDITED BY

James D. Wright

Larry Barnett, **Legal Construct, Social Concept: A Macrosociological Perspective on Law**

Vern L. Bengtson and W. Andrew Achenbaum, **The Changing Contract Across Generations**

Thomas G. Blomberg and Stanley Cohen (eds.), **Punishment and Social Control: Essays in Honor of Sheldon L. Messinger**

Remi Clignet, **Death, Deeds, and Descendants: Inheritance in Modern America**

Mary Ellen Colten and Susan Gore (eds.), **Adolescent Stress: Causes and Consequences**

Rand D. Conger and Glen H. Elder, Jr., **Families in Troubled Times: Adapting to Change in Rural America**

Joel A. Devine and James D. Wright, **The Greatest of Evils: Urban Poverty and the American Underclass**

G. William Domhoff, **The Power Elite and the State: How Policy is Made in America**

G. William Domhoff, **State Autonomy or Class Dominance? Case Studies on Policy Making in America**

Paula S. England, **Comparable Worth: Theories and Evidence**

Paula S. England, **Theory on Gender/Feminism on Theory**

George Farkas, **Human Capital or Cultural Capital? Ethnicity and Poverty Groups in an Urban School District**

Ronald F. Inglehart, Neil Nevitte, Miguel Basañez, **The North American Trajectory: Cultural, Economic, and Political Ties among the United States, Canada, and Mexico**

Gary Kleck, **Point Blank: Guns and Violence in America**

Dean Knudsen and JoAnn L. Miller (eds.), **Abused and Battered: Social and Legal Responses to Family Violence**

James R. Kluegel, David S. Mason, and Bernd Wegener (eds.), **Social Justice and Political Change: Public Opinion in Capitalist and Post-Communist States**

Theodore R. Marmor, **The Politics of Medicare** (*Second Edition*)

Thomas S. Moore, **The Disposable Work Force: Worker Displacement and Employment Instability in America**

Clark McPhail, **The Myth of the Madding Crowd**

Steven L. Nock, **The Costs of Privacy: Surveillance and Reputation in America**

Talcott Parsons on National Socialism (*Edited and with an Introduction by Uta Gerhardt*)

James T. Richardson, Joel Best, and David G. Bromley (eds.), **The Satanism Scare**

Alice S. Rossi and Peter H. Rossi, **Of Human Bonding: Parent-Child Relations Across the Life Course**

Joseph F. Sheley and James D. Wright: **In the Line of Fire: Youth, Guns, and Violence in Urban America**

David G. Smith, **Paying for Medicare: The Politics of Reform**

James D. Wright, **Address Unknown: The Homeless in America**

James D. Wright and Peter H. Rossi, **Armed and Considered Dangerous: A Survey of Felons and Their Firearms, (Expanded Edition)**

James D. Wright, Peter H. Rossi, and Kathleen Daly, **Under the Gun: Weapons, Crime, and Violence in America**

Mary Zey, **Banking on Fraud: Drexel, Junk Bonds, and Buyouts**

THE NORTH AMERICAN TRAJECTORY

Cultural, Economic, and Political Ties among the United States, Canada, and Mexico

Ronald Inglehart, Neil Nevitte, and Miguel Basañez

ALDINE DE GRUYTER
New York

About the Authors

Ronald Inglehart is Professor of Political Science and Program Director at the Institute for Social Research at the University of Michigan. Author of more than one-hundred publications, his book *Culture Shifts in Advanced Industrial Society* was published in five languages.

Neil Nevitte is Professor of Political Science at the University of Toronto and a principal investigator in the *Canadian National Election Survey* and the World Values Surveys.

Miguel Basañez is Professor of Political Science at the Instituto Autonomo Tecnologico de Mexico and President of MORI de Mexico, a major survey research organization in Mexico.

ALDINE DE GRUYTER
A division of Walter de Gruyter, Inc.
200 Saw Mill River Road
Hawthorne, New York 10532

This publication is printed on acid free paper ∞

Library of Congress Cataloging-in-Publication Data
Inglehart, Ronald.
    The North American trajectory : cultural, economic, and political ties among the United States, Canada, and Mexico / Ronald Inglehart, Neil Nevitte, and Miguel Basañez.
       p. cm. — (Social institutions and social change)
    Includes bibliographical references and index.
    ISBN 0-202-30556-2 (alk. paper) 0-202-30557-0 (paper)
    1. North America—Civilization—20th century. 2. United States—Relations—Canada. 3. United States—Relations—Mexico. 4. Canada—Relations—United States. 5. Mexico—Relations—United States. 6. Canada—Relations—Mexico. 7. Mexico—Relations—Canada. I. Nevitte, Neil. II. Basañez, Miguel. III. Title. IV. Series.
E40.I54 1996
970.05—dc20
                                          96-8795
                                          CIP

Manufactured in the United States of America
10 9 8 7 6 5 4 3 2 1

To Marita, Susan, and Tatiana
with love

Contents

Preface   ix

1 Cultural, Economic, and Political Change
   in North America   1

       Introduction   1
       Bringing Values Back In   5
       Value Compatibility and North American
              Cultural Cleavages   11
       Value Continuity and Change   14
       Is There A North American Value System?   17
       Economic and Political Correlates of Value Systems   21
       Value Change and North American Integration   23

2 Changing Patterns of World Trade and
   Changing North American Linkages   27

       Changing Patterns of World Trade   27
       Dilemmas   34
       Support for Free Trade   38

3 Compatibility and Change in the Basic
   Values of North American Peoples   47

       Changing Values among Western Publics   48
       Value Change in North America   52
       Broader Patterns of Cultural Change   60
       Predictable Patterns of Social Change   63
       Conclusion   81

4 Declining Deference to Authority and
   Rising Citizen Activism   83

      Declining Confidence in Established Institutions   87
      The Rise of Citizen Intervention in Politics   94
      Democratization and Economic Development in
         Mexican Politics   101

5 In Search of a New Balance between State
   and Economy, Individual and Society   105

      Is the Work Ethic Declining?   120
      Predicting Social Change: A Summary of Results   128

6 Political Integration in North America?   135

      Support for Political Union   138
      Advantages and Disadvantages   141
      Views about Political Integration: How Robust
         Are They?   144
      Political Union, Value Change, and Policy
         Convergence   149
      Economic and Political Integration:
         The Connections   151

7 Conclusions   165

      Key Findings   167
      The Outlook for North American Integration   170

   Appendix:
   The Value Systems of forty-four Societies
   in Comparative Perspective   173

   References   185

   Index   192

Preface

This book builds on several studies. Above all, it was made possible by the combined efforts of the eighty-three principal investigators who carried out the 1990 World Values Surveys in forty-four societies. The authors expresses their deep gratitude to Rasa Alishauskiene, Vladimir Andreyenkov, Soo Young Auh, David Barker, Elena Bashkirova, Marek Boguszak, Marita Carballo de Cilley, Pi-chao Chen, Hei-yuan Chiu, Eric de Costa, Juan Diez Nicolas, Karel Dobbelaere, Mattei Dogan, Javier Elzo, Ustun Erguder, Yilmaz Esmer, Blanka Filipcova, Michael Fogarty, Luis de Franca, Christian Friesl, Yuji Fukuda, Ivan Gabal, Alec Gallup, George Gallup, Renzo Gubert, Peter Gundelach, Loek Halman, Elemer Hankiss, Stephen Harding, Gordon Heald, Felix Heunks, Carlos Huneeus, Kenji Iijima, J. C. Jesumo, Fridrik Jonsson, Ersin Kalaycioglu, Jan Kerkhofs, Hans-Dieter Klingemann, Renate Koecher, Marta Lagos, Max Larsen, Ola Listhaug, Jin-yun Liu, Nicolae Lotreanu, Leila Lotti, V. P. Madhok, Robert Manchin, Carlos Eduardo Meirelles Matheus, Anna Melich, Ruud de Moor, Elisabeth Noelle-Neumann, Stefan Olafsson, Francisco Andres Orizo, R. C. Pandit, Juhani Pehkonen, Thorleif Petterson, Jacques-Rene Rabier, Andrei Raichev, Vladimir Rak, Helene Riffault, Ole Riis, Andrus Saar, Renata Siemienska, Kancho Stoichev, Kareem Tejumola, Noel Timms, Mikk Titma, Niko Tos, Jorge Vala, Andrei Vardomatski, Christine Woessner, Jiang Xingrong, Vladimir Yadov, Seiko Yamazaki, Catalin Zamfir, Brigita Zepa, Xiang Zongde, and Paul Zulehner. The World Values Surveys build on the 1981 European Values Systems Survey directed by Jan Kerkhofs, Ruud de Moor, Gordon Heald, Juan Linz, Elisabeth Noelle-Neumann, Jacques-Rene Rabier and Helene Riffault. Thanks are also due to Karlheinz Reif and Anna Melich of the Commission of the European Union, who directed the Euro-Barometer surveys, which constitute another major data source. Finally, we wish to acknowledge the contributions made by the participants in the two-wave Political Action study, Samuel Barnes, Dieter Fuchs, Jacques Hagenaars, Felix Heunks, M. Kent Jennings, Max Kaase, Hans-Dieter Klingemann, Jacques Thomasson, and Jan Van Deth.

Data from both the World Values Surveys and the Euro-Barometer surveys are available from the ICPSR survey data archive at the University of Michigan. The processing and documentation of these surveys was made possible by a National Science Foundation grant to Inglehart, SES 91-22433. Thanks are due to Julio Borquez, Georgia Aktan and Bettina Schroeder for skillful and effective research assistance, and to Judith Ottmar for outstanding secretarial and administrative assistance.

The authors would like to thank the Donner Canadian Foundation, whose generous support made the Canadian data collection and analysis possible. Fieldwork and analysis of the United States and Mexican surveys was supported by an anonymous foundation; we are grateful for their help.

1

Cultural, Economic, and Political Change in North America

INTRODUCTION

North America is steering a new course. Since the mid-1980s, the United States, Canada, and Mexico have been moving toward continental economic integration, culminating in the establishment of the North American Free Trade Agreement (NAFTA) in 1994. This book focuses on how changes in basic values among the publics of the United States, Canada, and Mexico are transforming economic, social, and political life, giving these countries an increasingly compatible cultural perspective. In the long run, these changes have important implications for economic and political cooperation between these countries.

North American integration has been highly controversial, with organized labor in the United States opposing it for fear that it would bring a massive loss of American jobs to Mexico (the "giant sucking sound" that H. Ross Perot said we would all hear). Conversely, some observers in Mexico have blamed NAFTA for the financial crisis linked with the 1994 devaluation of the peso. In Canada, NAFTA was evoked as an argument by both sides in the 1995 referendum on Quebec separatism: Opponents of secession argued that an independent Quebec would risk losing the advantages of free access to North American markets, while independence advocates took it for granted that they need not worry about the economic consequences of secession because Quebec is already part of an economic entity much larger than Canada. In the United States, perceptions of cultural differences and economic competition, in a time of high immigration flows and high unemployment rates, have given impetus to proposed curbs on immigration.

Nevertheless, our evidence indicates that the long-term trend in all three countries is toward an increasingly global perspective. A narrow nationalism that had been dominant since the nineteenth century is gradually giving way to a more cosmopolitan sense of identity. A North

American perspective makes sense because it is increasingly clear that the old economic boundaries are becoming outmoded.

In 1989, the United States and Canada, which already exchanged more trade than any other two countries in the world, ratified a comprehensive bilateral trade agreement. Almost immediately afterward, U.S. and Mexican officials began discussing a similar agreement, and by 1994 the three countries had established the North American Free Trade Agreement. Some see NAFTA as an initial step toward an even more ambitious project, a free-trading community that will encompass two continents stretching from Alaska to Cape Horn. But even if that vision is not realized, the North American trading bloc with its 360 million people and a combined annual production of $6 trillion constitutes the world's largest international economic power, its closest rival being the European Union with an internal market of 346 million people and $5 trillion in annual output.

For the United States, Canada, and Mexico, the move toward continental free trade represents a policy shift, one that raises a variety of fundamental, theoretical, and practical questions: Why are the three countries pursuing continental economic integration? What explains the timing of the policy shift? And can these three countries work together effectively?

The economic case for free trade is a powerful one. Some see NAFTA as a strategic response to the new realities of globalization and most particularly the economic face of globalization—the emergence of new trading blocs (Dominguez 1992; Ostry 1992). Today, the North American economies face a dynamic, prosperous, and expanding European Union, which is merging the economics of its member states into a single market. Having absorbed Greece, Spain, and Portugal in the 1980s and East Germany in 1990, the European Union admitted Sweden, Austria, and Finland to membership in the early 1990s, to constitute a fifteen-nation economic and political alliance. Czechoslovakia, Poland, Hungary, and Turkey are seeking admission. North Americans also confront the challenge of competing with the dynamic East Asian economies led by Japan, China, South Korea, Taiwan, Hong Kong, and Singapore.

From a continental perspective, NAFTA can also be seen as the logical extension of evolving patterns of closer commercial cooperation, the origins of which can be traced to the 1950s and 1960s (Smith 1988). And from the standpoint of neoclassical economics, the drive toward continental free trade is perfectly logical. The push to expand access to larger markets is a widely recognized means of stimulating economic growth: it is the strategy of choice for countries aiming to maximize returns from the economies of scale, for lowering costs, for increasing competitiveness, and for exploiting comparative advantages most efficiently. From this viewpoint the puzzling question is not Why are the United States, Canada, and Mexico pursuing free trade now? but Why didn't they do so decades ago? Much of the answer lies in psychological and cultural barriers.

Economic interests unquestionably are vital to the dynamics of integration. But economists were among the first to recognize that economic perspectives alone could not provide a complete or convincing account of why countries move toward economic integration. Economic explanations fall short not just because of the sizable gap between economic theory and behavior (Johnson 1965; Milner and Yoffie 1989) but also because they fail to take into account the crucial role that noneconomic factors play in the dynamics of economic interdependence (Cohen 1990). Investigators attempting to provide a more comprehensive account of integration have consequently focused on two questions: Which noneconomic factors are crucial? And precisely how do these noneconomic factors contribute to the process of integration?

In the 1960s and 1970s, theorists working from a variety of perspectives argued that no account of integration would be complete without considering the role of political factors. Functionalists, neofunctionalists, communications theorists, and revisionists made considerable progress toward bringing politics back in, although no consensus emerged about the relative importance of leadership, trade, levels of institutional coordination, or styles of decision-making (Etzioni 1965; Haas 1971; Nye 1968; Puchala 1971; Lindberg and Scheingold 1970). Since the late 1970s, realists, institutionalists, and others have further expanded those political perspectives by bringing the state back in. Those efforts draw attention to important strategic concerns, to the role that interest groups play, to the connection between state and societal factors, and to the interdependence of domestic and international decision-making (Milner 1988; Cohen 1990; Gourevitch 1986; Nye 1988; Putnam 1988).

This book builds on both classic and recent contributions to our understanding of the politics of integration but it takes these perspectives in a different direction. We argue that no explanation of North American economic integration is complete without considering the role that values play in the process of integration. More particularly, our focus is on the values of mass publics, and our goal is to move mass values from a marginal position to the center of analysis. We argue that mass values have shaped the politics of continental integration in significant ways and, further, that value change among the American, Canadian, and Mexican publics helps to explain why political leaders pursued NAFTA when they did. The book draws on a unique body of directly comparable cross-national and cross-time evidence to show that what Americans,

Canadians, and Mexicans want out of life is changing and that these changes, coupled with sociostructural transformations, are reshaping people's feelings about national identity, about trust, and about the balance between economic and noneconomic goals.

Values play a central role in the classic literature on integration, with a variety of theorists arguing that values are crucial because they help shape the dynamics of integration in significant ways (Deutsch et al. 1957; Haas 1958). Those theoretical perspectives provide a useful starting point for, as we will see, the North American evidence indicates that there is a good deal of empirical support for these original speculations. Contemporary perspectives on integration, particularly those examining how international and domestic factors interact to determine the outcomes of such trade policies as NAFTA, have drawn attention once again to the significance of public values for another set of reasons: they bring into focus their *political* significance (Krasner 1978; Katzenstein 1978). A particularly forceful explanation of why publics and their values count in the politics of integration is provided by Putnam, who suggests that the politics of international negotiations can be understood as a two-level game (1988:434). He argues:

> At the national level, domestic groups pursue their interests by pressuring governments to adopt favorable politics, and politicians seek power by constructing coalitions among these groups. At the international level, national governments seek to maximize their own ability to satisfy domestic pressures, while minimizing the adverse consequences of foreign developments. Neither of the two games can be ignored by central decision-makers, so long as their countries remain interdependent yet sovereign (p. 436).

The values of mass publics matter for two reasons: First, those negotiating trade agreements like NAFTA do not have independent policy preferences (ibid.). Second, for such agreements to be politically acceptable, they must satisfy not only the other parties at the negotiating table but also the relevant domestic constituencies they represent. They must satisfy them because these domestic constituencies can support or block ratification of these agreements. The mechanisms for ratification, Putnam points out (pp. 436–40), can be either formal or informal and in each case they also depend upon the institutional rules of the game and opportunities. Those who count as the relevant domestic constituencies also differ, depending upon a variety of factors such as how open or closed the given governing regimes are.

Classic analysis of international relations has tended to downplay the role of public opinion. But during the 1990s, it became increasingly clear that the beliefs and values of mass publics are coming to play a crucial role. For example, the fact that the Danish public blocked ratification of the Maastricht treaty in 1992 had a massive impact on efforts to move toward a common European currency, and on the political integration of the European Union more generally. In the Danish case, the tool for ratifying public support for Maastricht was a national referendum and the political significance of public opinion was clear and direct. The Danish public rejected the Maastricht proposals, which would have propelled Denmark toward greater integration with its European partners; in doing so, they threw the entire European Union into a crisis that was only partly resolved when the Danish public later approved a revised version of the referendum in 1993. In the United States, public preferences are given voice by the constitutional provision requiring that treaties be ratified by a two-thirds majority in the Senate. There is no equivalent constitutional requirement in Canada, but Canadian-U.S. relations are so highly charged that the Canadian government felt compelled to go to the people by calling a federal election in 1988 on the issue of the Canada-U.S. Free Trade Agreement. The Canadian public then ratified the Canada-U.S. Free Trade Agreement by returning the government to office. In Mexico, with a less open regime, the opportunities for ratification by the public were far more constrained and the size of the relevant public more limited. But even there, considerations of credibility and face-saving played a role.

In the United States, on the other hand, a dramatic increase in public awareness and involvement took place as NAFTA moved toward ratification by Congress in 1993. Until the final week, it was uncertain whether NAFTA would be accepted by the U.S. Senate, and President Clinton was able to swing sufficient votes for passage only by massive concessions to key constituencies. Because a vote against the trade agreement was considered politically safe, a majority of those who were elected by narrow majorities voted against NAFTA in the Senate. Most economists in the United States agreed that NAFTA was likely to have a favorable overall impact on the U.S. economy. But its narrow last-minute victory demonstrated that political considerations play a crucial role in global economics.

BRINGING VALUES BACK IN

The idea that values matter to integration is not new, though recent work in political economy sometimes loses sight of it. The political accounts of integration that emerged in the 1960s and 1970s all recognize that values play a role and that value compatibility between political units is conducive to integration. Some observers emphasize the importance of elite values. Schmitter, for example, argues that "the more complementary elites come to acquire similar expectations and attitudes toward the integrative process, the easier it will be to form transnational associations and to accept regional identities" (1971:253). Others, like Jacob, include entire communities: "For integration to occur among two or more existing communities," he argues, "requires that values shared with each become shared with each other" (1964:210). But the most comprehensive account of the role that values play in the integration process springs from a still earlier body of work.

More than forty years ago, a group of scholars concerned with the prospects of securing peace and prosperity in West Europe joined forces to explore a common question: how to achieve greater cross-national integration through strategic institution-building. From these efforts, and drawing on comparative historical evidence drawn mainly from European case studies, Deutsch and colleagues (1952, 1957, 1963) developed a social learning perspective linking cross-national transactions to economic and political integration. Deutsch argued that high levels of transactions between peoples (the movement of peoples, cross-border commerce, and communication flows) encourage greater similarities in main values. Similarities in main values interact and are conducive to greater mutual trust between different peoples. Higher levels of trust, in turn, encourage greater cooperation and economic integration. And economic integration, Deutsch concludes, is conducive to greater political integration. The essential chain of reasoning linking these elements is summarized in Figure 1.1. Deutsch's historically informed account of how values shape the process of integration is a plausible one and, indeed, the essential elements of that perspective remain influential; they are reflected in subsequent versions of integration theory (Lindberg and Scheingold 1970; Nye 1976; Diebold 1988). Moreover, some of the basic elements of this perspective have been tested in a number of settings and the weight of the accumulated evidence appears to work in ways that are consistent with that formulation.

In the North American context, for example, the signing of the Canada-U.S. Free Trade Agreement indicates a mutual commitment to greater economic integration between the two countries. Deutsch's perspective implies that the signing of that agreement should have been preceded by changes in cross-border transactions. It was. The volume of Canada-U.S. two-way border crossings (the movement of people) rose from seventy-two million visits in 1980 to ninety-four million visits in 1989 (Statistics Canada 1991). Commercial and financial transactions also increased sharply over the period leading up to the agreement (Schott and Smith 1988).

For Deutsch, the importance of the high frequency of cross-border

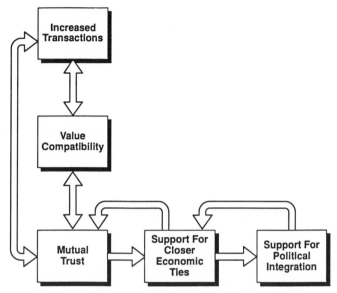

Figure 1.1. Values and the dynamics of integration.

transactions is that these exchanges are conducive to mutual responsiveness and trust (Deutsch et al. 1957). With increasing rates of trade, diplomatic exchanges, tourist flows, and other types of interaction, the expectation is that different nationalities will find each other increasingly predictable and hence trustworthy; it is a learning process in which positive reinforcement leads to positive expectations and behavior. This emphasis on the importance of mutual trust is also a central theme in the political culture literature. The idea that interpersonal trust plays an important role in both economic and political cooperation has been confirmed by a large body of research (Wylie 1957; Banfield 1958; Almond and Verba 1963; Pruitt 1965; Easton 1966; Hart 1973; Luhmann 1979; Hill 1981; Miyake 1982; Abramson 1983; Inglehart 1990).

Empirical research about trust between different nationalities is relatively scarce, but the available evidence indicates that trust between different nationalities is a relatively stable attribute (Deutsch et al. 1957; Merritt and Puchala 1968; Nincic and Russett 1979; Inglehart 1991). The trustworthiness of thirteen nationalities was rated by nine West European publics in 1976 and then again in 1986. The rankings were virtually identical over the ten-year period, with a modest tendency for all nationalities to become more trusted. Trust ratings are highest between pairs of nationalities who share a common language group and, as Deutsch would expect, between those who have democratic political institutions. Moreover, the more prosperous nationalities tend to be the most highly trusted. Each of these factors turn out to be significant at the .0001 level and together they explain 72 percent of the variance in cross-national trust (Inglehart 1991). The experience of being on the same or opposite sides in World War II left an enduring imprint on the orientations of European publics; for example, in the 1950s the French and German publics distrusted each other deeply (Merritt and Puchala 1968). But the experience of working together within a successful set of European institutions seems to have had a gradual but ultimately significant impact. By 1980, the French regarded the West Germans as their closest ally and the nationality they trusted *most* (Inglehart 1991).

Both Deutsch's theory and the lessons from the European Union experience lead one to expect that the rate of interactions generated by NAFTA would have a similar effect between the three North American countries. Feelings of trust or distrust are central because they encourage or present serious obstacles to integration. To what extent, then, do the North American publics trust each other? As Figure 1.2 shows, there are significant asymmetries. The American public feels a great deal of trust for Canadians: here, trust outweighs distrust by a ratio of 16:1. Trust is also strongly predominant in the feelings of the U.S. public toward the Mexicans, and of Canadians toward the Americans. But trust is significantly weaker in the orientations of Canadians toward the Mexican people, where uncertainty is widespread. And the pattern reverses itself in the feelings of the Mexicans toward the American people: more than twice as many Mexicans distrust Americans as trust them. The origins of feelings of distrust seem to be rooted in historical conflicts, and the fact that in 1846 the United States annexed over half of Mexico's territory. But it also seems to reflect the generally lower levels of interpersonal trust among the Mexican public. For feelings of trust only narrowly outweigh feelings of distrust in the Mexican public's attitudes toward Central Americans—people who have never threatened Mexico. In any event, the Mexicans' low level of trust for the American people may present a serious obstacle to North American integration.

If Deutsch's speculations are generalizable to non-European settings, we would expect to find that rising levels of cross-national trust between the three countries are linked with rising public support for closer economic ties. Evidence from the 1990 World Values Surveys strongly supports that expectation: in all three countries, we find that feelings of trust or distrust for a given nationality are closely linked with support for closer economic ties with that nationality. In the United States, for example, among those who do not trust the Mexican people at all, only 35 percent support closer economic ties with Mexico. Among those who trust the Mexican people completely, fully 85 percent support having

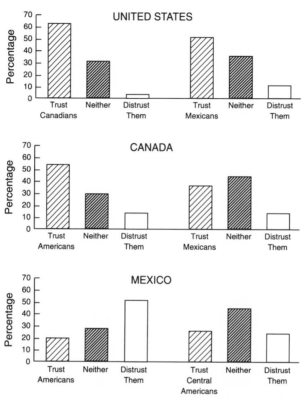

Figure 1.2. Feelings of trust among North American peoples. *Source:* 1990 World Values Survey. Note: "Trust them completely" or "Trust them a little" are grouped together as "Trust [nationality]"; "Do not trust them very much" and "Do not trust them at all" are grouped as "Distrust."

closer economic ties. As we will show, very similar patterns apply to American attitudes toward closer ties with Canada; to Canadian support for closer ties with the United States and Mexico; and to Mexican attitudes toward closer economic ties with the United States. In short, the North American evidence seems to point in the same direction as the West European findings, providing further support for Deutsch's contention that values play a crucial role in the dynamics of integration. Higher levels of trust are linked with greater support for integration.

The history of the European Community illustrates that economic integration tends to stimulate growth. That experience also provides support for another relationship that Deutsch identifies as central to the integration process, namely, that support for closer economic ties tends to bring closer political ties among the peoples involved. From that perspective it is no coincidence that as they move toward full economic union, the fifteen member states of the European Union are now discussing plans for political union as well. The process has been gradual. Almost forty years have elapsed since the birth of the six-nation European Common Market, and political union is still only slowly emerging. Nevertheless, after centuries of bitter rivalry, political union now *is* under serious discussion. A variety of benchmarks can be used for determining thresholds of political integration but it seems clear that high levels of effective economic integration are practically impossible to achieve without a reasonably well developed system of political cooperation. Although the process is slow and uneven, the European experience—the push toward a common currency, a shared bureaucracy, and coordinated foreign and domestic policies—raises the question of whether closer economic ties between the United States, Canada, and Mexico will unleash pressures for greater political coordination in North America. Once again, the World Values Survey evidence suggests that the lessons from the West European experience are relevant to the North American setting. In the United States, Canada, and Mexico, support for economic integration is related to support for closer political ties— though when the evidence is examined in detail (Chapter 6) we will see that the linkages between those orientations appear to be more complex than earlier perspectives suggest.

In the early days of European integration, Haas (1958), Ball (1968), and others developed a functionalist theory of regional integration, which held that economic integration has an inherent tendency to spill over into political integration, an idea that the founders of the European Common Market clearly had in mind. As it turned out, the process was less automatic than the functionalists had hoped: determined opposition by Charles de Gaulle blocked any movement toward political integration as long as he was in office. The European experience demonstrates that it is difficult to separate politics from economics. Successful economic integration was coordinated through supranational institution-building and through regular intergovernmental consultation. The early stages of American history illustrate the same theme. Here, thirteen originally independent and mutually suspicious states gradually merged to form a single economic-political unit.

But there have also been many cases of political disintegration instead of integration, for higher rates of economic and political interaction do not automatically bring people together. If feelings of trust and shared values do not develop, close interaction can lead to brutal conflict. The bloody breakdown of postcolonial India into India-Pakistan-Bangladesh, the contemporary conflicts in what used to be Yugoslavia, and the ethnic strife in the successor states to the Soviet Union provide dramatic examples of the potential costs of such conflicts. Centuries of living together have not eradicated Basque and Catalonian nationalism in Spain, or Welsh, Scottish, and Irish nationalism in the United Kingdom.

In the North American setting our focus is mainly on the aggregate value shifts of the three populations. But even here there are powerful reminders of cultural variations within each country: formal political borders are not a faithful reflection of such variations. Quebecois resistance to cultural integration to Anglophone Canadian norms has been fierce and their national aspirations have as much vitality today as at any time in Quebec history: the fact that in the 1995 referendum, the people of Quebec voted against separation from the rest of Canada by only the narrowest of margins makes that clear. Furthermore, centuries of European settlement have not eradicated the identities of North America's native peoples. Canadian native peoples may have more in common with American native peoples than with European Canadians. On the other hand, Americans in the Pacific Northwest probably have more in common with Canadians in British Columbia than with their fellow Americans in South Carolina. To say that transactions between states tend to go with closer political ties does not mean that one always leads to the other. Nor does it mean that closer political coordination will lead to the disappearance of cultural communities.

VALUE COMPATIBILITY AND NORTH AMERICAN CULTURAL CLEAVAGES

Increased levels of cross-border transactions, evidence that cross-national trust is related to support for closer economic ties, and evidence of linkage between support for economic and political ties add further weight to Deutsch's perspective on the dynamics of integration. The question of value compatibility is central to the analysis that follows, and it remains to be demonstrated. Deutsch claims that "mutual compatibility of main values is an essential condition for integration" (1968:58). Further, he identifies two value domains that are particularly crucial to successful integration: similarity in orientations toward democracy, and compatibility of economic perspectives (1968:126). If the success of North American integration depends on the extent to which publics in those states are culturally similar, then a central question is To what extent do Americans, Canadians, and Mexicans share common values? Or, more precisely, are the "main values" in each of these three countries compatible?

The weight of the historical evidence might lead one to assume that they are *not* compatible—and the gulf between the values of the Mexican people, on one hand, and those held by publics of the United States and Canada, on the other, appears to be particularly wide. One influential historical explanation for North American cultural variation is provided by Louis Hartz (1964), who argues that each of the three new societies was settled by very different founding peoples. In New Spain (Mexico) language, culture, religion, and political institutions were cohesively transplanted from the old world to the new, as they were in New France (Quebec). In contrast with the United States and Anglophone Canada, Mexican national identity welded together three themes: Hispanic greatness, colonial progress, and national struggle (Morse 1964). Mexico's primary cultural orientations are frequently interpreted as flowing from the contemplative Latin American Catholic tradition as opposed to the combative Anglo-Saxon Protestant tradition prevailing in the United States and Anglophone Canada (Basañez 1990). Mexico's political development featured many of the characteristics of other authoritarian regimes: low levels of popular mobilization, a limited role for interest groups, elite domination, and a decision-making style involving the arbitrary exercise of power (Coleman and Davis 1988). Mexico has been shaped by a tradition of patrimony, deference, and fatalism; it emphasizes the role of central authority (Craig and Cornelius 1980; Purcell 1975).

The differences between Mexico's Catholic tradition and the predominantly Protestant traditions of the United States and Canada are particularly striking when it comes to public virtues. Dealy (1977) suggests that the Anglo-Saxon virtues of labor, humility, frugality, service, and honesty stand in stark contrast to such Latin values as recreation, grandiosity, generosity, dignity, and manhood. These differences led to sharp contrasts in economically significant attitudes toward work, time, and the payment of taxes and also in orientations toward family and friendship (Basañez 1990).

This absence of a North American cultural consensus is not just a question of the cleavage between Mexico and her two northern neighbors, however. Seymour Martin Lipset, the foremost comparative analyst of the political cultures of the United States and Canada, in a series of influential studies carried out over a period of nearly three decades, has argued that the United States and Canada are divided by enduring differences in basic values and political styles (Lipset 1963, 1990):

> The two countries differ in their basic organizing principles. Canada has been and is a more class-aware, elitist, law-abiding, statist, collectively-oriented and particularistic (group-oriented) society than the United States. These fundamental distinctions stem in a large part from the Amer-

ican Revolution and the diverse social and environmental ecologies flowing from the division of British North America. (1990:8)

Lipset's pioneering work has generated considerable controversy, particularly among Canadian observers. The controversy involves conflicting interpretations of founding circumstances and competing judgments about whether these founding circumstances produced societies that were essentially alike or fundamentally different (Bell and Tepperman 1979; G. Horowitz 1966, 1978; Clark 1976). Vigorous debate also centers on divergent assessments of contemporary differences and similarities. Baer and colleagues, for example, find no significant differences between Americans and English Canadians on such dimensions as collectivism and support for equality of condition (Baer, Grabb, and Johnston 1990). Similarly, Gibbins and Nevitte (1985) discover no residues of Toryism or elitism separating the ideological worlds of new generations of Canadians from their American counterparts. The two interpretations are not entirely incompatible. Lipset is almost certainly correct in his insight that the United States and Canada were shaped by fundamentally different founding circumstances, and that these differences have left traces that still persist today; and it is the perception that there are significant differences that fires much of the contemporary nationalist opposition to NAFTA. But our evidence suggests that these differences have been gradually eroding.

We began by suggesting that the economic case for North American free trade is a powerful one. But at the same time, the historical and political reasons for resisting NAFTA also seem to be powerful, particularly for Canada and Mexico. The national histories of the United States, Canada, and Mexico are grounded in variations on a common theme: exceptionalism. Each society views itself as unique. For the United States, the case for exceptionalism is made by drawing sharp distinctions between the American vision and the visions of old European states that the revolutionaries rejected (Boorstin 1953). The Canadian and Mexican nation-building projects were forged against the backdrop of American influence and the United States provides the benchmark against which their exceptionalisms are measured. For Mexicans those exceptional founding principles are captured in the ethos of the Mexican Revolution, and for Canadians, the historical reference point is Canada's reaction to the American Revolution—the Canadian counterrevolution and the values it embodied.

The national traditions and identities of Canadians and Mexicans continue to be brought into focus and gain coherence by highlighting the contrasts between Canadian and American, or Mexican and American, experiences and values. And for both societies, relations with the

United States provide a useful outlet for dissatisfaction with problems in domestic political, social, and economic life. For contemporary nationalists, maintaining a political, social, and economic distance from the United States represents fidelity to these founding principles. Carlos Rico captures the sentiment succinctly. He argues that for Mexico, free trade with the United States "would be the equivalent of recognizing the failure of the aims of independence and sovereignty that are central to the ideology of the Mexican Revolution" (cited in Weintraub 1990:17). Almost identical concerns are echoed by Canadian nationalists. For nationalists who take these historical traditions to be fundamental, the relevant question is, Why is NAFTA being pursued at all?

VALUE CONTINUITY AND CHANGE

National historical experiences produce one set of expectations about NAFTA, while contemporary economic theories have quite another set of implications. The tension between economic and historical logics underpins dilemmas that are reflected in public debates about NAFTA in all three countries. We have suggested that conventional economic theory by itself is insufficient to account for why the three societies are pursuing open trade with each other. But so also is historical logic. Major changes have swept across all three societies since their founding eras, and the evidence indicates that the founding cultures are not frozen; there are strong indications that all three societies are changing—in some respects quite rapidly.

The sources of change can be traced to economic development, increased educational opportunities, a significant expansion of the middle class, and rising levels of social and geographic mobility. For Mexico, one consequence of those shifts has been changing political attitudes, a decline in deference toward authority, increased challenges to government and government policies, and the proliferation of independent interest groups (Coleman and Davis 1988). In the past decade, the expanded middle class has been at the forefront of the opposition to the entrenched party of government, the PRI. There is growing public commitment to democratization and social justice. Available evidence indicates that Mexican support for increased civil liberties—freedom of speech, a free press, public contestation, and organization—is high (ibid.). Another consequence of these changes has been increased tension between traditional and modern values (Alduncin 1986). To date, the empirical evidence of the scope and depth of these value changes has been incomplete and unsystematic (Cornelius 1986). The range of political and economic opportunities open to the average Mexican remains far more limited than what is available to publics in the United States or Canada. But as Etzioni (1968) has suggested, regional integration may well be the agent of a more open and participatory society by providing "new frameworks for transforming unresponsive societies" (1968:389).

There is also a large body of evidence indicating that important changes are taking place in Canada. Canada ceased to be a predominantly Anglo-Saxon society in the 1950s, and far-reaching demographic shifts are under way. Domestic birth rates have dropped to such a degree that it is only through immigration that Canada maintains its current population levels. Traditional West European sources of immigration have declined, while non-European sources have dramatically increased. Canada is less European than ever before. Founding circumstances may be important but we can ask, How relevant are such founding values as Toryism, collectivism, and elitism and such episodes as the counterrevolution to new Canadians from Eastern Europe, Asia, and the Caribbean?

Canada used to be distinguished from the United States by the presence of two main linguistic communities and the absence of a significant racial divide. These differences are fading. Racial conflict has moved from the margins to the center of political debate in Canada, while in the United States the influx of more than twenty million Hispanics, above all from Mexico, has given rise to public controversies about language politics and multiculturalism (Nevitte and Gibbins 1990). Moreover, long-standing structural differences between the U.S. and Canadian economies have also shrunk. Levels of postsecondary education, the size of the work force in the tertiary sector, rates of female employment, and so on are more similar now than ever before. During the past three decades, basic value changes have transformed the role of women throughout advanced industrial society; largely confined to the role of wife and mother a generation ago, most women in these societies now have full-time jobs outside the home. And in both countries there is evidence of a rising level of political participation, which in the European setting has been linked with support for closer integration of the European Community (Scheingold 1971; Inglehart 1990; Nevitte 1991).

The contrasting founding traditions have undoubtedly left their imprint upon contemporary value differences between the three North American societies. The claim that the United States is still characterized by an exceptional emphasis on certain key characteristics such as emphasis on individual achievement is supported by empirical evidence, for example. Table 1.1 shows responses to a World Values Survey question about how business and industry should be managed.

The options presented in these surveys ranged from the traditional capitalist model, in which the owners run their business or appoint

Table 1.1.   Support for Traditional Capitalist
Management of Industry (Percentage
Saying "Owners Should Run Their Own
Business or Choose the Managers")

United States	62%
Canada	58
Ireland	51
Britain	50
West Germany	47
Denmark	43
Iceland	43
Belgium	42
Japan	40
Norway	38
Argentina	34
Netherlands	32
Sweden	31
Italy	30
Mexico	28
Spain	25
South Korea	25
France	21

Source: 1981 World Values Survey.

managers, through joint employee-owner participation in management, to state ownership. As Table 1.1 indicates, the United States was the strongest bastion of support for the individualist capitalist model among the eighteen societies for which data are available from the 1981 World Values Survey. Though Canada proves to be only marginally more collectivist than the United States, the Mexican public differed drastically from their northern neighbors on this issue: only 28 percent of them favored full control by owners—in sharp contrast to Americans, who overwhelmingly emphasize the right of the individual owner to run his or her own enterprise, free from collective interference.

According to Lipset, two main themes in the American character—equality and achievement—emerged from the interplay between America's Puritan tradition and the revolutionary ethos. There is considerable evidence in support of his contention that the United States remains an exceptional society, characterized not only by an extreme emphasis on individual achievement, but also by an exceptional attachment to religion. "For almost a century, prominent European visitors who wrote on American life have been unanimous in remarking on the exceptional religiosity of the society," as Lipset points out (1990:23). Already in 1830, Tocqueville commented that "there is no country in the world where the

Christian religion retains greater influence over the souls of men than in America" ([1830 1955:61). Martineau in 1934, Trollope in 1860, Bryce in 1883, and Weber in 1904 all arrived at similar conclusions (Lipset 1963:160–61). Evidence from the 1981 World Values Survey indicates that this conclusion was still valid in the 1980s. The American public was characterized by much higher levels of religiosity than most other publics studied: they ranked high on church attendance and high on the percentage who believed in God, for example. Table 1.2 shows one particularly striking cross-national comparison: far more Americans said they believed in hell than did any other public in the 1981 World Values Survey. Though Mexicans were relatively close to the Americans on this variable, the two peoples were separated by a margin of more than 20 percentage points. And the Canadians were even further away, separated by a gap of 30 points.

IS THERE A NORTH AMERICAN VALUE SYSTEM?

To what extent do the peoples of the three North American countries share a common values system? One would certainly not expect to find

Table 1.2. Percentage of Public Saying They Believe in Hell

United States	73%
Mexico	52
Ireland	52
South Korea	48
Canada	43
South Africa	41
Australia	40
Spain	39
Argentina	37
Italy	36
Britain	30
Japan	28
Norway	23
Belgium	20
France	17
West Germany	16
Netherlands	15
Iceland	13
Hungary	12
Sweden	10
Denmark	7

Source: 1981 World Values Survey.

unanimity on all issues across the publics of the three societies that make up NAFTA, but in view of the remarkably high rates of exchanges they have experienced, in trade, mass media, and people, one might expect to find that on key value dimensions the publics of these societies would hold relatively similar basic values. Indeed, if they do not, the prospects for long-term political integration are probably dim. The question, To what extent do the North American publics share a common culture? immediately points to the need for some yardstick by which to measure their similarity. Quite obviously, these societies are not identical. But it is conceivable that, in global perspective, the basic values of the Canadians, the Americans, and the Mexicans may be more similar to each other than they are to those of the Chinese, the Swedes, the Nigerians, or the peoples of other regions. Is there a North American culture in this sense? And if so, how distinct is it?

To test these hypotheses, let us examine data from the 1990–1991 World Values Survey, drawn from forty-four nations throughout the world, representing 70 percent of the world's population and covering the full range of economic and political variation.[1] These data provide an unprecedented opportunity to view the basic values of North Americans in a global empirical perspective. As we will see, the evidence provides clear answers to the questions we have just posed. On crucial topics, the core values of the American public are significantly closer to those of the Canadians and even to those of the Mexicans than they are to those of the Japanese, Indians, Nigerians, or Russians.

This generalization does not (and could not) apply to every conceivable issue. But it does apply to two broad dimensions that reflect most of the key values examined in the 1990 World Values Survey. Since hundreds of questions were asked in these surveys, it would not be feasible to compare the values of all forty-four publics on each topic separately. Instead, we will compare the orientations of these publics on two particularly important dimensions that sum up the cross-national variation on scores of narrower values. These two dimensions tap:

1. *Traditional authority vs. rational-legal authority.* This dimension is based on a large number of items that reflect emphasis on obedience to traditional (usually religious) authority, and adherence to communal obligations and norms of sharing; vs. a worldview in which authority is legitimated by rational-legal and secular norms, linked with an emphasis on economic accumulation and individual achievement.

2. *Scarcity values vs. postmodern values.* This reflects the fact that in postindustrial society, historically unprecedented levels of wealth and the emergence of the welfare states have given rise to a shift from scarcity norms, which emphasize hard work and self-denial, to postmodern

values, which emphasize the quality of life, emancipation of women and sexual minorities, and related postmaterialist priorities such as emphasis on self-expression. The Appendix gives fuller detail on the items underlying these two respective dimensions.

Figure 1.3 sums up an immense amount of information. It is based on the responses to scores of questions given by more than sixty thousand respondents in forty-four societies. Our first major finding is that there is a great deal of constraint among cultural systems. The pattern found

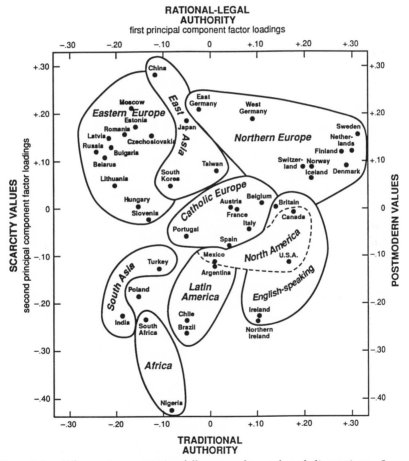

Figure 1.3. Where given societies fall on two key cultural dimensions. *Source:* 1990–1991 World Values Survey. Positions are based on the mean scores of the publics of the given nation on each of the two dimensions.

here is anything but random. The first two dimensions that emerge from the principal components factor analysis depicted in Figure 1.3 account for fully 51 percent of the cross-national variation among these forty-seven variables! Additional dimensions explain relatively small amounts of variance. And these dimensions are robust, showing little change if we drop some of the items, even high-loading ones. The horizontal axis depicts the polarization between a cluster of items labeled Scarcity Values and another cluster labeled Postmodern Values; the vertical axis reflects the polarization between traditional-religious authority and ra-tional-bureaucratic authority. The scales on the borders of Figure 1.3 indicate each item's loadings on these two dimensions.

Figure 1.3 shows the location of each society on the two dimensions we have been examining. To make this possible, dummy variables were created for each of our forty-four societies; these variables were mapped onto the two dimensions shaped by the worldviews of the respective publics.

Given groups of nations take coherent positions on the two dimen-sions. The four Latin American societies fall into one coherent cluster. Though surveyed independently, they produce relatively similar results. The same is true of the United States and Canada, of the two African societies, and of the four East Asian societies. Their people's values were measured separately, by different organizations and by people who had no idea what the others were finding; nevertheless, the results from the four Latin American societies, the two African societies, and the United States and Canada are much more similar to each other than they are to other societies. They are not identical: excellent books have been written about the cultural differences between the United States and Canada, for example. But virtually all informed observers (including the authors of those books) would consider Canada to be culturally more similar to the United States than to almost any other country, except perhaps Britain or Australia. The empirical findings are remarkably coherent. The peoples of the United States and Canada clearly have distinct values, but in global perspective they are as similar to each other as are the people of East Germany and West Germany—and considerably closer than the Germans and the Austrians.

Similarly, the Northern European societies form another cluster, with the five Nordic societies concentrated at one end and East and West Germany at the other; Catholic Europe constitutes another cluster, adja-cent to Northern Europe but distinct from it. The four English-speaking societies form another cluster, with Britain being next to the Northern European cluster but also very near to Canada.

Most of the twelve Eastern European societies fall into a common cluster. Poland clearly *is* an outlier: though geographically located in

Eastern Europe, it is an intensely Catholic society and the worldview of the Polish people emphasizes traditional cultural norms to a far greater extent than is true of other Eastern European societies—or other industrial societies more broadly. The other predominantly Roman Catholic societies of the Eastern European group (Lithuania, Hungary, and Slovenia) deviate in the same direction, but not to the same degree.

One of the most interesting features of Figure 1.3 is the fact that, when examined in global perspective, the three North American societies are characterized by relatively similar values. The two English-speaking nations of North America are culturally quite close to each other, with Canada also being closely similar to Great Britain. But in global perspective, the Mexican value system is reasonably close to that of its two English-speaking neighbors. This is particularly true concerning the traditional vs. rational-legal values tapped by the vertical dimension: all three North American societies are characterized by relatively traditional religious values in comparison with those prevailing in Northern Europe, Eastern Europe, or East Asia. This is less true of the scarcity vs. postmodern values tapped by the horizontal dimension: the Mexicans are clearly less postmodern in their outlook than are the Canadians or Americans. As we will see, this dimension is strongly linked with a society's level of economic development; consequently, as economic development takes place, the values of the Mexican public may move toward those of the Canadians and Americans.

ECONOMIC AND POLITICAL CORRELATES
OF VALUE SYSTEMS

As both the Weberian and Marxist versions of modernization theory claim, the decline of traditional values is strongly linked with economic growth: the growth rates of these societies from 1965 to 1990 show a .62 correlation, with emphasis on rational-legal authority, rather than traditional authority. This linkage is too strong to be due to chance (it is significant at the .0001 level) and it suggests that an important component of modernization theory was correct. Countries with cultures that place them high on the vertical axis have had much higher growth rates than those that rank lower. This could reflect either (1) the influence of culture on economic growth (a phenomenon similar to that hypothesized by Weber in *The Protestant Ethic and the Spirit of Capitalism*), or (2) the fact that a society's culture is determined by its economic institutions, as Marx alleged. We will not attempt to sort out the causal direction in the limited space available here, but analyses by Granato,

Inglehart, and Leblang (1997) and Inglehart (1997) indicate that cultural factors play an important role in economic growth.

While the modernization process is linked with high rates of economic growth, postmodernization is not. Quite the contrary, relatively high growth rates show a modest linkage with scarcity values rather than with postmodern values. This may reflect the fact that postmaterialists do not emphasize economic growth; and they tend to give priority to protecting the environment, if forced to choose. Nevertheless, there is a very strong correlation between postmodern values and a society's level of wealth ($r = .82$): rich countries are far more likely to have postmodern values.

Finally, the postmodernization process has important political implications. Inkeles and Diamond (1980), Inglehart (1990), and others have argued that economic development is linked with cultural changes that are conducive to democracy, an argument that has been hotly disputed by dependency theorists, neo-Marxists, and some rational-choice theorists. Our data show no correlation whatever between the modernization axis and the number of years for which a given society has been democratic. Industrialization, urbanization, etc., can give rise to either democratic or authoritarian regimes.

But there is an extremely strong correlation between the postmodernization dimension and democracy: $r = .91$, significant at the .0000 level. The empirical linkage is astonishingly strong: high levels of subjective well-being, coupled with postmodern values, including interpersonal trust, tolerance, and postmaterialist values are closely linked with stable democracy. One could argue that this cultural syndrome is conducive to democracy; or that democracy somehow gives rise to a culture of trust, tolerance, subjective well-being, and postmaterialist values; or that the cultural syndrome and the political institutions are mutually supportive. Space does not permit us to untangle the causal linkages here, but it seems clear beyond any reasonable doubt that they tend to go together [for an attempt to untangle the causal linkages, see Inglehart, Ellis, Granato, and Leblang (1996) and Inglehart (1997)].

The evidence from the World Values Surveys indicates that socioeconomic change is not random and unpredictable, with each society following an idiosyncratic course. On the contrary, change tends to follow clear configurations, in which specific clusters of cultural characteristics go together with specific types of political and economic change. The familiar modernization syndrome of urbanization, industrialization, and mass literacy tends to have foreseeable consequences such as increasing mass mobilization. And, as we have seen, modernization is linked with specific cultural changes, such as the shift from traditional to bureaucratic authority.

Similarly, the emergence of advanced industrial society, with an increasing share of the public having higher education, being employed in the service sector, and feeling assured that their survival needs will be met, gives rise to a process in which high levels of subjective well-being and postmodern values emerge—and in which a variety of attributes, from equal rights for women to democratic political institutions, become increasingly likely.

Significant value differences undoubtedly continue to divide North Americans today. Impressionistically, everyone "knows" that the peoples of these three countries differ from each other in important ways. But these impressions are usually fuzzy, incomplete, heavily influenced by stereotypes, supported by sketchy evidence, and may be out of date. Everyone also "knows" that important transformations have taken place in all three societies. The critical questions for the analysis that follows are: Do the basic goals of these three peoples really differ? If so, in exactly what ways and by how much? What are the trajectories of value change? And are the "main values" of publics in the three societies now more compatible? To answer these questions we rely on systematic evidence: the first cross-national survey of basic values and goals ever carried out in all three countries. Our data were gathered in two waves, with a first survey in spring 1981 and a second in spring 1990. With these data we analyze the value changes that took place during the 1980s, the period leading up to the NAFTA negotiations.

VALUE CHANGE AND NORTH AMERICAN INTEGRATION

The major story told in this book is that the value systems of the three North American societies are gradually shifting and the direction of value change is consistent with the broad transformations that are taking place in most advanced industrial states. North Americans are on a common trajectory of change moving toward:

1.   free-market economics,
2.   democratic political institutions,
3.   globalization.

Each of the three processes is more complex than these labels indicate. North Americans, like publics elsewhere, are moving toward free-market economics but not back to laissez-faire capitalism: the trend seems to be toward a model in which government regulation will play a crucial, though limited role, and where welfare state institutions will have an important function. Existing social security programs enjoy widespread support, and efforts to abolish them, or threats to their integrity from North American policy integration, would generate opposition and renewed social conflict.

Similarly, there is evidence that the evolution of advanced industrial society has an inherent tendency to make democratic institutions more likely, for two reasons: first, because they are the most effective way of coordinating technologically advanced societies; and second, because the publics of these societies are becoming increasingly likely to *want* democratic institutions, and increasingly adept at getting them. This transformation does not come easily, or automatically. Determined elites, in control of the army and police, can resist pressures for considerable periods of time. But as they mature, industrial societies develop characteristics conducive to democratization, such as increasingly specialized and educated labor forces. It is impossible to develop a technologically advanced economy without a highly educated work force, and once it emerges, it is relatively articulate and adept at organizing to exert political pressure. These changes are also evident in North America, which means that publics in all three countries are better equipped and more inclined to bring their interests to bear on decision-makers charting the course of continental integration.

We have labeled the third basic trend "globalization" but in fact, it reflects a withdrawal of support from established state institutions in *two* directions, moving to broader but looser configurations. The rise of the global economy makes traditional state boundaries less important than they once were. Traditional national boundaries, our evidence suggests, are also becoming less important. They clearly have become less important to Quebecois and native North Americans (Nevitte 1996). The slogan Think Globally, Act Locally suggests what is happening. On the one hand, increasingly global communications networks, as well as the value changes and rising educational levels just mentioned, are giving rise to an increasingly cosmopolitan outlook among the publics of advanced industrial states. But at the same time, an increasing emphasis on self-determination feeds demands to decentralize decision-making away from hierarchical national institutions toward more immediate levels. Often that process pumps new life into old regional ethnic cleavages and claims for collective autonomy. Quebec provides an example within North America: Canada's French-speaking ethnic minority is seeking increased autonomy for the province of Quebec. But as we will see, the drive toward autonomy is not a unique feature of small language communities; moreover, that search does not reflect the traditional parochial ethnocentrism that was characteristic of many agrarian or early industrial societies. Quite the contrary, the Quebecois have an increasingly cosmopolitan outlook and they are significantly more favorable to NAFTA than are Canadians in general.

Values change and so do public perceptions of "interests." As Nye argues, the shifting perceptions of interests held by citizens demanding accountability from public officials can be a decisive force in shaping decisions like the North American Free Trade Agreement, where domestic and international environments and interests intersect (1988:238–39). Early efforts to explain European integration focused on two interests: peace and prosperity. In the North American setting, one set of questions to emerge is, Prosperity for whom? And at what cost? But another theme also emerges. North American perceptions of interest have shifted away from a preoccupation with material gain and toward post-material concerns. As Scheingold suggested twenty years ago, the increased relevance of nonmaterial interests provides a very different set of standards for evaluating and interpreting integration, standards that are much broader than affluence (1971:388). Scheingold speculated that the relevant issues now are whether the expanded communities are likely to be responsive to demands for a more egalitarian and participatory system (pp. 388–89). The North American evidence clearly demonstrates that these noneconomic issues *are* critical.

As the following chapters demonstrate, a great deal of social, economic, and political value change is taking place in all three societies—and many of the changes conform to a predictable pattern. We find a systematic intergenerational shift. This means that we can actually predict most of the changes that took place from 1981 to 1990, from patterns that are visible in the 1981 baseline data. As we will see below, thirty-four variables shifted in a predictable direction from 1981 to 1990. Using the same strategy, we may be able to forecast further value changes that are likely to take place during the coming decades.

In Chapter 2, we set the stage for our analysis by examining the place of each economy in its global and continental setting. First, we further develop this economic theme by examining public support for the idea of free trade and closer ties with North American partner countries. Second, we show that economic interests shape support for North American free trade in predictable ways.

Chapter 3 examines the shift from materialist to postmaterialist orientations in each of the three publics and analyzes the causes of that intergenerational value shift, which is a core element in the much broader postmodern shift. We suggest that the shift has its origins in the formative experiences of the younger generation throughout advanced industrial societies. The historically unprecedented prosperity that has characterized Western societies since World War II, together with the safety net provided by the welfare state in the past few decades, has given rise to a situation in which a growing share of the public no longer gives top priority to the quest for economic and physical security. Instead, there has been growing concern for the quality of life.

This shift in basic value priorities has far-reaching implications. In Chapters 4 and 5 we demonstrate that it is linked with generational changes in prevailing motivations to work, in religious outlook, in sexual norms, and in political goals. It has also led to a gradual erosion of traditional nationalism and ethnocentrism, giving rise to an increasingly cosmopolitan sense of identity. Chapter 6 demonstrates that these orientations shape support for economic and political integration among all three publics.

North America is steering a new course. Changing values among the publics of the United States, Canada, and Mexico are transforming economic, social, and political life in ways that have important implications for economic and political cooperation between these countries.

NOTE

1. The World Values Surveys were carried out from March 1990 to January 1991 in forty-one societies; later surveys were completed in Slovenia (1992), Romania (1993), and Taiwan (1994). Representative national samples were used in all cases except East Germany, Northern Ireland, and the greater Moscow region (surveyed *in addition* to the entire Russian republic). The quality of the samples varies from country to country. Surveys in Western countries were carried out by professional survey organizations with a great deal of experience. In Eastern Europe they were carried out by the respective national academies of sciences or university-based institutes, some of which had carried out few previous surveys. The surveys from low-income countries generally have larger error margins than those from other countries. The samples from India, Nigeria, and China overrepresent the urban areas and the more educated strata. Since these groups tend to have orientations relatively similar to those found in industrial societies, our data probably underestimate the size of cross-national differences involving these countries. Nevertheless, these three countries frequently show very distinctive orientations. The data from the 1990–1991 surveys were released through the ICPSR survey data archive in July 1994; for details concerning fieldwork, see the ICPSR codebook, available from the Institute for Social Research, University of Michigan.

2

Changing Patterns of World Trade and Changing North American Linkages

CHANGING PATTERNS OF WORLD TRADE

Since the Second World War, the General Agreement on Tariffs and Trade (GATT) has provided the framework for regularizing the multilateral trading practices of most advanced industrial states. In a series of agreements, starting with the Geneva talks of the 1940s and including the Tokyo and Kennedy rounds of the 1960s and 1970s, major trading nations negotiated massive reductions in tariffs on manufactured goods. On average, tariffs fell from about 40 percent to about 5 percent. That trade liberalization, coupled with the development of fully convertible currencies and the emergence of effective machinery for managing international exchange, encouraged a remarkably rapid expansion in world trade. Between 1950 and 1975, global output increased by some 200 percent, while the volume of trade expanded by about 500 percent. In one spurt, starting in the mid-1960s, the exports of advanced industrial states grew 80 percent faster than industrial production—a rate that was about twice as fast as the expansion of the GDP (Stewart 1984).

By most benchmarks, GATT's performance in promoting freer trade through multilateral negotiation has been an enormous success, particularly during its first twenty-five years. But further progress toward multilateral trade liberalization started to lose momentum by the 1970s and the Uruguay round, which began in 1986, appeared to have completely stalled by 1990. Two broad recent trends are noteworthy. First, since the 1970s, major trading nations have increasingly resorted to a variety of protectionist strategies including import and export restraints, antidumping safeguards, countervailing duties, price fixing, and the use of informal and formal quotas. This shift from "open" to "managed" trade has been accompanied by a shift from multilateral trading patterns to the formation of regional groupings. The European Union has emerged as the most coherent trading bloc in the world; it has, by far, the largest volume of internal trade and its potential to play a dominant role in the world economy has been further accelerated by the restructuring of Eastern Europe and the reunification of Germany. The Asia-Pacific region, particularly Japan and the Four Little Dragons—South Korea, Taiwan, Singapore, and Hong Kong—forms a second even more dynamic, though less coherent network. North America represents a potential counterweight to them (see Figure 2.1).

The resurgence of protectionism and the regionalization of the global economy in the last two decades do not mean that multilateralism has failed. Nonetheless, declining confidence in the multilateral framework encourages trading nations to search for complementary alternatives. The economic logic guiding countries into trading blocs, particularly those with small economies, is driven by stark choice: countries outside such blocs can stand alone and face the prospect of competing with nations that enjoy guaranteed access to huge integrated markets such as that of the European Union; or they can join together, forming groupings like the European Community and solidify the advantages gained from twenty-five years of trade liberalization while searching out new profit niches.

The regionalization of the global economy may well be the most significant force behind the movement toward North American free trade, but the particular national economic circumstances and concerns of each of the three partners to NAFTA are also important factors. The United States emerged from the Second World War as the undisputed leader of the noncommunist world and although GATT was inspired by American

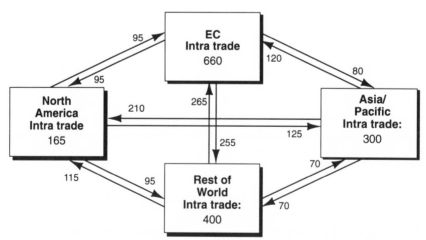

Figure 2.1. World trade flows, 1989 (figures rounded to the nearest billion). *Source: Economist* 316 (7673, September 22), 1990 (originally extracted from GATT and OECD).

proposals, it is doubtful that the United States was the main beneficiary of the multilateral strategies pursued by GATT. By most broad indicators the relative position of the United States in the world economy has declined substantially. In 1945, the United States' share of the world GNP stood at 50 percent; by 1980 it had dropped to 21 percent (Maira 1983). In 1950, Americans enjoyed the highest per capita gross domestic product in the world. By 1982, five European states enjoyed a higher per capita standard of living (Katzenstein 1988). At the same time, the United States has also become much more open and much more dependent on the world economy. More than 20 percent of U.S. industrial output is exported and one in six manufacturing jobs depends on foreign markets. Forty percent of American farmland produces for export and about one-third of the profits of American corporations come from exports and foreign investment. Imports account for more than half of most important raw materials, and between 1970 and 1980 the contribution of trade to the United States GDP doubled (Bergsten 1982).

The gradual erosion of America's relative economic status and its increased vulnerability can be measured against a variety of other benchmarks as well. American vulnerability due to its dependence on external sources of oil was increased by the emergence of OPEC and the wild price fluctuations that resulted form the creation of that cartel. In 1970, for example, imported oil cost the United States $3 billion. By 1980, the bill had jumped to over $80 billion. Japan has emerged as an economic superpower that rivals and in some respects has surpassed U.S. technological preeminence. One result has been a widespread call to reassess U.S.-Japanese trade relations. Many observers express alarm at the apparent decline in the competitiveness of American management and research and development. Other countries have overtaken the United States in more traditional economic spheres. American exports of manufactured goods are less than those of Germany, which has one-third as large a population. The U.S. proportion of international monetary reserves has declined significantly; it is much smaller than that of either Saudi Arabia or Germany. At the same time, the United States has also become more dependent than ever before on foreign investment (Fry 1980). Challenges to the economic status of the United States have come not only from other nations but also from other international economic actors. One of the most striking transformations of the international economy in the postwar period has been the rise of multinational corporations. How multinationals figure in the erosion of national sovereignty and the increasingly prominent roles they play in the economies of advanced industrial states including North America, as well as in the third world, have been amply demonstrated elsewhere (Vernon 1977; Moran 1974; Cardoso and Faletto 1979). By one estimate, multinational corporations now account for $2 trillion of offshore production. Private international banks have also emerged as crucial nongovernmental economic actors.

The two central themes characterizing America's economic evolution in the postwar period—declining relative importance and increased vulnerability—work together. American jobs, economic growth, prices, and overall economic stability are now far more dependent than ever before on events outside the United States. At the same time, the United States is less able than before to dictate the course of these events. The promise of North American continental economic integration cannot restore the United States to its postwar position as the world's preeminent economic power, but it can help that country to consolidate its position as the dominant actor within one major region of an increasingly multipolar world. NAFTA would provide stable access to large markets, promote increased efficiency, and reduce transaction costs. It could also ensure secure access to large reserves of such strategic natural resources as oil, natural gas, metals, and hydroelectric power, which are available in Canada and Mexico.

One response to the changing place of the United States in the world economy has been increased domestic pressure for economic protectionism. That strategy would be profoundly dangerous to the Canadian and Mexican economies because of the extensive and powerful economic bonds that tie the three continental economies together (Figure 2.2). About two-thirds of Canada's exports go to the United States and about the same proportion of Canada's imports come from the United States. The proportions are very similar for Mexico; and Canada and Mexico combined account for about one-quarter of all U.S. exports. The basic distribution of intra–North American trade, moreover, has been quite stable over the past forty years. One major reason for American influence on the continental economy, of course, stems directly from differences in population size, market size, and economic performance. The population of the United States is ten times that of Canada and nearly three times that of Mexico. Simply put, the United States has a large, well-established economy, while Canada and Mexico have relatively small and unevenly developed economies. The relationships between the American and the two other economies have been characterized as "complex interdependence" (Keohane and Nye 1977). They are also asymmetrical and the realities are plain; large economies set the beat and small economies dance to it.[1]

The details of the deep and extensive economic linkages between the United States and Canada, as well as between Mexico and the United States, have been documented in detail elsewhere (Stern 1989; Rugman 1987; Diebold 1988; Reynolds, Wanesman, and Bueno 1991). Even so, it

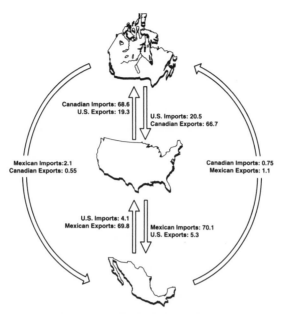

Canadian Imports: 68.6
U.S. Exports: 19.3

U.S. Imports: 20.5
Canadian Exports: 66.7

Mexican Imports:2.1
Canadian Exports: 0.55

Canadian Imports: 0.75
Mexican Exports: 1.1

U.S. Imports: 4.1
Mexican Exports: 69.8

Mexican Imports: 70.1
U.S. Exports: 5.3

Figure 2.2. North American trade patterns: percentage imports and exports. *Source: Yearbook of International Statistics* (New York: United Nations, 1988), and *Estadísticas Históricas de México,* Val. II (Mexico City: INEGI, 1985, pp. 665–669).

is useful to highlight some of the central themes that structure these relationships. Canada began this century as a newly independent state that was heavily reliant upon capital from its former colonial patron, Britain. But by 1926, the United States had surpassed Britain as the major holder of direct and portfolio capital in Canada, and in the short span of another twenty years the American share of Canada's total foreign liabilities leaped to 72 percent. By 1964, the United States held about 80 percent of Canada's foreign investment and the $12.9 billion invested by American corporations accounted for 31 percent of all U.S. direct foreign investment—more than the total of all U.S. direct foreign investment in Europe or Latin America (Redekop 1978). Along with massive capital inflows has come a concentration of American economic activity in key sectors of the Canadian economy. By the mid 1970s, over 90 percent of Canada's petroleum, coal, and rubber industries were foreign owned; over 80 percent of transportation equipment and chemical products and over 70 percent of machinery manufacturing were also foreign owned. In the last fifteen years, cross-border investments accelerated. By 1986, Canadian investment in the U.S. economy rose to $18 billion, while U.S. direct investment in Canada exceeded $50 billion. In other respects, the status quo changed only marginally. Over 60 percent of all Canadian manufacturing still remains in foreign, mostly American hands (Schott and Smith 1988).

These are the characteristics of a "branch plant" economy and the evolution of that economy, ironically, can be largely explained as a result of a series of Canadian national economic polices aimed at establishing a domestic manufacturing economic base (Stairs and Winham 1985). Branch plant economies have their own dynamics, which typically are shaped by relations. In the Canadian case, 50 percent of all export sales by subsidiaries are made to and 70 percent of all imports come from their parent corporations. Much of the expansion of the Canadian branch plants has been serviced by borrowing at preferential interest rates, rates obtained because of the security provided by parent corporations. In one seven-year period during the 1960s, the profits remitted to parent corporations exceeded Canada's entire net capital inflows (Levitt 1970). Branch plant reliance on parent corporations also extends to technology, research and development, management, and marketing. The Canadian economy still relies upon the export of raw and semiprocessed goods much more heavily than other states of comparable wealth.

Canada and Mexico differ in size, in levels of economic development, and in per capita wealth. Despite those important differences, there are striking parallels between the structures of Canadian-U.S. and Mexican-U.S. economic relations. These parallels go beyond the balance of trade with the United States; they also apply to the economic dynamics linking the two countries (Gilpin 1974). A very large proportion of Mexico's imports involve commercial transactions between subsidiaries trading with parent corporations, typically themselves U.S. subsidiaries. Like Canada, Mexico is short of capital and relies heavily on foreign investment and external financial markets to raise capital and to service debt. About two-thirds of foreign investment in Mexico comes from the United States, and American commercial banks hold a substantial portion of Mexico's external debt (Weintraub 1990). To a large extent the cost and availability of capital to Mexico is determined by externally driven interest rates and external evaluations of risk.

As in Canada, the American economy also exercises a powerful influence on Mexico's industrial sector, a sector that is critical to domestic economic performance. Manufacturing activity is labor intensive and Mexico, with its massive labor surplus, is hobbled by chronic unemployment. The United States imports more than 60 percent of all Mexico's manufactured exports (ibid.), and like Canada, Mexico relies heavily on imported technology, research and development, and marketing.

The United States is, by far, the largest trading partner for both Canada and Mexico; conversely, Canada is America's largest trading partner and Mexico ranks immediately after Japan as the United States' third largest trading partner. The sheer volume of economic transactions between the three economies and the intricate structural ties linking the three economies provide powerful economic incentives for further rationalizing continental free trade through NAFTA. To these economic incentives can be added a variety of noneconomic incentives. All three countries share strategic interests that stem from occupying the same continent. There are complementary sociodemographic dynamics as well. The Mexican population is young, the populations of Canada and the United States are aging. Mexico has a labor surplus, Canada and the United States have labor shortages. Geographic proximity and population and media flows also provide a measure of de facto transborder integration. Currently, Canadians make forty-two million visits per year to the United States, and about forty-eight million American visits were made to Canada. U.S.-Mexican legal border crossings now approach three hundred million annually, the largest volume of transboundary migrations between any two countries in the world. Long-standing migration from both Canada and Mexico to the United States, and to a lesser extent from the United States, has produced strong cross-border kinship networks.

Against this backdrop, the macroeconomic case for continental free trade seems a compelling one. Economists argue that the expansion of trade promotes increased efficiency and contributes to national and global economic welfare. For them, the liberalization of trade is not viewed as a zero-sum game in which the winnings of one country come at the expense of others. Rather, free trade is seen as a net *and* joint gain.

From this abstract economic standpoint, it is difficult to see why the prospects of free trade could spark any opposition at all. But the reality is that they do. Both historical and contemporary experience shows that public debates about free trade, not only in North America but also in Europe and elsewhere, have been deeply divisive. The macroeconomic perspective is only one viewpoint through which the dynamics of liberalizing trade can be seen. When social and political perspectives are added to the picture, the balance between advantages and disadvantages of expanding trade becomes much more complex. Trade liberalization, and in particular the push toward a continental economy through NAFTA, produces political opposition because it brings into sharp focus both long-standing and newly emerging dilemmas. As we will see, these dilemmas spring from discontinuities between economic and noneconomic values.

DILEMMAS

NAFTA might well be seen as a logical extension of the economic momentum that has shaped the North American continental economy for the last forty years. Why, then, has free trade inspired such heated public debate, particularly in Canada and Mexico? One explanation is that freer trade affects powerful economic interests in varying ways. Freer trade may produce aggregate economic gains, but citizens do not live in an aggregate economic world and changes to the economic status quo raise fundamental redistributive issues. As Rogowski (1989) has shown, liberalizing trade has significant consequences for domestic economic and political alignments. At stake are several issues: How will the net gains be distributed? Who stands to win and who stands to lose? What counts is how well endowed given societies are with the crucial factors of production: land, labor, and capital. Within any society, protection benefits (and liberalization harms) owners of factors in which, relative to the rest of the world, that society is poorly endowed. It has a similar impact upon producers who use that factor intensively (ibid.). Conversely, protection harms (and liberalization benefits) the holders of those factors that are relatively abundant and producers who use these locally abundant factors intensively. Thus for "a society rich in labor but poor in capital, protection benefits capital and harms labor; and the liberalization of trade benefits labor and harms capital" (p. 3). Those anticipating gains from freer trade can be expected to mobilize to support it and potential victims will mobilize to oppose it.

That logic can easily be applied to the North American setting, and when the particular national resources in capital and labor are taken into account, it produces specific and intuitively clear expectations. For example, it helps to explain why large corporations with advantages in capital support free trade. Free trade provides these enterprises with the opportunity to rationalize continental economic activities free from uneconomic national constraints. The result? Lower unit costs and higher profits. It explains why Canadian labor, which reaps the benefits of relative labor shortages (and higher levels of unionization) within Canada, mobilized to resist freer trade. At the same time it also helps to explain why Mexican labor, for precisely the opposite reason, would support freer trade. Mexican labor is in surplus and with greater access to large markets that are short of labor, Mexican labor stands to gain.

Economics is undoubtedly the driving force behind free trade and most analyses of free trade focus primarily on the economic consequences of liberalizing continental trade. But economic forces do not work in isolation from social and political factors nor can they be evaluated without reference to human values. Our central concern, and the focus of the analysis that follows, is upon the interplay between economic forces and human values. Economic prosperity is an instrumental goal, not an end in itself. Free trade is a hotly debated issue not just because it leads to redistributive economic conflicts but also because it brings into play dilemmas grounded in the tension between two imperatives: the drive to attain economic prosperity through maximizing economic efficiency, and the drive to achieve noneconomic human goals. Economic welfare is one horn of the dilemma, with a nation's status and autonomy being the other. At stake is the tension between economic rationality and the capacity to make public choices that are rooted in noneconomic values.

For the United States the dilemmas are related to the declining position of its place in the world economic political order and its increased vulnerability to events beyond its control. For Canada and Mexico, the dilemmas are grounded in the more immediate positions of those states within North America.

Traditionally, Canadian and Mexican relations with the United States have been a lightning rod for domestic political, economic, and social life. In both countries, the reasons have deep historical roots: the Canadian and Mexican nation-building projects were forged against the backdrop of American influence. The premises underpinning founding national ideals were cast in bold relief by contrasting them with American ideals—a strategy that emphasizes differences in founding values. For contemporary economic nationalists, maintaining economic, social, and political distance from the United States represents fidelity to these originating principles. Carlos Rico captures the sentiment succinctly. He argues that for Mexico, free trade with the United States "would be the equivalent of recognizing the failure of the aims of independence and sovereignty that are central to the ideology of the Mexican Revolution" (cited in Weintraub 1990:17). These very same concerns are echoed by Canadian nationalists. For them, the historical reference point is not, of course, the Mexican revolution, but Canada's reaction to the American Revolution—the Canadian counterrevolution and the values it embodied.

If free trade stirs similar old debates about national autonomy, it does so in quite different national contexts. In Canada, free trade with the United States is controversial because Canadian and American national values seem so similar that Canadian identity is threatened. Canada has a fragile national consensus, one fractured by historical linguistic, cultural, and regional divisions and further aggravated by contemporary political disputes about how those cleavages should be constitutionally managed. In Mexico, the free-trade controversy is rancorous not because of a fragile national culture but because the options for economic development seem so limited. Today, they may even have been narrowed to just one: Should Mexico hitch its economic wagon to that of its historical rival, the United States? For Canada and Mexico, free trade holds out the promise of prosperity, but prosperity that comes at a price; economic nationalists in both countries argue that the price—the loss of national autonomy—is too high (Fuentes 1991). The fear is that closer ties with the United States mean greater dependence, increased exposure to inequalities, and greater vulnerability; and that these forces will limit the ability of national governments to pursue social and economic welfare policies that reflect unique national values.

From these perspectives, the decisions by Canadian and Mexican governments to pursue free trade with the United States represent major historic departures from long-standing practice. The economic reasons for pursuing NAFTA are clear, but to some extent these reasons have existed for decades. One reason for the sudden shift toward mutual free trade might be that all three countries are simultaneously reacting to the growing impact of global economic change. But another equally important possibility is that the national values of these three publics and goals they aspire to are not as different as they once were. Debates about the conflict between prosperity and autonomy, the dilemmas posed by increased economic integration and the loss of national independence, are typically conducted from the perspective of one specific nation. But an emerging body of evidence suggests that in the last two decades another dilemma has gained salience and that dilemma springs primarily not from concern about national autonomy but from the increased value publics attach to *individual autonomy*. The drive toward greater and more meaningful participation in public life and increased democratization conflicts with traditional institutions that are based on hierarchical patterns of authority. The recent transformations in the former Soviet Union and in Eastern Europe provide the most dramatic evidence of sweeping changes toward democratization. But these changes are not limited to the former Communist bloc. A growing body of cross-national empirical evidence demonstrates that Western states are also experiencing pervasive shifts in the prevailing patterns of authority and conflict. Citizens are becoming less passive, less deferential, and less satisfied with the status quo and with traditional hierarchical institutions that inhibit active public participation. Today, the average citizen is better educated, more articulate, more cosmopolitan, more knowledgeable about politics, more concerned about public policymaking, increasingly demanding of public officials, and the expanding and politically articulate middle classes command more resources than ever before. The once large gap between the political skills of elites and publics has narrowed and traditional, hierarchical authority patterns are under siege.

One measure of the success of the new economic course charted by the three countries is provided by purely economic indicators: investment, economic growth and security, employment, and prosperity. But an equally important measure of success is the extent to which the human goals and aspirations of citizens in the three countries are served. At the moment, one can only speculate about whether citizen values in the three countries will be enhanced or hobbled by NAFTA. The decision to pursue a continental economic agreement, however, may indicate that significant changes in national values have taken place in each of the three countries. And we are well placed to examine how the value landscapes of these publics have changed in the last decade. Drawing on representative national surveys carried out in the United States, Canada, and Mexico first in 1981 and then replicated in 1990, this book will present the first empirical analysis ever conducted of changing values and attitudes among these three publics.

Conditions change and so do values. Contemporary Americans, Canadians, and Mexicans are inheritors of three different national traditions, but to what extent have these national traditions survived these remarkable changes? Do contemporary national values still bear the imprint of the founding ideals? Do the stereotypes that were valid even twenty-five years ago still apply? These questions are both fundamental and controversial. At issue are competing judgments about the direction and scope of value change.

Our goal in the following chapters is to address these and related questions, to do so systematically and with direct comparative evidence. The answers to these fundamental questions, we suggest, will have a significant bearing upon the kind of joint future that publics in North America can expect to face. They will also have a significant impact upon the opportunities for harmonizing common public choices. As the next three chapters demonstrate, the basic values and attitudes of all three publics *are* undergoing massive change. Thus far, these changes have largely escaped the notice of most observers: partly because they are taking place gradually, and partly because they remain invisible unless we set out to deliberately track them through survey research. Whether or not we observe them, however, these changes are taking place and they have important implications for an emerging North American free-trade area.

The most directly relevant change is the fact that there has been a gradual but persuasive decline in nationalism and feelings of attachment to the existing nation-state among the publics of all three countries. Furthermore, many of the cultural differences that have long divided Mexico, Canada, and the United States seem to be eroding: in their basic values, the publics of these three societies seem to be coming closer.

Evidence of these changes will be presented and explored in the next three chapters. We note them here in order to point out their crucial relevance to the question of free trade.

SUPPORT FOR FREE TRADE

Let us set the stage for our analysis of North American values by examining public attitudes toward the issue that underpins continental economic integration: free trade. We would not expect the publics of all three countries to be equally enthusiastic about the principle of free trade. After all, some countries have prospered more than others under open trade environments. Furthermore, if the attitudes of economic elites in the three countries are a reliable measure of the orientations of their corresponding publics, then we may well expect to find significant variations in citizen orientations to open trade (Harvard Business Review 1991). One recent comprehensive survey of economic elites, for example, found that support for "free trade between nations" is weaker among Mexican business leaders (69 percent) than among their Canadian (81 percent) or American (78 percent) counterparts. It also found that American business elites are more likely (38 percent) than Mexican (20 percent) or Canadian (32 percent) elites to want "limits on the amount of foreign ownership of corporate assets" (ibid.).[2] The values that economic elites as leaders of powerful interest groups bring to free trade are important, but so are public attitudes. Following Putnam's (1988) reasoning, we would expect weak public support for free trade to make it harder for political leaders to craft trade accords that would satisfy domestic publics positioned to ratify agreements. What, then, are the levels of support for free trade among the North American publics?

The World Values Surveys in these three countries were conducted in June 1990, when trilateral negotiations for NAFTA were being publicly debated. The surveys asked representative national samples of publics in the United States, Canada, and Mexico the following set of questions:

> Most countries like our own depend on trade. Here is a list of various ways of dealing with trade issues. Please tell me how much you agree or disagree with the following statements:
> 1.   There should be no restrictions on the free flow of goods and services across international borders.
> 2.   We should allow goods and services to flow *more* freely across our borders as long as (Americans/Canadians/Mexicans) don't lose jobs.
> 3.   We should give countries free access to our markets only if they give us free access to theirs.

The responses to the three questions are reported in Figure 2.3. The answers given to the first statement provide a benchmark: they indicate levels of public support for the most general and unrestricted form of free trade: free trade with no strings attached. As the left side of the figure illustrates, there are substantial cross-national variations in orientations to open trade. In 1990, support was clearly highest among the Mexican public, to whom the mass media (guided by the government) had presented an overwhelmingly positive picture of the future that NAFTA would bring. A slim majority of Canadians endorsed completely open trade (55 percent) but only 40 percent of Americans did so.[3]

Completely open trade, like total protectionism, represents an ideal: No modern states are completely open, nor are they entirely protectionist. In practice, few free-trade deals are struck without any conditions whatsoever, and we would expect citizens, like other economic actors, to support or oppose the lowering of free-trade barriers depending upon how they expect free trade to affect them (Milner and Yoffie 1989). For understandable reasons, public debate in all three countries reflects concern about the impact that freer trade would have on their jobs. As one would expect, when respondents were asked if they would support freer trade if it meant that they would not "lose jobs" (the second alter-

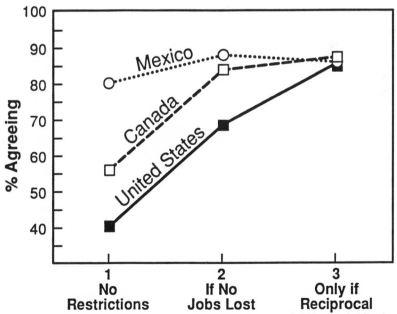

Figure 2.3. Support for free trade, under three circumstances. *Source:* 1990 World Values Survey.

native) support for more open trade increased among all three publics and it did so most dramatically among Canadians and Americans.

The third alternative, "We should give countries free access to our markets only if they give us free access to theirs," presents the idea of reciprocity and draws attention to the link between economic and political considerations. Reciprocity involves such values as good faith, fairness, and the preparedness to make equivalent concessions (Keohane 1986; Rhodes 1989). The norm of reciprocity, evidence suggests, has become an increasingly important guide to enterprises pursuing strategic trade policies (Milner and Yoffie 1989) as well as for government-to-government relations (Axelrod 1984). Moreover, it has been argued that reciprocity is particularly crucial to the negotiation of trade agreements between states, like the North American ones, whose relationships are highly interdependent, asymmetrical, and continuing (Yarborough and Yarborough 1986). Reciprocity may be the governing norm for large enterprises charting strategic trade positions and for governments looking for closer collaboration with other states, but do the same norms influence *public* support for expanding trade arrangements? Are public attitudes to open trade also shaped by good faith, fairness, and the preparedness to make equivalent concessions? The World Values Surveys suggest that they are, and the evidence is striking. When the guarantee of a level playing field is introduced, more than 80 percent of all three publics support free trade. Only 15 percent of Americans, Canadians, and Mexicans resist free trade under the condition of reciprocity.

When these responses are analyzed in more detail, and the cultural and economic backgrounds of respondents are considered, substantial variations between groups emerge. For example, French Canadians, many of whom aspire to constitutional independence from Canada, are clearly more enthusiastic about free trade than are their English Canadian counterparts. African-Americans, who make up a disproportionate share of the American underclass, are also consistently more favorably disposed to free trade than are their white American counterparts. But surprisingly, although Mexicans are the *most* enthusiastic about free trade, Hispanic-Americans turn out to be the *least* enthusiastic.

Endorsing the general idea of free trade is one thing, but there is no guarantee that support for the principle of free trade automatically turns into support for close economic ties between the partner countries to a NAFTA. Given trade asymmetries, vulnerabilities, and the cultural-political freight that ties with the United States have historically carried for Mexicans and Canadians, we might anticipate that support for closer economic trade with the United States could well be more muted for the Mexican and Canadian publics. Publics in each country were asked specific questions about economic ties with each of the other countries in

North America. Respondents were asked, "In your opinion, should America (or Canada or Mexico) have closer, or more distant economic ties with Canada (or Mexico or the United States)?"

Respondents were presented with a four-point scale, on which 1 indicated much closer ties and 4 indicated much more distant ties. Surprising as it may seem, the responses consistently reveal majority support for closer or much closer ties to the other two countries among all three publics. But they also show significant national variations when only the more emphatic response, much closer ties, is considered. The data presented in Figure 2.4, for example, suggest that the Mexican public is more supportive of much closer ties with Canada and the United States, but they also show that Americans and Canadians do not reciprocate. American and Canadian support for much closer ties with Mexico is lukewarm. For example, 40 percent of the Mexican public wanted much closer economic ties with the United States, while only 20 percent of the Americans reciprocated. Conversely, only 17 percent of Mexicans reported wanting more distant economic ties with the United States while more than one in four Americans wanted more distant ties with Mexico. On the other hand, nearly 30 percent of Canadians want more distant

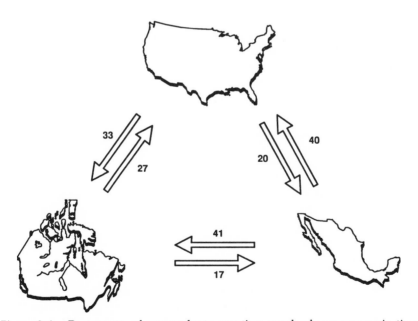

Figure 2.4. Percentage of respondents wanting much closer economic ties: United States, Canada, and Mexico. *Source:* 1990 World Values Survey.

ties with the United States while less than 10 percent of Americans want more distant ties with Canada.

As it turns out, support for the principle of free trade *is* related to attitudes toward closer economic ties with the other North American countries, though there are also predictable variations in the extent to which these orientations are connected. For Americans who are located in the North American "hub" economy and who are generally less enthusiastic than Mexicans about closer ties, attitudes to free trade are a better predictor of closer ties with Mexico ($r = .21$) than with Canada ($r = .14$). For Mexicans and Canadians occupying the "spokes" on the economic wheel, free-trade orientations predict closer economic ties with the United States equally well ($r = .2$). But for publics in the two-spoke economies, free-trade attitudes are far less salient. Indeed, for Canadians, attitudes to free trade in general are all but irrelevant ($r = .07$) when it comes to predicting support for closer economic ties with Mexico.[4]

Proponents of continental free trade make the case for NAFTA by emphasizing the aggregate advantages of expanding trade environments to the publics in the three national economies. The conventional reasoning is that the country as a whole stands to gain because of the complementary comparative advantages that will flow from large markets. Large markets mean economies of scale. Economies of scale drive down unit costs. Lower unit costs mean lower prices to consumers, and the competitive position of North American products in foreign markets improves. The result? Each country is better positioned to take a larger share of world markets. At the same time, it has also been demonstrated that changing trade conditions produce dislocations and adjustments, and expanding trade environments have quite different impacts on different sectors within national economies. This perspective predicts that one's support for or opposition to free trade will be shaped by the gains or losses anticipated from the new trading arrangement. The evidence summarized in Figure 2.5 supports this prediction. In the U.S. case, for example, those in big and small businesses anticipate gains from free trade with Canada; they are the strongest supporters of closer ties with that country. As expected, big business is also most supportive of closer economic ties with Mexico. The comparative advantages in the agricultural sector work in a different direction. If the American and Canadian plains are North America's breadbasket, then Mexico has become its salad bowl. A stable climate, cheap land, low-cost labor, reforms in the communal farms, and greater application of technology to Mexican agriculture have resulted in dramatic increases in food production. Mexican food exports to the United States doubled between 1985 and 1990; Mexico is now America's largest foreign source of food, accounting for

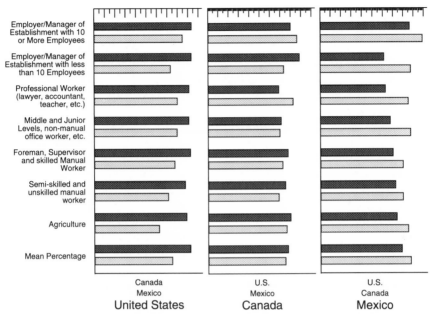

Figure 2.5. Support for closer economic ties, by occupation sector. *Source:* 1990 World Values Survey.

25 percent of all the produce Americans eat. For the same reason, cheap labor and low-cost agricultural products present a challenge to American farmers and unskilled labor—and accordingly, these groups are least supportive of closer economic ties with Mexico.

The sectorial impact of economic incentives for free trade in Canada operates in different ways and the survey evidence reflects those differences. Canadian business has always been hobbled by a severe domestic disadvantage: a small market. Closer economic ties to the United States and Mexico provide Canadian businesses, both large and small, with the opportunity to gain greater access to markets that are fifteen times larger than their own. It comes as little surprise, then, to discover that Canadian business supports closer economic ties with both the United States and Mexico. At the same time, the service sector accounts for a very substantial and growing proportion of Canadian-U.S. commercial transactions. Here, Canadian professionals face a severe challenge. The American service enterprises already enjoy the advantages of greater size and greater specialization and they are well positioned to reap major gains in the Canadian service market at the expense of their Canadian counterparts. Canadian professionals, accordingly, are least supportive of closer ties to the United States. Mexico presents no such challenge to this group and the Canadian professional class along with big business are the strongest supporters of closer economic ties with Mexico. As with the United States, Mexican economic advantages in agriculture and lower costs of labor place Canadians in the semiskilled and unskilled labor pools at a relative disadvantage. For that reason they are much less enthusiastic about the prospects of closer economic ties with Mexico.

For Mexicans, the average level of support for closer economic ties with their North American partners is much higher than for their American and Canadian counterparts. From the economic perspective alone, it is easy to see why: Mexicans stand to gain the most. Per capita income in Mexico is only one-seventh as high as in the United States and Canada. Bringing the Mexican economy even approximately into line with those of the United States and Canada would represent a massive accomplishment. Not surprisingly, business support for closer economic ties with the United States and Canada is high. Indeed, for those in larger enterprises it is unanimous. Nor is it surprising to discover that Mexicans in the agricultural sector are more enthusiastic than most others about closer economic ties with the United States. For them, the American market is critical to this increasingly export-oriented sector. In Mexico, support for closer economic ties with the United States is weakest among those employed in two sectors: small business and the professions. Existing small businesses are typically not well placed to take best advantage of new opportunities, and the Mexican professions, as in Canada, are the domain of cultural elites who have resisted closer ties with the United States for both economic and noneconomic reasons.[5]

Two key findings emerge from this overview of orientations toward free trade and attitudes about closer economic ties with specific North American partners. First, there are significant and predictable variations in public attitudes toward continental economic integration within each country. To a large extent, where one stands on free trade depends on where one sits in the economy.

The second basic finding is that Canadians and Mexicans are clearly more eager supporters of freer trade than Americans; they are also more supportive of closer economic ties with the United States than are the Americans themselves. In light of the historical anxiety and resentment that both countries have expressed toward the powerful influence that the American economy has had on them, the levels of Canadian and Mexican support that we find here are impressive and striking. Indeed, they are surprising: in the past, nationalistic fear of being swallowed by their larger neighbor seems to have been the historically predominant pattern. Though there is little survey evidence to document the strength or depth of those sentiments in the past (Sigler and Goresky 1976), the historical record suggests that throughout most of the past two hundred years, the United States was quite willing to merge with Canada or Mexico; it was the smaller partners who typically resisted integration. To an astonishing extent, these traditional forms of nationalism seem to have vanished. The next three chapters will explore some of the reasons *why* this has happened.

NOTES

1. As Nye's (1976) analysis of postwar Canadian-U.S. bargaining shows, economic asymmetries do not automatically translate into equivalent asymmetries of political influence. Wagner's (1988) perceptive examination of interdependence and bargaining suggests why this might be so.

2. The *Harvard Business Review* (1991) study also indicates that strong support for preferential treatment for domestic firms is considerably higher in Mexico (26 percent) and the United States (22 percent) than Canada (12 percent).

3. General ideological considerations aside, there are strategic reasons that could explain national differences in support for the principle of free trade. For smaller economies, like Canada and Mexico, where it is more difficult for domestic enterprises to reach the economies of scale, access to foreign markets is more critical. For large economies, like the United States, operating in an environment of imperfect competition (North America) in which other governments have a record of economic intervention, unconditional support for free trade becomes less attractive (Milner and Yoffie 1989).

4. In the Canadian version of the survey, publics were asked if they supported the recently ratified Canada-U.S. Free Trade Agreement. As we would expect, support for the principle of open trade is correlated ($r = .22$) with support for that free-trade deal. On balance, 54 percent of Canadian respondents supported the agreement. More surprisingly, one-third (33 percent) of those who favored open trade opposed the Canada-U.S. Free Trade Agreement.

5. Mexican attitudes to closer economic ties with Canada are much more variable, reflecting perhaps the relatively small role that Mexican–Canadian trade plays in the overall performance of those economies. Even so, Mexican labor is supportive of closer economic ties with that country.

3

Compatibility and Change in the Basic Values of North American Peoples

The North American dilemma lies in the fact that there are strong economic incentives for the United States, Canada, and Mexico to merge their economies into one powerful North American free-trade zone; but doing so will probably lead to closer political and cultural ties between these countries. What will be the impact on the peoples of these three societies?

Will free trade with the United States swamp Canadian cultural identity, as Canadian opponents of the 1989 Free Trade Agreement with the United States have argued? This argument implicitly assumes (1) that Canadians have political and cultural values and goals that differ in major ways from those prevailing in the United States, and (2) that economic integration will cause these differences to erode. These assumptions may or may not be true, but they have never been demonstrated empirically. This book will do so. In this and the next two chapters, we will compare the basic values of the Canadian, American, and Mexican publics in order to determine how much they differ and where. We will also explore the degree to which they are changing—and whether they are moving in different directions, or along a common trajectory.

Mexican opponents of free trade with the United States have argued that it will bring Mexico increasingly under the economic, political, and cultural domination of the United States. American opponents of free trade have argued that it will encourage massive Hispanic immigration, which would endanger their country's cultural and political institutions. To some extent, such questions reflect sheer xenophobia or outmoded stereotypes, but we should also recognize that they express legitimate concerns. It is conceivable that Canadians (or Americans or Mexicans) really *are* different from other North Americans in important respects that have significant behavioral consequences. To simply deny, a priori, that such differences exist will not convince the opponents of North American integration—moreover, it may blind those who favor integration to genuine problems.

47

Many previous studies of cultural differences have relied largely on impressionistic evidence, some of it dating back to the eighteenth century. Writers' and travelers' impressions are sometimes insightful, as Alexis de Tocqueville's writings demonstrate. But on the whole, this kind of evidence is neither systematic nor reliable; for every brilliant insight, one can find scores of misperceptions. Worse still, even insights that were accurate some decades ago may be outmoded today, for culture changes. Stereotypes live on, however, long after they have ceased to accurately depict the real world.

In the following chapters, we will examine the results of interviews with representative national samples of the publics of the United States, Canada, and Mexico. We will not assume that what was true at one point in time holds true forever. Instead, we will compare results from cross-national surveys carried out in 1981 with the responses to the same questions in 1990 surveys.

This enables us to address another set of questions. We will not only ask, Do the basic values of Mexicans, Canadians, and Americans differ in significant ways? but also Are these differences growing larger over time or are the goals of North American peoples converging?

The possibility that the basic values of these publics may be changing is not a matter of idle speculation. A massive body of evidence indicates that, in at least some important respects, the basic values and goals of the publics of advanced industrial society *have* been changing, in a gradual but pervasive fashion. Let us examine this evidence.

CHANGING VALUES AMONG WESTERN PUBLICS

The basic values of the publics of advanced industrial societies have been undergoing a gradual intergenerational shift during the past several decades. Though given countries have shifted at varying rates, processes of economic and technological change seem to have had a generally similar impact across industrial societies.

The possibility of intergenerational value change was first explored by Inglehart (1971), who hypothesized that the basic value priorities of Western publics had been shifting from a materialist emphasis toward a postmaterialist one—from giving top priority to physical sustenance and safety, toward heavier emphasis on belonging, self-expression, and the quality of life. His investigation was guided by two key hypotheses:

1. *A scarcity hypothesis.* An individual's priorities reflect the socioeconomic environment: one places the greatest subjective value on those things that are in relatively short supply.

2. *A socialization hypothesis*. The relationship between socio-economic environment and value priorities is not one of immediate adjustment: a substantial time lag is involved for, to a large extent, one's basic values reflect the conditions that prevailed during one's preadult years.

The scarcity hypothesis is similar to the principle of diminishing marginal utility, and it suggests that the recent economic history of advanced industrial societies has significant implications. For these societies are historically exceptional: most of their population does *not* live under conditions of hunger and economic insecurity. This seems to have brought a gradual shift in which needs for belonging, self-expression, and an autonomous role in society became more prominent. Prolonged periods of prosperity tend to encourage the spread of postmaterialist values; economic decline seems to have the opposite effect.

But there is not a simple one-to-one relationship between economic level and the prevalence of postmaterialist values. These values reflect one's *subjective* sense of security, not one's economic level per se. While rich people tend to feel more secure than poor people, one's sense of security is also influenced by the cultural setting and social welfare institutions in which one is raised. Thus, the scarcity hypothesis must be supplemented with the socialization hypothesis.

One of the most pervasive concepts in social science is that a basic human personality structure tends to take shape by the time an individual reaches adulthood, and undergoes relatively little change thereafter.

Taken together, these two hypotheses generate a set of predictions concerning value change. First, while the scarcity hypothesis implies that prosperity is conducive to the spread of postmaterialist values, the socialization hypothesis implies that neither an individual's values nor those of a society as a whole will change overnight. For the most part, fundamental value change takes place as younger birth cohorts replace older ones in the adult population of a society. Consequently, after a period of sharply rising economic and physical security, one should find substantial differences between the value priorities of older and younger groups: they have been shaped by different experiences in their formative years.

This hypothesis was first tested in surveys carried out in 1970 with representative national cross sections of the publics of Great Britain, France, West Germany, Italy, The Netherlands, and Belgium. Samples of each public chose the goals they considered most important among a set of goals designed to tap economic and physical security, on one hand, or self-expression and the nonmaterial quality of life, on the other hand. Those whose top two priorities were given to the former goals were classified as pure *materialists;* those whose top priorities were given exclusively to the latter goals were classified as pure *postmaterialists.* Those who chose some combination of these goals were classified as *mixed* types.

We find the predicted skew by age group, as Figure 3.1 demonstrates. The pattern is similar in all six Western European countries included in the 1970 survey: among the older groups, materialists outnumber postmaterialists enormously; as we move to younger groups, the proportion of materialists declines and that of postmaterialists increases. Thus, among the oldest cohort, materialists outnumber postmaterialists by a ratio of more than twelve to one; among the youngest cohort, the bal-

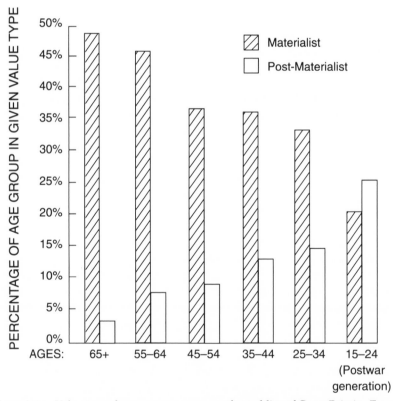

Figure 3.1. Value type, by age group, among the publics of Great Britain, France, West Germany, Italy, Belgium, and The Netherlands in 1970. *Source:* European Community Survey of February, 1970; based on original 4-item Materialist/Postmaterialist values battery. Reprinted from Inglehart (1990:76).

ance has shifted dramatically: Postmaterialists are about as numerous as materialists.

The age-related differences shown in Figure 3.1 are striking. But does this pattern reflect life cycle effects, birth cohort effects, or some combination of the two? The theory predicts that we will find birth cohort differences, but these differences between the priorities of young and old could reflect some life cycle effect. Does aging make one place ever-increasing emphasis on economic and physical security?

Fortunately, we now have a sufficient time series database to answer this question. The battery used to measure materialist/postmaterialist values has become a standard feature of surveys carried out in the European Community countries. Figure 3.2 traces the balance between materialists and postmaterialists within given birth cohorts from 1970 to 1993, using the pooled data from all six Western European nations (more than 235,000 interviews). Each cohort's position at a given time is calculated by subtracting the percentage of materialists in that cohort from the percentage of postmaterialists. Thus, the zero point on the vertical axis reflects a situation in which the two groups are equally numerous (this is where the cohort born in 1946–1955 was located in 1970). In this figure, the proportion of postmaterialists increases as we move up on the vertical axis; the proportion of materialists increases as we move down. If the age differences reflected a life cycle effect, then each of the

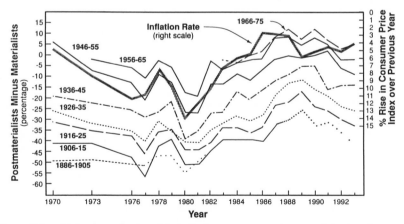

Figure 3.2. Cohort analysis with inflation rate superimposed (using inverted scale on right): Postmaterialists (%) minus materialists (%) in six West European societies, 1970–1993. *Source:* Based on combined weighted sample of European Community surveys carried out in West Germany, France, Britain, Italy, The Netherlands, and Belgium, in given years, using the four-item materialist/postmaterialist values index (N = 235,085).

cohort lines should move downward, toward the materialist pole, as we move from left to right across this twenty-three-year period.

We find no such downward movement. Instead, the younger birth cohorts remain more postmaterialist throughout the period from 1970 to 1993: given cohorts do *not* become more materialist as they age—indeed, most of these cohorts are actually a little *less* materialist at the end of this period than they were at the start. Some striking period effects are evident: there was a clear tendency for each cohort to dip toward the materialist pole during the major economic recession of the mid-1970s and again during the recession of the early 1980s (these effects are consistent with the theory, which links postmaterialist values with economic security). But these period effects are relatively transient; they disappear when economic conditions return to normal. In the long run, the values of a given birth cohort seem remarkably stable. Abramson and Inglehart (1995) carry out a detailed cohort analysis of these data, controlling for the effects of other variables such as education. They conclude that these age differences reflect a long-term process of intergenerational value change.

A great deal of population replacement has taken place since 1970. Are these demographic shifts reflected in the distribution of materialists and postmaterialists in Western Europe? Very much so. In 1970, materialists outnumbered postmaterialists overwhelmingly in all of these countries. But by 1993, in both The Netherlands and the United States, postmaterialists had become more numerous than materialists; in West Germany and Britain, the two groups were about equal; and in France, Belgium, and Italy, the balance had shifted markedly toward postmaterialist values. In 1970–1971, within the six Western European nations as a whole, materialists outnumbered postmaterialists by a ratio of almost four to one. By 1993, this ratio had fallen to four to three. Postmaterialists had become almost as numerous as materialists.

VALUE CHANGE IN NORTH AMERICA

Are the United States, Mexico, and Canada undergoing a process of value change similar to what is occurring in other Western countries? An affirmative answer to this question implies (1) that a meaningful materialist/postmaterialist dimension exists in each of these countries—in other words, that their publics polarize along this dimension, with some people consistently giving top priority to the goals of economic and physical security, while others consistently give priority to self-expression and the quality of life; and (2) that a gradual shift is taking place, with emphasis moving from the materialist goals to the postmaterialist ones.

An abundant body of evidence demonstrates that both propositions hold true for the United States (Inglehart 1977, 1990), but only fragmentary evidence is available for Mexico and Canada. The four-item values battery has been administered on at least one or two occasions in each country, but the full dimensional structure has not been examined, and long-term shifts have never been demonstrated. Because the Canadian socioeconomic situation is rather similar to that of the United States, it seems likely that the Canadian public may be undergoing a similar shift. The Mexican situation, however, is sufficiently different that it is uncertain whether its public would be undergoing the same process of cultural change.

On one hand, Mexico has experienced substantial economic growth during the past fifty years, growing at an impressive mean rate of 6.5 percent annually from 1941 to 1981—but with virtually no economic growth since 1982. Theoretically, the shift from materialist to post-materialist values results from rising levels of economic and physical security, which suggests that value change may be taking place in Mexico, though the negative economic situation of the past decade would tend to retard it. Other considerations also make it seem somewhat doubtful whether Mexico would be moving toward postmaterialism. Mexico's economic level is much lower in absolute terms than that of either the United States or Canada: while the United States had a per capita GNP of $22,240 in 1990, and Canada had one of $20,440, the Mexican level was only $3,030—about one-seventh the income of its North American neighbors. Moreover, the Mexican economy has experienced severe difficulties in recent years. This would lead us to expect fewer postmaterialists in Mexico than in the United States or Canada—if they are present at all. Let us examine the empirical evidence to see what the actual situation is.

Figure 3.3 shows the results of factor analyses of the 1990 World Values Survey data from the United States, Canada, and Mexico. Those goals that are chosen together appear near each other in Figure 3.3; those items that do *not* tend to be chosen together appear relatively far apart. As one can see at a glance, our respondents' choices tend to polarize into two distinct clusters: people *either* focus on the postmaterialist goals (shown in italics) *or* they emphasize the materialist goals (shown in bold face type). The results demonstrate that the materialist/postmaterialist dimension is meaningful in all three countries, for the response patterns are strikingly similar: *All six* of the materialist items (dealing with economic growth, a stable economy, fighting rising prices, maintaining order, strong defense forces, and the fight against crime) have negative polarity in all three countries; and all six of the post-materialist items have positive polarity in all three countries. This means that some respondents consistently give high priority to the former

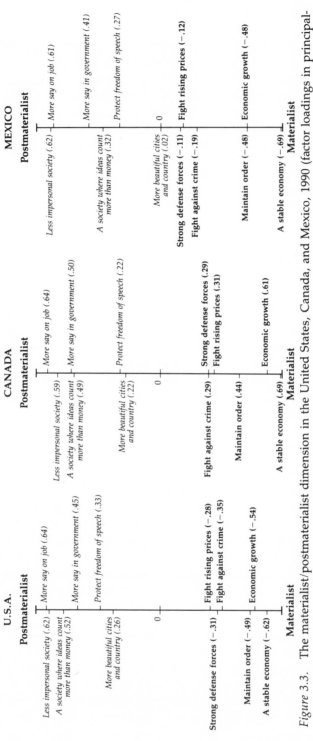

Figure 3.3. The materialist/postmaterialist dimension in the United States, Canada, and Mexico, 1990 (factor loadings in principal-component analysis). Source: Representative national samples of publics of the three respective countries, interviewed in May–June 1990 as part of the 1990 World Values Survey. Fieldwork carried out by the Gallup Organization (U.S.), *N* = 1839; Gallup-Canada, *N* = 1730; and by Centro de Estudios de Opinion Publica (CEOP), *N* = 1531.

group, while others consistently give high priority to the other group—in other words, some are materialists while others are postmaterialists. These 1990 U.S. results are almost identical to those from other U.S. surveys carried out in 1973, 1974, and 1981: the pattern is stable over time, indicating that this is an enduring axis of polarization among the American people.

Under closer examination, however, a significant cross-national difference emerges. Though the basic pattern in Mexico is similar to what we find in the United States and Canada, it has crystallized less sharply. In Mexico, the average loading on the materialist/postmaterialist dimension is weaker than in the other two countries (and weaker than those found throughout Western Europe). Some of the items have loadings so weak that they barely fall into the appropriate cluster; this is especially true of the priority given to "Trying to make our cities and countryside more beautiful" (abbreviated in Figure 3.3 as "More beautiful cities and country"), which has a neutral loading. This particular item has consistently shown relatively weak loadings on the materialist/postmaterialist dimension in surveys throughout Western Europe and the United States (though over time, it has gradually moved more clearly into the postmaterialist cluster). One might conclude that the responses of the Mexican public resemble those of other Western societies, but are at an earlier point on the trajectory. Postmaterialism exists in Mexico, but it seems to have emerged more recently and had less time to crystallize than in economically more developed countries. Accordingly, postmaterialist values have a somewhat different meaning in Mexico—with the environmental question in particular being less clearly linked with postmaterialism than it is elsewhere.

Are postmaterialist values more prevalent among the young in North America, as is the case in other industrial societies? Figure 3.4 shows one piece of evidence, based on the minimal four-item values battery. Though this gives a less accurate measure of the underlying dimension than the broader twelve-item materialist/postmaterialist values battery, it has been widely used, so we will examine its results. As Figure 3.4 demonstrates, the young are less likely than the old to emphasize materialist values in all three countries. In the United States, for example, among the oldest cohort surveyed in 1990, materialists are almost as widespread as postmaterialists, which produces an index of slightly above zero on the vertical axis; but in the youngest U.S. cohort, postmaterialists outweigh materialists by two to one (11 percent are materialists, and 22 percent are postmaterialists, with 66 percent falling into the various mixed categories, so we obtain a score of +11). There is a slight overall upward slope in Figure 3.4, but the correlations with age are weak in all three countries.

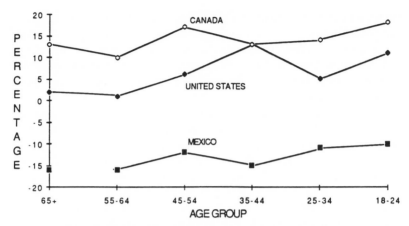

Figure 3.4. Materialist/postmaterialist, by age: the four-item battery. Vertical axis is the postmaterialist (%) minus materialist (%). The value in Mexico's 65+ group is missing because the Mexican sample contains fewer than 30 cases over 65 years of age. *Source:* 1990 World Values Survey.

Already in the earliest surveys on this topic, the United States (and Great Britain) showed age-related differences that were only half as large as those found in Germany, Italy, or France. This reflected the fact that the two English-speaking countries (together with Canada) had industrialized earlier than other countries, and were already, by the late nineteenth century, the richest nations in the world. This relative advantage continued through the 1940s: while Germany, France, and Italy were invaded and heavily devastated during World War II, Britain and the United States suffered much less.

Subsequently, however, the English-speaking countries showed much lower rates of economic growth than other Western countries. Germany, Italy, and France, in particular, experienced economic miracles that moved them ahead of Britain in per capita wealth. In countries like Germany or Italy, the younger generations have been raised under conditions radically different from those of the older cohorts; these differences between the formative experiences of younger and older groups are much greater than those found in the English-speaking countries— so the latter show smaller intergenerational value differences.

This phenomenon has been compounded by a tendency for age-related difference to shrink in *all* of these countries. As Figure 3.4 demonstrates, the two oldest (and by far most materialistic) cohorts had largely vanished from our samples by 1990. They were replaced by younger cohorts that were only a little less materialist than the other postwar cohorts (indeed, the very youngest cohort hardly differs at all from the next older one). Consequently, although a good deal of value change has taken place in the past twenty years, the pace of change is now slowing down.

Figure 3.5 gives another perspective on intergenerational value change in these countries. It is rather similar to Figure 3.2, but it is based on the twelve-item values battery, which provides a more accurate measure of the underlying values. As we reduce error in measurement, the correlation with age becomes stronger, particularly in the United States and Canada. In the United States, for example, we now find a pattern in which, among the oldest cohort, materialists outnumber postmaterialists by more than two to one—while among the youngest group, the two types are about equal. The index rises much more steeply than in Figure 3.4 (reflecting the fact that the correlation with age is about twice as strong as with the four-item values battery). In Canada, materialists clearly outnumber postmaterialists among the oldest cohort—but the situation is reversed among the youngest group, where postmaterialists are considerably more numerous than materialists; Accordingly, the index for Canada rises from −8 to +16 on the vertical axis. In Mexico, among the oldest group, materialists are 1.6 times more numerous than postmaterialists, but among the youngest group, the two types are equally numerous.

If our theory is correct, intergenerational population replacement should be producing a gradual shift toward postmaterialist values as

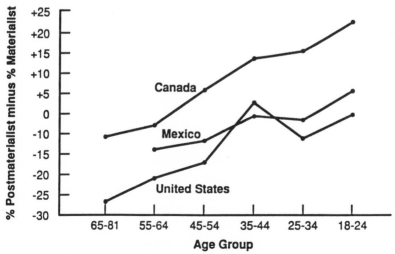

Figure 3.5. Values by age in North America. Scores of 0–2 are treated as materialist and 4–6 as postmaterialist. A score of 3 = mixed. The oldest group in Mexico contains fewer than 30 cases and is not shown.

younger (and more postmaterialist) cohorts replace older, more materialist ones in the adult population. Has this been taking place? As Figure 3.6 demonstrates, the answer is yes. In all three countries, we observe significant shifts in the balance between materialist and postmaterialist since 1981. By 1990, postmaterialists had become more numerous than materialists in both the United States and Canada. There was less of a shift in Mexico; even in 1990, materialists still outnumbered postmaterialists there by two to one, but a significant shift toward postmaterialist values had taken place. These shifts are all in the predicted direction, but the shifts in the United States and Canada are so large that they cannot be attributed to intergenerational population replacement alone. In these two countries, population replacement effects seem to have been compounded by period effects: the impact of rising prosperity during the 1980s moved in the same direction as the effects of population replacement from 1981 to 1990. Experiencing severe economic problems throughout most of the 1980s, Mexico has not had period effects that reinforced the effects of generational change. Nevertheless, it is clear that a shift toward postmaterialist values has been taking place in all three North American countries.

The speed of this transformation varies from country to country. Mexico shows a correlation between values and age that is only half as strong as that in the United States. Postmaterialist values have only begun to emerge in Mexico; though a materialist/postmaterialist axis of polarization is discernible in Mexico, it is less clearly crystallized than in other Western countries, and is a less important basis of sociopolitical cleavage. In view of the fact that Mexico has a much lower per capita income than the United States or Canada and in view of the stagnant economy Mexico experienced during the 1980s, this is precisely what our theory would lead us to expect: these findings demonstrate that the young are not automatically less materialistic than the old. The age differences emerge in advanced industrial societies as a consequence of the different formative experiences that shape older and younger cohorts.

At the time of the 1990 survey, the Mexican economy was beginning to regain some of the vigor it had shown in earlier decades. Mexico's joining the North American common market was expected to stimulate more rapid growth, but these expectations were disappointed in the short term. At present, the Mexican economy is undergoing a crisis. Nevertheless, we expect that Mexico will eventually enter the ranks of the advanced industrial societies. If this proves to be the case, then the impact of postmaterialist values should become an increasingly important factor in Mexican politics, reshaping parties and issues as they have already reshaped the politics of other Western countries.

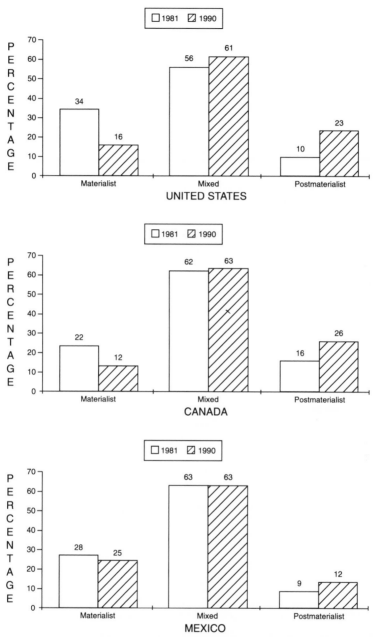

Figure 3.6. Materialist/postmaterialist values in North America: changes from 1981 to 1990 (distributions based on four-item index). Note: Because this battery was not asked in the United States in the 1981 World Values Survey, we use the results from the CPS 1980 National Election Study for the cross-time comparison in the United States. All other results are from the 1981 and 1990 World Values Surveys.

BROADER PATTERNS OF CULTURAL CHANGE

This change is part of a still broader cultural transformation that is
gradually changing the worldviews of Western publics. Throughout
most of history, most people have lived in the shadow of insecurity;
even today, a majority of the world's population faces real danger of
going hungry. But for the past several decades, an increasing share of
the world's population has lived in industrial societies in which the
threat of death from starvation has receded. Mean life expectancies have
risen dramatically in these countries. This change in formative experiences has given rise to changes that go well beyond the value shift we
have been discussing so far.

The rise of postmaterialism is only one aspect of a still broader process of cultural change that is reshaping the political outlook, religious
orientations, gender roles, and sexual mores of advanced industrial society. These changes are related to a common concern: the need for a
sense of security that religion and absolute cultural norms have traditionally provided. In the decades since World War II, the emergence of
unprecedentedly high levels of prosperity, together with the relatively
high levels of social security provided by the welfare state, have contributed to a decline in the prevailing sense of vulnerability. For the general
public, one's fate is no longer so heavily influenced by unpredictable
forces as it was in agrarian and early industrial society. This has been
conducive to the spread of orientations that place less emphasis on
traditional religious and cultural norms—especially insofar as these
norms conflict with individual self-expression.

There are two main reasons for the decline of traditional religious
social and sexual norms in advanced industrial societies. The first is that
an increasing sense of security brings a diminishing need for absolute
norms. Individuals under high stress need rigid, predictable rules. They
need to be sure of what is going to happen because their margin for error
is slender—an unexpected turn of events could be fatal. Postmaterialists
reflect the converse phenomenon: under conditions of relative security,
one can tolerate more diversity; one does not need the security of absolute rules that religious sanctions provide. Consequently, we would expect postmaterialists to accept cultural change more readily than others.

The second reason is that societal and religious norms usually have a
function. Such basic norms as "Thou shalt not kill" help restrict violence
to narrow, predictable channels. Without such norms, a society would
tend to tear itself apart. Many religious norms such as "Thou shalt not
commit adultery" or "Honor thy father and mother" are linked with
maintaining the family unit. This particular function has become less
crucial than it once was. As long as divorce threatens its children's

survival, society is apt to view divorce as intolerable. It threatens the long-term viability of society. Although the family was once the key economic unit, in advanced industrial society people's working life is now overwhelmingly outside the home and most education now takes place outside the family. Furthermore, the welfare state has taken over responsibility for sheer survival. Formerly, whether children survived depended on whether their parents provided for them; and parents depended on their children in old age. The family's life or death function has been softened by the rise of the welfare state. Today, the new generation can survive if the family breaks up. One-parent families and childless old people are far more viable under contemporary conditions than they once were.

Norms linked to the maintenance of the two-parent heterosexual family clearly are weakening, for a variety of reasons, ranging from the rise of the welfare state to the drastic decline of infant mortality rates (which means it is no longer necessary to produce four or five children in order to maintain the population). Together with the development of birth control technology, these changes have made it functionally feasible for these societies to relax some of the absolute norms that have governed family and sexual behavior for centuries.

We would expect younger cohorts to abandon traditional norms more readily than older groups, because the young are still relatively flexible. However, for the old, these norms have become part of an elaborate belief system that they began to build up during their early decades. Figure 3.7 indicates that this hypothesis holds true for a coherent set of norms spanning homosexuality, divorce, abortion, and prostitution. In all three countries, the older groups hold much less permissive attitudes toward each of these topics. These four attitudes are strongly intercorrelated: those who take a nonpermissive stand on one of them tend to take a similar stand on each of the other three questions as well. Also, the young are much more permissive than the old on all four topics. Thus, we can sum up the relationship between age and sexual permissiveness in general by using a composite index, as is done in Figure 3.7.

These results are based on the 1981 survey. The same questions were replicated in the 1990 survey and they show a similar pattern, with the old being far less permissive than the young, in all three countries. But we use the 1981 data here, because they serve as the basis for a prediction: Inglehart (1988, 1990) found strong differences between the values of young and old throughout the 1981 World Values Survey, and interpreted them as reflecting a pervasive process of intergenerational value change. If he was correct, this process should produce a coherent cultural shift from 1981 to 1990. In the present case, for example, we expect that as younger respondents, with more permissive values, replace old-

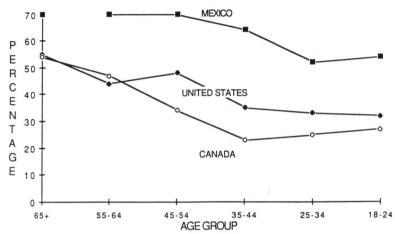

Figure 3.7. Sexual restrictiveness, by age group. Percentage saying that homosexuality, prostitution, divorce, and abortion are never or almost never permissible. On a scale from 1 to 10, where 1 means "never permissible" and 10
means "always permissible," these respondents give a mean rating of 2.25
to these four forms of behavior. The value in Mexico's 65+ group is missing
because the Mexican sample contains fewer than 30 cases over 65 years of
age. *Source:* 1981 World Values Survey.

er, less permissive ones in the adult population as a whole, we will find
an overall shift toward greater sexual permissiveness. Thus these results
from 1981 imply that our 1990 sample should show a higher level of
sexual permissiveness. We will test this prediction below, but first we
examine another aspect of the data.

As Figure 3.8 demonstrates, those who hold postmaterialist values
show markedly less sexual restrictiveness than those with materialist
values. This finding is far from self-evident, for nothing in the battery of
questions used to measure postmaterialist values has anything to do
with sexual norms. In face content, the two sets of variables are entirely
distinct. But as we have argued, they *do* share a set of common causes:
the relative security that has characterized the formative experiences of
the postmaterialists has also been conducive to more permissive views
concerning divorce, abortion, and homosexuality. There is not a one-to-
one relationship between the two sets of values. Some materialists have
puritanical values concerning sex, and some materialists are highly permissive. But on the whole, there is an astonishingly strong tendency for
postmaterialists to hold more permissive attitudes toward sexual behavior than do materialists. Coupled with the fact that both orientations are
more widespread among younger than older respondents, this suggests
that they are both part of a broader syndrome.

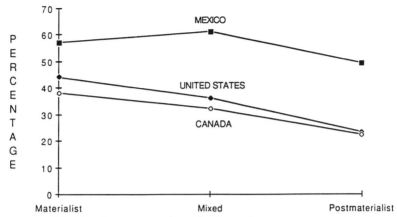

Figure 3.8. Sexual restrictiveness, by value type. Percentage saying that homosexuality, prostitution, divorce, and abortion are never or almost never permissible. On a scale from 1 to 10, where 1 means "never permissible" and 10
means "always permissible," these respondents give a mean rating of 2.25
to these four forms of behavior. Because these values were not measured in
the 1981 U.S. survey, we show the 1990 results for that country. *Source:* 1981
World Values Survey.

PREDICTABLE PATTERNS OF SOCIAL CHANGE

By itself, the fact that the young have different attitudes from the old
does not necessarily mean that any change is taking place: the age differences could simply reflect life cycle effects. But if we find sizable differences between the attitudes of young and old *and* these attitudes show a
consistent correlation with materialist/postmaterialist values, we then
have reason to believe that the age differences reflect an ongoing cultural shift, based on differences between the formative experiences of given
birth cohorts.

This is an important and unusual point. Successful prediction in the
social sciences is rare, but our theory of intergenerational value change
generates a set of systematic predictions, which we are now in a position
to test. These predictions apply only when a specific set of conditions is
present, but (as we will see) these conditions apply to a surprisingly
wide range of cases.

We predict that we will find gradual value shifts, in a predictable
direction, whenever a basic value (1) shows substantial differences
across age groups and (2) shows significant differences between materialists and postmaterialists in a consistent direction (that is, the postmaterialists differ from materialists in the same direction as the young

differ from the old). When both of these conditions are met, we predict that we will find a gradual shift from 1981 to 1990 toward the values espoused by the younger and more postmaterialist respondents.

This prediction is based on population replacement effects. The fact that a given attitude (sexual permissiveness, for example) is correlated with materialist/postmaterialist values is taken as an indicator that the age-related differences reflect differences in the degree of security different birth cohorts experienced during their formative years. We do not assume that people are becoming more permissive in their attitudes toward sexual behavior *because* they are postmaterialist, but because the two orientations share common causes.

Thus, if a given attitude varies across age groups but is unrelated to materialist/postmaterialist values, we would not predict that it will change over time: there is no indication that the age differences reflect differences in formative experiences—they may simply reflect life cycle effects. Conversely, if a given attitude is correlated with materialist/postmaterialist values, but not with age, no clear prediction is possible: there *might* be an intergenerational shift, in which the age relationship is concealed by life cycle effects superimposed on the generational differences. But in such cases, a one-shot survey does not enable one to discern what is happening—time series data are needed. Obviously, if an attitude is uncorrelated with either age or values, we would have no reason to predict changes in any specific direction.

Short-term economic events (or political or social events) might also have an impact on these attitudes, but there would be no reason to predict a systematic long-term shift. As Figure 3.2 indicates, short-term fluctuations or period effects can have an impact on the values of mass public even when a long-term intergenerational shift *is* occurring: the impact of current events is superimposed on the long-term trend at any given moment. This means that our predictions will not always come true: if period effects are sufficiently strong, they can neutralize the effects of intergenerational change. In the long run, however, our predictions should stand up fairly well. Though negative period effects will tend to conceal an underlying intergenerational shift, positive period effects will tend to magnify it. And in the long run, negative and positive period effects will tend to cancel each other out so that the underlying trend will become visible.

The period from 1981 to 1990 is not very long from the perspective of intergenerational population replacement, but it is long enough that at least moderate amounts of systematic change should become visible. We have found sizable differences between the sexual restrictiveness of young and old in all three countries; *and* these attitudes show a consistent correlation with materialist/postmaterialist values. Consequently, we predict a gradual shift toward the values of the young and post-materialists—that is, a decline in sexual restrictiveness.

Figure 3.9 confirms this interpretation, for it shows that from 1981 to 1990, sexually restrictive attitudes became significantly less widespread in all three countries—precisely as predicted. The absolute levels of permissiveness vary from country to country, with Mexico being the most restrictive society at both time points, and Canadian society the least restrictive one, both in 1981 and 1990. But the three countries seem to be moving on a common trajectory, with the U.S. public in 1990 taking approximately the same position that the Canadians held in 1981—and with Mexico showing particularly rapid changes. Though far less permissive than the U.S. public in 1981, the Mexican public had almost converged with the Americans by 1990.

These changes over time vary somewhat among French-speaking Canadians and English-speaking Canadians; and among blacks and whites in the United States. Each of these groups moved toward more permissive sexual norms from 1981 to 1990, but two groups showed particularly rapid changes: the Mexicans and the English-speaking Canadians. Obviously, intergenerational population replacement alone does not explain everything that happened, for some groups changed more rapidly than others. The impact of specific events, affecting some groups more than

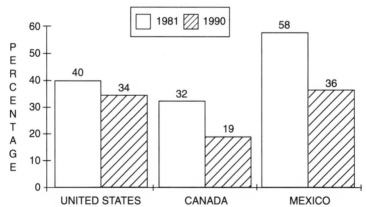

Figure 3.9. Sexual restrictiveness in 1981 vs. 1990. Percentage saying that homosexuality, prostitution, divorce, and abortion are never or almost never permissible. On a scale from 1 to 10, where 1 means "never permissible" and 10 means "always permissible," these respondents give a mean rating of 2.25 to these four forms of behavior. *Source:* 1981 and 1990 World Values Surveys.

others, seems to be superimposed on the component of change that is due to intergenerational population replacement.

How much of the observed change is due to population replacement and how much reflects period effects? We can make a rough estimate of the change due to population replacement over a ten-year period by simply removing the oldest cohort from our sample and replacing it with a new cohort at the youngest end. We can do the latter by simply doubling the size of the youngest cohort already in the sample: this assumes that the incoming youngest cohort will have the same values as the present youngest cohort. This is a conservative assumption, since so far the youngest cohorts have nearly always shown *more* permissive values than the next older cohorts. This procedure may tend to underestimate shifts, but it gives at least a rough first approximation of what to expect. Using this procedure with the 1981 data, we generate an estimated value shift that is right on target for the United States: our estimate for 1990 is that 35 percent of the U.S. sample will be "high" on sexual restrictiveness, and the figure that we actually observe is 34 percent. But the observed changes in both Canada and Mexico are considerably larger than those projected: in both countries, it seems that from 1981 to 1990 period effects were at work that *reinforced* the effects of population replacement. We will not attempt to explain the specific period effects that were at work here. For present purposes, our point simply is that the values of all these groups *did* move in the predicted direction.

This may be true of norms concerning sexual behavior, but does a pattern of intergenerational value change appear in other realms as well? The answer is yes—again and again. With impressive regularity, we observe a pattern in which a wide variety of basic social norms show age-related differences that are linked with materialist/postmaterialist values in a coherent fashion: the young differ from the old in the *same* direction as the postmaterialists differ from the materialists. Furthermore, these differences have predictive power: again and again, we observe shifts in prevailing values from 1981 to 1990 in which the values of the younger, more postmaterialistic cohorts become increasingly widespread over time.

This pattern is not absolute. We find one major exception to this rule: a domain in which the values espoused by the younger and more postmaterialistic types do *not* become more widespread over time, but instead became less widespread from 1981 to 1990. This is a significant phenomenon, which is discussed below. It reflects the fact that intergenerational population replacement is not the *only* factor that influences change—period effects are also at work. But on the whole, the prevailing pattern is one in which the age differences and the differences between the values of postmaterialists and materialists that we find in

1981 *do* generate accurate predictions of the direction in which values actually changed in all three countries from 1981 to 1990.

Figure 3.10 provides evidence concerning one such shift. Like most other variables analyzed in this chapter, this figure sums up the responses to a whole series of questions, rather than being based on a single item. Since these responses tend to be correlated in a systematic fashion, this not only enables us to summarize a number of responses at once, it also provides more reliable measures of the given values. In this case, the questions tapped the values people consider important in child rearing. Our respondents were told: "Here's a list of qualities which children can be encouraged to learn at home. Which, if any, do you consider to be especially important?"

They were shown a list of eleven qualities, ranging from good manners to unselfishness. Among these eleven items, five are of particular interest, for it turns out that people tend to emphasize *either* the goals of independence, imagination, and determination, *or* the goals of obedience and good manners. Those who choose one item in the first group are likely to emphasize the other items in that group as well, but they are *not* likely to emphasize obedience or good manners. It is easy to see why the two groups of goals tend to be emphasized by different people: Such values as independence, imagination, and determination reflect a high

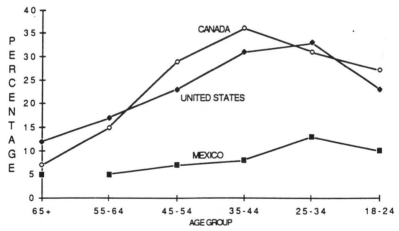

Figure 3.10. Emphasis on autonomy over obedience as child-rearing values, by age group. Percentage who mention independence, imagination, or determination more frequently than obedience or good manners as values that it is important to teach a child. The value in Mexico's 65+ group is missing because the Mexican sample contains fewer than 30 cases over 65 years of age. *Source:* 1981 World Values Survey.

value on encouraging a child to think for itself. They emphasize *autonomy*. Those who choose obedience and good manners are stressing an opposite set of virtues—conformity to established authority and respect for established social norms.[1]

As Figure 3.10 demonstrates, in all three countries the younger cohorts tend to emphasize autonomy more strongly than do the older groups. Longitudinal research carried out in the United States has demonstrated that from the 1950s to the 1980s, there was a gradual decline in the American public's emphasis on conformity to authority in child rearing, and there was a corresponding rise in emphasis on autonomy (Alwin 1986). This suggests that the age-related differences reflected in Figure 3.10 reflect a process of intergenerational value change (the alternative interpretation would be that they reflect a life cycle effect, by which one gradually becomes more authoritarian as one ages).

As we see from Figure 3.11, emphasis on independence, imagination, and determination seems to be linked with postmaterialist values. Though we lack 1981 data for the United States, in both Canada and Mexico the postmaterialists are about twice as likely to emphasize autonomy as are materialists. Since we know that there has been an intergenerational shift from materialist to postmaterialist values, this too suggests that a related shift may be taking place in child-rearing values.

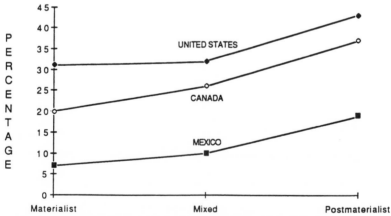

Figure 3.11. Emphasis on autonomy over obedience as child-rearing values, by value type. Percentage who mention independence, imagination, or determination more frequently than obedience or good manners as values that it is important to teach a child. Because these values were not measured in the 1981 U.S. survey, we show the 1990 results for that country. *Source:* 1981 World Values Survey.

As Figure 3.12 demonstrates, this does indeed seem to be the case. Shifts in the relative emphasis on independence, imagination, and determination versus obedience and good manners took place in all three countries from 1981 to 1990—with all three publics moving in the direction predicted by the correlations with age and postmaterialist values. In both the United States and Canada, emphasis on the three autonomy values showed a substantial jump during the past decade; but the change that took place in Mexico was even more dramatic. In 1981, the Mexicans were less than half as likely to emphasize autonomy values as were their North American neighbors. By 1990, they had almost caught up with them. Here again, Mexico seems to be undergoing particularly rapid change.

We do not believe that all of this change is due to intergenerational population replacement. In both the United States and Mexico, the observed shifts are larger than what population replacement alone would produce (in Canada, the shift is about right). And Mexican society, in particular, seems to be changing much more rapidly than the other two countries: it seems clear that other, nation-specific factors are also involved. These effects seem to be reinforcing population replacement. But again, in all three countries, an entire set of responses shows changes over time that move in the *direction* that is predicted from the relationship with age and materialist/postmaterialist values in 1981.

This pattern of intergenerational change is not limited to child-rearing

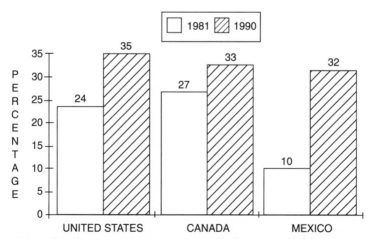

Figure 3.12. Emphasis on autonomy over obedience as child-rearing values, 1981 vs. 1990. Percentage who mention independence, imagination, or determination more frequently than obedience or good manners as values that it is important to teach a child. *Source:* 1981 and 1990 World Values Surveys.

values. It is part of a global change in attitudes toward authority that is reshaping the cultures of all three countries.

In 1981 and again in 1990, representative national samples of the Mexican, Canadian, and U.S. publics were asked: "Here is a list of various changes in our way of life that might take place in the future. Please tell me for each one, if it were to happen, whether you think it would be a good thing, a bad thing, or don't you mind?" One of the possible changes mentioned was "greater respect for authority."

As Figure 3.13 demonstrates, in all three countries, in 1981 the young were less likely than the old to say that greater respect for authority would be a good thing. The difference across age groups was relatively small in Mexico and quite steep in Canada. By itself, this does not prove anything about intergenerational change: one can easily imagine explanations for this pattern that would be based on a life cycle interpretation: the old are likelier than the young to *be* in positions of authority, so of course they will be more favorable to it. One could counter that most members of the oldest group (those sixty-five to eighty-five years of age at the time of the survey) are no longer in positions of authority, yet they are, on the whole, the ones who are *most* favorable to greater respect for authority. The debate could go on endlessly, but fortunately it does not need to: we are able to test the two competing interpretations.

Figure 3.14 shows a significant piece of supplementary evidence: the way these attitudes relate to materialist/postmaterialist values. As we

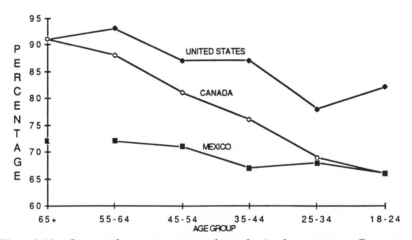

Figure 3.13. Support for greater respect for authority, by age group. Percentage saying greater respect for authority would be a good thing. The value in Mexico's 65+ group is missing because the Mexican sample contains fewer than 30 cases over 65 years of age. *Source:* 1981 World Values Survey.

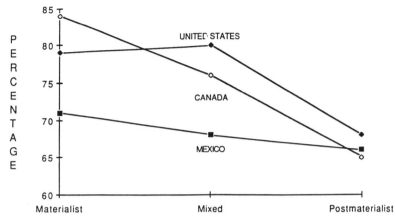

Figure 3.14. Support for greater respect for authority, by value type. Percentage saying greater respect for authority would be a good thing. Because these values were not measured in the 1981 U.S. survey, we show the 1990 results for that country. *Source:* 1981 World Values Survey.

would expect, in all three countries the postmaterialists are less likely to endorse greater respect for authority than are materialists. Again, the relationship is of modest strength in Mexico but quite pronounced in Canada, with the United States falling in between.

Once again, our two sets of indicators give converging signals, with the young differing from the old in the same direction that the post-materialists differ from the materialists. According to our model, this points to a process of intergenerational value change and predicts that support for greater respect for authority should gradually decline, from 1981 to 1990. Is our prediction correct?

As Figure 3.15 illustrates, the answer is yes. In all three countries, we find less emphasis on authority in 1990 than in 1981. The decline is relatively modest in Mexico (which also showed the weakest linkages with age group and value type in 1981). The change is largest in Canada (where the correlations with age and value type were strongest). Once again, our 1981 data generate an accurate prediction of the direction in which things changed during the following nine years. As the next chapters show, this is true of a great many other attitudes concerning very different topics including political participation, confidence in gov-ernment institutions, church attendance, and attitudes toward how businesses should be managed.

We do not find such a clear and regular pattern with all orientations, however. There is one striking exception. To examine this phenomenon, we turn to a battery of questions concerning the ties between parents

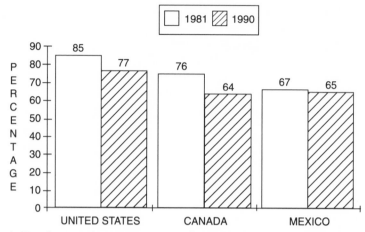

Figure 3.15. Support for greater respect for authority, 1981 vs. 1990. Percentage saying greater respect for authority would be a good thing. *Source:* 1981 and 1990 World Values Surveys.

and children. The text of these questions appears in the legend to Figure 3.16; they concern whether a child needs both a father and a mother, whether a woman needs children in order to be fulfilled, and a child's duties toward one's parents and parents' duties toward their children.

One's first impression from examining Figure 3.16 is that the younger cohorts place less emphasis on maintaining the traditional two-parent family with children than do the older ones. On the whole, this is true, and it fits well with a good deal of widely known evidence concerning the decline of the nuclear family: during the past few decades, there has been a striking decline in the number of children born per woman, a sharp rise in divorce rates, and an even sharper rise in the number of children raised by single mothers. The fact that the young place less emphasis on family ties than do older groups might be interpreted as evidence of an intergenerational change linked with this basic cultural shift.

But when we examine Figure 3.16 more closely, we find an interesting anomaly: In both the United States and Canada, the youngest cohort *does not* seem to follow the overall trend. Rather than placing less emphasis on family duty than the next older cohort, it emphasizes family values *more* heavily. This is a small enough deviation that it might be dismissed as due to sampling error, especially since in all three countries postmaterialists emphasize family duty more heavily than the materialists do (see Figure 3.17).

But this reversal of age-related trends in both the United States and

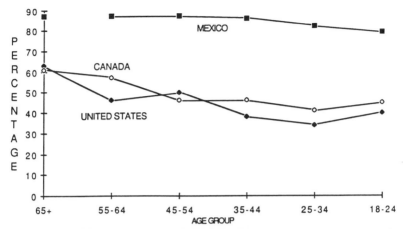

Figure 3.16. Emphasis on family duty, by age group. Percentage ranking high on Family Duty Scale. Percentage agreeing with the position in boldface type on at least 3 of the 4 following statements:

1. If someone says a child needs a home with both a father and a mother to grow up happily, would you tend to **agree** or disagree?
2. Do you think that a woman **has to have children in order to be fulfilled** or is this not necessary?
3. With which of these two statements do you tend to agree? (A) **Regardless of what the qualities and faults of one's parents are, one must always love and respect them.** (B) One does not have a duty to respect and love parents who have not earned it by their behavior and attitudes.
4. Which of the following statements best describes your views? (A) **Parents' duty is to do their best for their children, even at the expense of their own well-being.** (B) Parents have a life of their own and should not be asked to sacrifice their own well-being for the sake of their children.

The value in Mexico's 65+ group is missing because the Mexican sample contains fewer than 30 cases over 65 years of age. *Source:* 1981 World Values Survey.

Canada becomes all the more interesting when we examine Figure 3.18. For we find that in both the United States and Canada, there was an *increase*, rather than a decrease in emphasis on family duty from 1981 to 1990. The rise is modest in both countries, but it runs counter to the trends that would be predicted by most of the evidence in Figures 3.16 and 3.17. Only the Mexican public moves in the expected direction from 1981 to 1990, with a sizable *decline* in emphasis on family duties.

The pattern here is complex. In contrast with the consistent pattern found with most age-related variables, the increase over time did *not* move in the same direction as the trend across age groups (at least not in

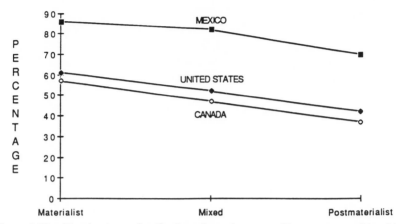

Figure 3.17. Emphasis on family duty, by value type. Percentage ranking high on Family Duty Scale. Percentage agreeing with the position in boldface on at least 3 of the 4 statements cited in Figure 3.16. Because these values were not measured in the 1981 U.S. survey, we show the 1990 results for that country. *Source:* 1981 World Values Survey.

the United States and Canada). The observed anomalies are small. Both the rise in emphasis on family duty that we find from 1981 to 1990 for the United States and Canada *and* the reversal in the age pattern for those two countries are small enough that either (or both) could be attributable to sampling error. But they are also consistent with the interpretation

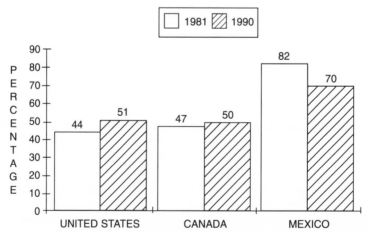

Figure 3.18. Emphasis on family duty, 1981 vs. 1990. Percentage ranking high on Family Duty Scale. Percentage agreeing with the position bold on at least 3 of the 4 statements cited in Figure 3.16. *Source:* 1981 and 1990 World Values Surveys.

that the prevailing trend for several decades *has* been toward declining emphasis on family values, but that this trend is now leveling off and may be reversing itself. After all, no trend can continue forever. De-emphasis on the family may have moved about as far as it can: the nuclear family may still have a vital function to fulfill.

Our failures in prediction may be just as significant as our successes. The very fact that our model usually does accurately predict the direction in which changes moved from 1981 to 1990 makes the clear-cut reversal of patterns that we find for both the United States and Canada in 1990 particularly interesting. We suspect it may indicate a turning point in the decline of a sense of family duty (if it does, then Mexico—which showed much higher levels in both 1981 and 1990—has not yet reached that point). Throughout advanced industrial society, the past few decades have been characterized by a striking decline in birth rates, a rise in divorce rates, a decline in marriage rates, and a rise in the number of single-person households. All these have been seen as indicators of a breakdown of the traditional family unit.

In purely economic terms, the necessity of the family unit undoubtedly *has* become less crucial. But there are certain psychological functions that the family unit fills and that thus far no other institution seems able to fill equally well. It is too early to say whether the reversal of expectations that we find in Figure 3.18 represents a turning point in the decline of family ties, but it seems to be a possibility worth considering.

Now let us turn to another cluster of attitudes on which the evidence is somewhat mixed: a group of attitudes that we refer to as "civil permissiveness." This cluster involves attitudes toward buying stolen goods, driving a stolen car, accepting a bribe, and threatening workers on strike. Like the clusters of attitudes that make up our other indices, attitudes toward these four kinds of behavior tend to go together. Consequently, we have used them to construct the civil permissiveness index that is analyzed here.

To avoid burying the reader in excessive detail, from this point on we will usually not present figures showing the exact relationship between the dependent variable (civil permissiveness, in this case) and age and materialist/postmaterialist values. The reader is by now familiar with the fact that many variables show coherent relationships with both age and values, in which the attitudes of the young differ from those of the old in the same way as the postmaterialists differ from the materialists. We will simply ask the reader to take our word for it that civil permissiveness is one more variable that fits this pattern, though with some nuances.

The young are more permissive than the old in all three countries, as was true with attitudes toward sexual behavior, and the postmaterialists tend to have slightly higher levels of civil permissiveness than do materialists. Here, the pattern is much less clear-cut than it was with sexual permissiveness. Canadian postmaterialists are slightly higher on civil permissiveness than are the materialists in that country, but the difference is much smaller than the one linked with sexual permissiveness. In Mexico, the postmaterialists are actually less permissive than the materialists. While 1981 data on values are not available for the United States, 1990 data indicate that U.S. postmaterialists are slightly more permissive than materialists.

The age group pattern suggests that we should find a shift toward greater civil permissiveness from 1981 to 1990, but only in Canada is there a clear relationship with materialist/postmaterialist values.

As Figure 3.19 demonstrates, the pattern of changes over time is also ambiguous. In the United States and Canada, we find some shift toward greater civil permissiveness from 1981 to 1990, but the change is small. In Mexico, on the other hand, the change is large—but it cannot be attributed to intergenerational population replacement: most of it seems to reflect nation-specific-period effects (as we will see in Chapter 4, during the late 1980s there was a sharp decline in trust in government and a sharp rise in mass politicization in Mexico—apparently coupled with rising opposition to the continued dominance of Mexican politics by the PRI).

These findings indicate that the shift toward sexual permissiveness that we observed earlier is *not* a shift toward permissiveness in gener-

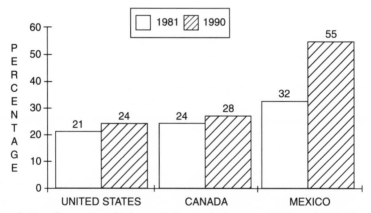

Figure 3.19. Percentage high on civil permissiveness, 1981 vs. 1990. Those saying it is sometimes permissible to do two or more of the following: (1) buy stolen goods, (2) drive a stolen car, (3) accept a bribe, (4) threaten workers who strike. *Source:* 1981 and 1990 World Values Surveys.

al—at least not in the United States and Canada. We are not dealing with a nihilistic trend toward the feeling that "anything goes" (including theft and bribes). Instead, the trend toward greater sexual permissiveness reflects increasing acceptance of certain specific forms of behavior linked with individual self-expression. They point toward decriminalization of what is sometimes referred to as "victimless crime." Recent changes in Mexico seem very distinctive, but both the United States and Canada remain nonpermissive toward this cluster of attitudes.

To conclude this chapter, let us examine a set of attitudes that, for most of our respondents, may well be the most central and important component of their worldview: their attitudes toward religion. Whether or not one believes in God is a powerful predictor of a wide range of other orientations. Religion has remarkably broad ramifications. More than forty of the questions included in the 1981 survey show strong correlations with a religiosity dimension. The four most sensitive indicators of this dimension are (1) whether the respondents say that God is important in their lives (rated on a ten-point scale), (2) whether they describe themselves as religious, (3) whether they say they get strength and comfort from religion, and (4) whether they sometimes pray. These attitudes are strongly correlated with age. In all three countries, the young place far less emphasis on religion than do the older respondents. In the United States and Canada, the members of the oldest cohort are about twice as likely to rank high on religiosity as are the members of the youngest cohort; in Mexico, the differences are almost equally striking.

The age-linked differences connected with religiosity are stronger and more consistent than those found with attitudes toward family duty or civil permissiveness. Religiosity is also linked with materialist/postmaterialist values in the expected direction: in all three countries, postmaterialists place less emphasis on religion than do materialists. Here, the indicators all point in the same direction. As Figure 3.20 demonstrates, we find precisely those changes over time that these correlations with age and values predict. In all three countries, there was a decline in religiosity from 1981 to 1990. The change was slight in the United States, but sizable in both Canada and Mexico.

This observed decline in religiosity confirms our predictions, but it tends to contradict a thesis long upheld by some eminent sociologists of religion: Andrew Greeley (1972) has argued that there is no evidence of a long-term decline in mass attachment to religion. Greeley bases his case mainly on evidence from the United States, and he mainly relies on church attendance statistics to buttress his argument.

Overall, we find rather convincing evidence of a long-term decline in religiosity among Western societies, but the data examined thus far are based on subjective orientations toward religion and not on church at-

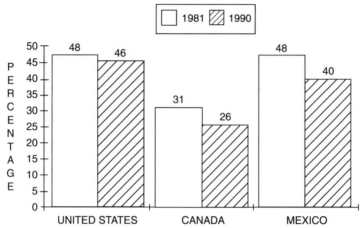

Figure 3.20. Religiosity in North America, 1981 vs. 1990. Percentage ranking importance of God in their lives at 10 on a scale from 1 = not important at all, to 10 = very important; *and* who also describe themselves as religious people, say they get strength and comfort from religion, and that they sometimes pray. *Source:* 1981 and 1990 World Values Surveys.

tendance. It is conceivable that inward feelings of devoutness might be gradually disappearing, but outward manifestations such as church attendance were persisting largely unchanged. After all, church attendance is partly a social ritual that does not necessarily reflect one's inward state. To some extent, people attend church in order to meet their friends and neighbors, to hear the music, or to observe social traditions that have become largely secular.

To what extent are attitudes and behavior on the same trajectory? Our 1981 surveys show that, in all three countries, church attendance rates were substantially lower among the young than among the old. These age differences were paralleled by consistent differences across value types: Postmaterialists attend church less frequently than do materialists. This suggests that we can*not* count on a given cohort to become more faithful in their church attendance as they grow older: The age differences may reflect different formative experiences, which have left the younger generations with a weaker attachment to religion. An old adage has it that there are no atheists in foxholes. More generally, we would argue that people who live in danger and insecurity have a powerful need for the absolute certainty provided by religion. Conversely, those raised under conditions of historically unprecedented prosperity, reinforced by the welfare state, feel less need for traditional religion than those who have lived through devastating wars and the threat of starvation.

Our 1981 data predict declines in church attendance from 1981 to 1990. As Figure 3.21 demonstrates, we find confirming evidence in all three countries. The change is very modest in the United States: it falls well within the range of normal sampling error, and would not be worth mentioning if it did not occur in the broader context of confirming indications found here. In both Canada and Mexico, on the other hand, we find relatively large declines in church attendance.

Greeley was right, as far as his evidence goes: if we limit ourselves to evidence concerning church attendance only and if we deal only with data from the United States, then there are only faint signs of a decline in mass attachment to religion. Examined in broader perspective, however, there is evidence of a pervasive process of secularization. Insofar as religion mainly fills the function of providing reassurance against fears rooted in economic and physical insecurity, it seems to be declining and is likely to decline further.

But providing a sense of security in an insecure world is not the only function of religion. Historically, it has also provided answers to the questions, Where are we going? Where do we come from? and Why are we here? In modern times, people have increasingly turned to the physical sciences or to ideologies such as Marxism for answers to these questions. Today, apparently, those who turn to religion are mainly driven by a sense of insecurity. The emergence of advanced industrial society and the rise of the welfare state have made this a dwindling base for recruitment. But, at the same time, we would expect the shift toward postmaterialist values to bring a growing concern for the meaning and

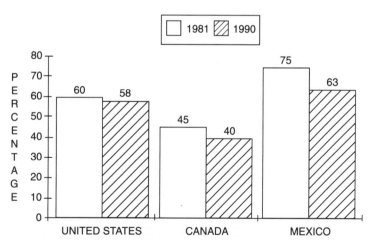

Figure 3.21. Percentage attending church at least once a month, 1981 vs. 1990. *Source:* 1981 and 1990 World Values Surveys.

purpose of life. Theoretically, these are prototypically postmaterialist concerns. Moreover, M. Inglehart, McIntosh, and Pacini (1990) have shown that although postmaterialists are less likely to hold traditional religious beliefs than are those with mixed or materialist values, they are *more* likely to emphasize "religious seeking" (cf. Kotejin 1988). The 1981 World Values Survey data confirm this interpretation. In each nation, our respondents were asked, "How often, if at all, do you think about the meaning and purpose of life?" The responses are related to value types in the three North American countries.

Though postmaterialists are less likely to say they believe in God, in virtually every society for which we have data, they are significantly *more* likely to say that they spend time thinking about the meaning and purpose of life. This holds true *despite* the fact that older people are more likely to say they do so than are younger ones (and the postmaterialists, of course, tend to be young). It seems likely that this reflects a life cycle effect: the old are more apt to spend time thinking about the meaning of life because they are nearing the end of their lives, not because they were born at an earlier point in history. If this is the case, then we apparently have a life cycle effect superimposed on a generational change, suppressing the age relationship. If so, we would expect the spread of postmaterialist values to bring a growing tendency for people to spend time thinking about the meaning and purpose of life. This is precisely what we find, as Figure 3.22 demonstrates.

The change from 1981 to 1990 is only slight in the United States, but in both Canada and Mexico we find strong increases in the percentage of the public who "often" think about the meaning and purpose of life.

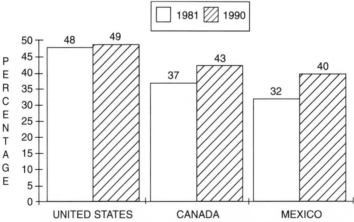

Figure 3.22. Percentage who "often" think about the meaning and purpose of life, 1981 vs. 1990. *Source:* 1981 and 1990 World Values Surveys.

As long as most churches base their appeal on the need for absolute, predictable rules, their decline is likely to continue. Conceivably, religion could also respond to needs that seem to be becoming more salient, helping provide a sense of the meaning and purpose of life—but it has not yet adapted to this task in a world where scientific explanations command more authority than do traditional formulations, devised in pastoral and agrarian societies.

CONCLUSION

As we have seen, some of the most basic values of the peoples of the United States, Canada, and Mexico are gradually changing. What is the overall pattern? On the whole, the three publics seem to be moving in parallel—they are on a common trajectory, changing in the same direction. Earlier assumptions that "the United States only shows Canada the image of her own future" (Horowitz 1978) seem unrealistic in the light of these findings. In many ways, Canada seems to be ahead of the United States, though moving in the same direction. The overall pattern is not one in which all three are converging toward a common model, which is the United States. What we seem to be witnessing is neither divergence nor Americanization, but a complex process of modernization that is transforming all three societies in a broadly similar fashion.

NOTE

1. This battery of questions uses a "grab bag" format: the respondent is shown a list and is free to choose as many alternatives as he or she likes. Such questions are very sensitive to how aggressively the interviewer encourages the respondent to give additional choices, so they tend to be unreliable for cross-national comparisons: in one country the fieldwork staff may elicit only two or three mentions per respondent, while in another country they may elicit six or seven choices per respondent. To control for this problem, in constructing our index we do *not* sum up the raw scores; instead, we calculate the relative *balance* between two contrasting types of choices.

4

Declining Deference to Authority and Rising Citizen Activism

Political values, as well as social values, are changing in North America. The preceding chapter presented evidence of widespread change in social norms. This chapter examines systematic intergenerational changes in political attitudes and behavior. A long-term shift is making the publics of all three North American societies more likely to act in autonomous, elite-challenging ways.

Confidence in established political and societal institutions is eroding, but the participant potential of the American, Canadian, and Mexican publics is gradually rising. Here, as with most of the changes examined in the preceding chapter, the three publics seem to be moving on a common trajectory. With many of these changes, either the Canadians or the Americans lead, but the Mexican public is moving on the same trajectory and generally at a faster pace—the net result being a tendency toward convergence.

The changes we find are profoundly important. They consist of two related shifts: (1) the erosion of institutional authority, and (2) the rise of citizen intervention in politics. Established institutions that have shaped Western society for generations are losing their authority over the average citizen. Public confidence is declining, not only in key governmental institutions such as parliament (Congress), police, civil service, and armed forces, but also in churches, educational systems, and the press. There is even evidence of a weakening sense of attachment to that most basic of all Western institutions, the nation-state itself.

Evidence of such changes has usually been attributed to the fact that the specific government in office at the time was less honest or effective than previous governments. And there is little doubt that unpopular governments *do* evoke less confidence than popular ones. But we believe that a long-term component is involved here, and not just the fluctuations linked with specific officeholders. The decline of trust in government is by now a well-known theme in American politics. Starting in the mid-1960s, a steep decline took place in the American public's feeling that it could trust the government in Washington (Miller 1974). This decline leveled off in recent years and has even shown some recovery, but it has never returned to the high levels registered in the 1950s and early 1960s.

This phenomenon is by no means limited to the United States. In Canada, for example, the popularity level of Canada's Prime Minister Mulroney dropped to 15 percent in 1990—the lowest level ever recorded in Canadian history—and his successors have had a difficult time in holding the country together. In Mexico, the Institutional Revolutionary Party (or PRI), which under various names has dominated Mexican politics since 1929, winning 94 percent of the presidential vote as recently as 1976, was barely able to win 50 percent of the vote in the presidential elections of 1988. Though the party made a partial recovery in the 1993 elections, it is currently experiencing immense political and economic difficulties. By 1995, President Zedillo's approval level had fallen to 15 percent. It is not just specific political leaders or specific parties that are losing the public's confidence. We find a pervasive tendency toward a loss of confidence in *all* established institutions. Moreover, this tendency appears consistently in several countries (and not just in one specific setting): we seem to be dealing with something structural, and not simply the consequences of the ineptness (or charisma) of whoever currently holds office.

Short-term fluctuations in these variables will certainly continue to occur. After the Gulf War, for example, the U.S. public's confidence in the military showed a spectacular resurgence, moving it far above any other institution, but this was probably an isolated anomaly. The evidence examined in this chapter suggests that we are witnessing an enduring trend that is weakening the authority of established institutions, with the authority of governmental institutions undergoing the most substantial erosion of all.

Broadly speaking, this erosion of political authority can be traced to some of the same factors that have been examined in the previous chapter. It has often been observed that in time of national danger the public tends to seek the security of strong leaders and strong institutions. Thus, during the traumatic insecurity of the Great Depression a wave of upheavals took place in which newly established democracies in Italy, Germany, Hungary, and Spain gave way to the rule of such authoritarian leaders as Mussolini, Hitler, Horthy, and Franco. Even in the United States, a country with deep-rooted democratic institutions, the American people rallied behind Franklin Delano Roosevelt, a strong leader who exercised exceptional powers and was reelected for an unprecedented four terms.

Long-enduring security may pave the way for the reverse phenomenon: gradually, the public sees less need for the discipline and self-denial demanded by strong governments and other social institutions. A postmaterialist emphasis on self-expression and self-realization becomes increasingly central. There are potential dangers in this evolution, such as the possibility that societal institutions will become too atrophied to cope with a national emergency if one should emerge. But there are positive aspects as well. We find a declining sense of nationalism, which bodes well for the future evolution of international cooperation, and for a potential North American free-trade zone in particular. In the very long term, it may even open the way for world government. Moreover, the erosion of state authority has been accompanied by a rising potential for citizen intervention in politics. Partly this is due to a shift in values, with a weakening emphasis on the goals of economic and physical security, which favor strong authorities; but an equally important precondition favoring rising citizen intervention is the long-term rise in educational levels and in mass political skills that have characterized all industrial societies. This process has been described as "cognitive mobilization" (Inglehart 1977).

The institutions that mobilized mass political participation in the late nineteenth and early twentieth century—labor union, church, and mass political party—were hierarchical organizations in which a small number of leaders or bosses led masses of disciplined troops. These institutions were effective in bringing large numbers of newly enfranchised citizens to the polls in an era when universal compulsory education had just taken root and the average citizen had a low level of political skills. But while these elite-directed organizations could mobilize large numbers, they produced only a relatively low *level* of participation, rarely going beyond mere voting.

By itself, voting is not necessarily a very effective way for citizens to exert their control over national decisions. It can be, and often is, manipulated by elites. An extreme example is the people's democracies of the Communist world, which regularly attained far higher levels of electoral participation than did any liberal democracy—in an institutional framework that kept real decision-making entirely in the hands of the elites. Voting *can* be an effective step toward empowering the citizens—but it is not a very discriminating one. Essentially, it means that the citizens get to choose one set of elites or another, and then let them make the actual decisions until the next election.

A newer elite-directing mode of participation is emerging that expresses the individual's preferences with far greater precision than the old. It is issue oriented, and based on ad hoc groups rather than on established bureaucratic organizations, and it aims at effecting specific policy changes rather than simply supporting the leaders of a given group. This mode of participation requires relatively high skill levels.

Let us take one's formal education as an indicator of political skills. On this scale, sheer literacy seems sufficient to produce voting. Most citizens of Western democracies reached this threshold generations ago. But while mere literacy may be sufficient to produce high rates of voting, for citizens to take the initiative at the national level seems to require at least a secondary education, and probably a university education.

The rise of postindustrial society or information society (Bell 1973, 1976) leads to a growing potential for citizen participation in politics. Increasingly, not only one's formal education but one's job experience as well develop politically relevant skills. The traditional assembly-line worker produced material objects, working in a hierarchical system that required very little autonomous judgment. Workers in the service and information sectors deal with people and concepts; operating in an environment where innovation is crucial, they need autonomy for the use of individual judgment. Innovation cannot be prescribed from above. Accustomed to working in less hierarchical decision structures in their job life, people in the information and service sectors are relatively likely to have both the skills and the inclination to take part in decision-making in the political realm as well.

As cognitive mobilization proceeds, traditional kinds of organizations become progressively less effective. With a wide range of alternative channels of information and input, people rely less and less on permanent organizational networks such as labor unions, churches, and old-line urban political machines. Both union membership rates and church attendance have been falling in most Western countries, and traditional political party ties have also been weakening. This can have the effect of *depressing* voting turnout, which is heavily dependent on elite-directed mobilization, and may require little or no cognitive response to current issues. At the same time, however, elite-challenging types of participation, aimed at influencing specific policy decisions, are becoming more widespread.

The iron law of oligarchy is weakening. Inglehart (1990) presents longitudinal survey evidence that throughout advanced industrial society, Western publics are becoming more politicized and more articulate. For example, in eight of the nine European Community countries surveyed regularly since 1973, the frequency with which people discuss politics rose gradually but steadily from 1973 to 1987 (Inglehart 1990:355). Similar evidence has been found for Canada (Nevitte 1990).

Political participation remained dependent on permanently established organizations as long as most of the people with bureaucratic skills held positions within these institutions. But today, ad hoc organizations can be brought into being virtually overnight, because the public now contains an unprecedentedly large proportion of nonelites who nevertheless have high levels of political skills. A balance between elites and mass that was upset centuries ago is in the process of being redressed.

A determined and cohesive political elite can repress demands for more autonomy and broader participation in decision-making, but it does so at the risk of economic and political stagnation. During the long years of Brezhnev's reign, precisely this was happening in the Soviet Union, with a resulting decline in productivity and economic growth and a general deterioration of morale. Western societies, on the other hand, have repeatedly been forced to respond to various waves of demands for increased mass participation in politics. These demands led to the enfranchisement of the working class around the turn of the century, followed by the movement for women's suffrage, the birth of the welfare state, and a wave of activism in the 1960s that resulted in the extension of civil rights to blacks in the southern United States and the extension of the vote to eighteen-year-olds throughout Western countries. In the 1960s, Canadian political activism rose sharply, particularly in Quebec, where public mobilization was so striking that it has been described as a quiet revolution. The 1960s were also a time of rising political activism in Mexico, when public opposition to the dominant PRI began to manifest itself more openly than in the past. The process of cognitive mobilization continues today, with such contemporary phenomena as the environmentalist movement, the women's movement, and the Gay Liberation movement.

DECLINING CONFIDENCE IN ESTABLISHED INSTITUTIONS

Let us turn to some evidence from the 1981 and 1990 surveys, to demonstrate the claims we have just laid out. Figure 4.1 shows the percentages of respondents who, in 1981, expressed "quite a lot" of confidence in *each* of the following groups in their country: (1) the armed forces, (2) the police, (3) parliament (or Congress), and (4) the civil service.

Ratings of these four groups tend to go together in all three countries: that is, those who express high levels of confidence in their country's civil service also tend to express high confidence in their country's parliament, police, and armed forces; those who have little confidence in one tend to have little confidence in the others. Consequently, we com-

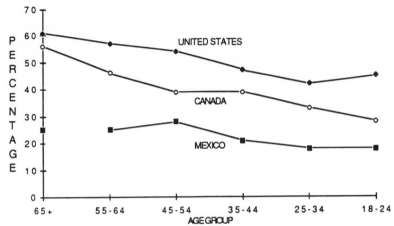

Figure 4.1. Percentage expressing "high" confidence in government institutions, by age group. Respondents were asked how much confidence they had in their country's (a) armed forces, (b) police, (c) parliament, and (d) civil service. Shown above are the percentages with an average score of 2 or lower, where 1 = "a lot," 2 = "quite a lot," 3 = "not very much," and 4 = "no confidence at all." *Source:* 1981 World Values Survey.

bine ratings for each of these institutions into one broader and more reliable index of confidence in the governmental institutions of one's country.

As Figure 4.1 makes clear, the American public expresses slightly higher levels of confidence in its governmental institutions than does the Canadian, and *much* higher levels than those indicated by the Mexican public. These cross-national differences seem to reflect objective realities: almost anyone familiar with Mexican political institutions would probably agree that they provide relatively little reason to *have* confidence in them. But for present purposes, the key point to be drawn from this figure is the fact that, in all three countries, the old express markedly higher levels of confidence than do the young. The age-related effects are remarkably consistent.

Could these age-related differences be a symptom of a generational change, similar to what we found in the previous chapter? We suspect that it is—and this inference is strengthened by the fact that postmaterialists tend to register lower levels of confidence in these institutions than do materialists. The Canadian data show this pattern clearly. The 1981 Mexican data are ambiguous and 1981 data on values are not available for the United States. The materialist/postmaterialist battery *was* included in the 1990 U.S. survey, however, and postmaterialists in the United States show lower levels of confidence in government institutions than materialists. Moreover, though the 1981 results from Mexico are ambiguous, the 1990 results are in the expected direction. Overall, postmaterialists tend to show less confidence in government than do materialists.

These findings are consistent with our argument that a sense of insecurity tends to motivate support for strong institutions—and for strong political authority in particular. Having experienced a relatively high sense of economic and physical security throughout their formative years, postmaterialists feel less need for strong authority than do materialists. Moreover, postmaterialists place relatively strong emphasis on self-expression—a value that inherently conflicts with the authority patterns of hierarchical bureaucratic organizations.

The familiar conjunction of age-related differences, together with value-related differences, points to the possibility of a shift over time, toward the outlook of the younger and more postmaterialist respondents. Do we find it? As Figure 4.2 demonstrates, the answer is yes. In all three countries, we find lower levels of confidence in government institutions in 1990 than those that existed in 1981. The decline is relatively modest in Mexico, where both the age-related and the value-related differences in 1981 were relatively small. But the Mexican public's confidence in government institutions was already so low in 1981 (with only 20 percent expressing confidence) that there was little room for it to drop lower. In fact, it did decline somewhat, and in 1990 only 18 percent expressed confidence. This was remarkably low in comparison with U.S. or Canadian levels of confidence in government—or in comparison

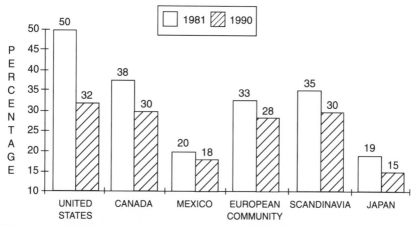

Figure 4.2. Percentage expressing "high" confidence in government institutions, 1981 vs. 1990. (See legend to Figure 4.1.) *Source:* 1981 and 1990 World Values Surveys.

with Mexican trust in nongovernmental institutions. The decline is sizable in Canada, and even more so in the United States, where the proportion expressing high levels of confidence fell from 50 percent in 1981 to only 32 percent in 1990. The detailed pattern of how the ratings for each of the respective groups changed from 1981 to 1990 is shown in Table 4.1.

The data tell a similar story concerning confidence in *non*governmental institutions. Based on ratings of churches, educational institutions, the legal system, and the press, the index used here reflects another cluster of empirically related responses. Again, in all three countries we find the young expressing lower levels of confidence in these institutions than do the old; and we find postmaterialists manifesting lower levels of confidence than materialists.

Once again, we find the symptoms of an intergenerational shift that seems to reflect the higher levels of economic and physical security that shaped the formative years of the younger cohorts, and once again, we find that the data from 1981 enable us to predict the changes that take place from 1981 to 1990. In both the United States and Canada, we find significant declines in levels of confidence registered for nongovernment

Table 4.1. Confidence in Government Institutions in 1981 vs. 1990[a]

	1981	1990
1. Armed Forces		
U.S.	36	29
Canada	19	11
Mexico	21	9
2. Police		
U.S.	27	21
Canada	30	24
Mexico	12	7
3. Congress/Parliament		
U.S.	14	8
Canada	8	6
Mexico	10	6
4. Civil Service		
U.S.	16	12
Canada	8	6
Mexico	8	4

Source: 1981 and 1990 World Value Surveys.
[a] Percentage expressing "a lot" of confidence.

institutions, as Figure 4.3 demonstrates. The Mexican data show little change from 1981 to 1990: here again, the impact of intergenerational change seems weaker in Mexico than in its neighbors to the north. Table 4.2 provides a detailed breakdown of how ratings of each of the nongovernmental institutions changed over time.

The erosion of institutional authority is a pervasive phenomenon that extends to the nation-state itself. In 1981, 79 percent of the U.S. public said that they were very proud to be Americans; they ranked significantly higher than the Canadians (63 percent of whom described themselves as very proud to be Canadians) and the Mexicans (66 percent of whom were "very proud" of their nationality). Though these are interesting cross-national differences, the most striking and significant differences are those linked with age cohort. In 1981, fully 90 percent of the Americans aged sixty-five and over said that they were "very proud" to be Americans. Among the youngest group, the figure was only 68 percent. In Canada, the percentage expressing a strong sense of national pride falls from 77 percent among the oldest group to 56 percent among the youngest. And in Mexico, the figure falls from 78 percent among the oldest group to 60 percent among the youngest.

Are these life cycle differences, or do they reflect a historic change linked with changing formative experiences? The evidence suggests that

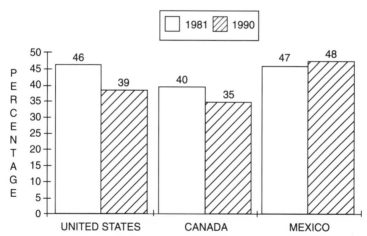

Figure 4.3. Percentage expressing "high confidence in nongovernment institutions, 1981 vs. 1990. Respondents were asked how much confidence they had in their country's (a) armed forces, (b) police, (c) parliament, and (d) civil service. The percentages are shown with an average score of 2 or lower, where 1 = "a lot," 2 = "quite a lot," 3 = "not very much," and 4 = "no confidence at all." *Source:* 1981 and 1990 World Values Surveys.

Table 4.2.   Confidence in Nongovernmental
Institutions in 1981 vs. 1990[a]

	1981	1990
1. Churches		
U.S.	45	46
Canada	30	24
Mexico	48	46
2. Educational System		
U.S.	27	22
Canada	16	19
Mexico	41	32
3. Legal System		
U.S.	17	12
Canada	14	10
Mexico	24	16
4. Press		
U.S.	12	7
Canada	6	5
Mexico	14	10

Source: 1981 and 1990 World Value Surveys.
[a] Percentage expressing "a lot" of confidence.

the latter is the case, for again, we find a consistent set of contrasts across value types that parallels the differences across age groups. In all three countries, the postmaterialists are significantly less likely to express a strong sense of national pride than are the materialists.

Before going on to see whether the differences found in 1981 enable us to predict the changes that take place from 1981 to 1990, let us note an additional point: one's sense of national pride is not an isolated attitude. It is part of a pervasive *syndrome* of attitudes related to established authority. For example, one's sense of national pride is clearly linked with how much confidence one has in governmental institutions. This linkage is considerably stronger in the United States and Canada than it is in Mexico, but all three countries show the same basic pattern: those who have low confidence in government institutions *also* tend to have relatively weak feelings of national pride.

It is not terribly surprising that one's sense of national pride is linked with one's confidence in government institutions. What is much less obvious is the fact that national pride is also linked with one's confidence in *non*governmental institutions. Here the linkage is about equally strong in all three nations.

This syndrome of attitudes is broader still. In each country, our respondents were asked: "In political matters, people talk of 'the left' and 'the right.' How would you place your views on this scale, generally speaking?" They were shown a ten-point scale, with the words *left* at the left and the word *right* at the opposite end. One's sense of national pride has become an important part of whether one considers oneself to be on the left or the right, in broad ideological terms. Again, the linkage is weaker in Mexico than in the United States or Canada, but in each country those who place themselves on the left are less likely to express a strong sense of national pride than are those who consider themselves to be on the right.

The fact that national pride is associated with the right is a familiar finding. Less obvious is the fact that national pride is even *more* strongly related to the strength of one's religious convictions than it is to one's sense of being on the left or on the right. Table 4.3 demonstrates this point. It is based on an index of religious intensity; our respondents are categorized in four groups, which correspond (roughly) to the least religious quintile, followed by the second and third quintiles, and then by the top 40 percent. This last group consists of all those who (1) described themselves as religious; (2) selected point 10 on a ten-point scale, indicating that God is *very* important in their lives; and (3) said they *do* get comfort and strength from religion. Across the three countries, nearly two-fifths of the respondents (38 percent, to be precise) chose this same response pattern.

As Table 4.3 shows us, those who score high on strength of religious convictions are much likelier to express a strong sense of national pride

Table 4.3. Percentage "Very Proud" of Nationality by Religious Intensity[a]

		Score on Index of Religious Intensity		
		United States	*Canada*	*Mexico*
Lowest	20%	58	52	42
2nd	20%	70	60	54
3rd	20%	75	64	49
Top	40%	83	70	67
Gamma		.33	.20	.23

Source: 1990 World Values surveys.

[a] Index is based on respondent's responses to these questions: "Independently of whether you go to church or not, would you say you are: (1) a religious person, (2) not a religious person, (3) a convinced atheist?"; "How important is God in your life? Please indicate on this scale: 10 means very important and 1 means not important at all." "Do you get comfort and strength from religion?" The three items were weighted equally and summed.

than those who have relatively weak religious convictions. The linkage is rather strong in all three countries.

As Table 4.4 demonstrates, the intensity of one's religious convictions is the strongest predictor of national pride, among all the orientation we have examined. Confidence in government institutions also plays an important role, controlling for the effects of the other variables; the same is true of materialist/postmaterialist values and of left-right self-placement. The responses to these items do *not* reflect a narrow evaluation of one's nation or one's political system. Instead, we seem to be dealing with a pervasive syndrome of response to authority in general. This syndrome is characterized by consistent linkages with age and materialist/postmaterialist values, with the young and the postmaterialists showing relatively low levels of national pride and all the other elements of the syndrome.

From 1981 to 1990, feelings of national pride moved on the same trajectory as did the other elements of this syndrome—a trajectory that is accurately predicted by the relationships with age and materialist/postmaterialist values. In all three countries, we find a decline in the percentage expressing strong feelings of national pride, as we see in Figure 4.4. The decline was modest in Canada, larger in the United States, and larger still in Mexico, where the percentage who were "very proud" to be Mexican fell from 66 percent in 1981 to 56 percent in 1990.

THE RISE OF CITIZEN INTERVENTION IN POLITICS

One of the well-established findings about *conventional* political participation is the fact that it is characterized by strong life cycle effects. Both

Table 4.4. Predictors of National Pride in North America: Multiple Classification Analysis

	Beta
Index of religious intensity	.14
Confidence in government institutions	.12
Materialist/postmaterialist values	.11
Left-right self-placement	.10
Respondent's age	.09
Confidence in nongovernment institutions	.08
Respondent's occupation	.07
Respondent's educational level	.07
Family income	.05
Respondent's sex	.02

$R = .35$

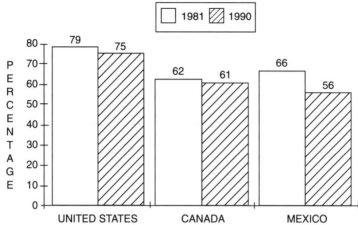

Figure 4.4. Percentage saying they are "very proud" to be (American/ Canadian/Mexican), 1981 vs. 1990. *Source:* 1981 and 1990 World Values Surveys.

Milbrath and Goel (1977) and Verba, Nie, and Kim (1978) found that the youngest group of adults surveyed virtually always showed lower levels of voting turnout and political interest than the next older group (generally, those in their thirties). The *oldest* groups also showed relatively low rates of conventional participation, producing a curvilinear pattern. These authors attributed this pattern to a combination of life cycle effects and enduring cohort differences: the young were less politicized because they were not yet fully integrated into political life, but the old showed lower rates of participation because they had lower educational levels than younger cohorts. Inglehart (1990) followed given cohorts over a period of nearly two decades and confirmed this interpretation: the low politicization of the young clearly *does* reflect a life cycle phenomenon. As it aged, the youngest adult cohort showed rising levels of participation, reaching the level of the most politically active cohort by the time it was in the mid-thirties age range. The oldest cohorts, on the other hand, showed no tendency to rise or decline in participation as they aged: the fact that, at any given time the oldest group showed lower rates of political participation than the younger group was an enduring attribute, reflecting the fact that the oldest group was less educated than younger groups. The implication is that as the younger, more highly educated cohorts gradually replace the older, less educated ones in the adult population, we should witness a gradual rise in conventional political participation rates. Evidence from nine West European societies demonstrates that this change does seem to be taking place: In eight out of the nine countries studied (that is, every country but Italy), rates of political discussion rose from 1973 to 1987 (Inglehart 1990).

Figure 4.5 shows the rate at which the three North American publics engage in three closely correlated forms of behavior: (1) discussing politics, (2) being interested in politics, and (3) having signed a political petition. For the United States and Canada, this figure shows a curvilinear pattern across age groups, in keeping with previous findings— with the youngest and oldest groups falling below the participation levels of the middle-aged. The Mexican public is heavily concentrated among the younger age groups because of rapid population growth, and our sample contains too few respondents over sixty-five years of age for reliable analysis; if it did, we suspect that we would observe a curvilinear pattern there, as in the United States and Canada.

Postmaterialists are markedly more likely to engage in conventional political activities than are those with materialist values. In the United States, for example, only 40 percent of the materialists rank "high" as compared with 65 percent of the postmaterialists. In Canada, the figures are 29 and 52 percent, respectively; and in Mexico they are 8 vs. 18 percent. This pattern reflects the fact that postmaterialists consist of those who have been raised under conditions of relative economic and physical security. They tend to take immediate survival needs for

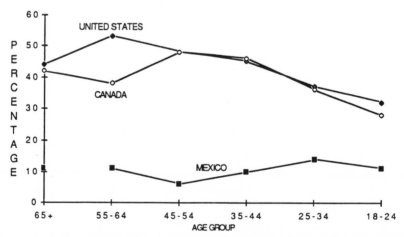

Figure 4.5. Percentage "high" on conventional participation, by age group. Those for whom at least two of the following are true: (1) discuss politics with their friends "frequently," (2) are "interested" or "very interested" in politics, (3) have signed a political petition. The value in Mexico's 65+ group is missing because the Mexican sample contains fewer than 30 cases over 65 years of age. *Source:* 1981 World Values Survey.

granted, and have more time and energy to expend in more remote and abstract activities—such as politics. Here the younger groups do *not* show higher levels of conventional political participation than the older groups. We attribute this to life cycle effects, which suppress evidence of an underlying generational change, for the postmaterialists *do* show relatively high levels of participation. The fact that postmaterialist values are linked with higher rates of conventional political activity should reinforce the trend by which higher educational levels tend to produce a gradually rising potential for mass political participation.

Do we find rising rates of conventional political participation? As Figure 4.6 indicates, the answer is a clear-cut yes. In all three countries, levels of political interest, political discussion, and signing of political petitions rose significantly from 1981 to 1990. The changes over time are dramatic. In the United States, the percentage who did at least two of these three activities rose from 41 percent in 1981 to 50 percent in 1990. In Canada, the rise was even steeper—from 38 to 53 percent. But Mexico shows the most dramatic changes of all: starting from a base of only 11 percent in 1981, the figure more than *doubled*, rising to 25 percent in 1990.

Thus, conventional political participation reflects a pattern of inter-generational change in which the higher participant *potential* of the younger cohorts is obscured (in any given cross section) by a life cycle effect: their higher underlying participant potential can be revealed only through longitudinal analysis. It is there, nevertheless, and contributes to a gradual rise in active forms of mass political participation over time. This applies to the three forms of conventional participation dealt with

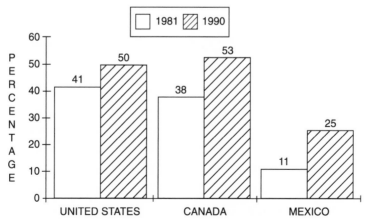

Figure 4.6. Percentage "high" on conventional participation, 1981 vs. 1990. (See legend to Figure 4.5.) *Source:* 1981 and 1990 World Values Surveys.

here, but not to forms of participation such as voting, which are largely shaped by elite-led bureaucratic organizations.

How do we explain the well-known phenomenon of declining rates of voter turnout, in the light of these findings? Here, we are dealing with two distinct and seemingly contradictory trends. Despite the fact that the younger, better educated birth cohorts show higher political discussion rates than do their elders, they have lower levels of political partisan loyalty. Surveys carried out in a number of West European countries reveal that throughout the 1970s and 1980s, the older birth cohorts reported considerably higher rates of political party loyalty than the postwar cohorts (Inglehart 1990:357–58). This finding parallels a pattern of intergenerational decline in party identification that has been found among the American electorate during the past two decades (Nie, Verba, and Petrocik 1979; Pomper 1975; Abramson 1979). What makes this finding seem paradoxical, however, is the fact that the better educated and those who are most involved in politics are *most* apt to identify with some political party. The younger cohorts are better educated and, as we have seen, more apt to be interested in politics, to discuss politics, and to sign petitions—but they are distinctly *less* likely to have a sense of party loyalty.

Though their education and politicization predispose them to identify with *some* political party, they have less incentive to identify with any specific political party, among the available choices. The established political parties came into being in an era dominated by social class conflict and economic issues, and tend to remain polarized on this basis. For the older cohorts, religion and social class provided powerful cues in establishing one's political party loyalties. The younger cohorts are less polarized according to social class, and religion plays a less important role in their lives. Moreover, in recent years, a new axis of polarization has arisen based on cultural and quality of life issues. Today, the established political party configuration in most countries does not adequately reflect the hottest contemporary issues; and those who have grown up in the postwar era have relatively little motivation to identify with any of the established political parties.

Thus, the 1970s and early 1980s saw a decline of political party loyalties in most Western countries—and partisan loyalties and party organizations are the most potent factors involved in producing a high electoral turnout. Hence, we find two divergent trends: on one hand, the highly bureaucratized or elite-directed forms of participation such as voting have stagnated; while the individually motivated or elite-challenging forms of participation have risen steadily.

Unlike the trend toward rising rates of political discussion, there is no reason to expect the decline of partisanship to continue indefinitely. A realignment of political party systems that makes party polarization correspond more closely to issue polarization could bring the decline to a gradual halt. Such a realignment already seems to be taking place in some Western countries. But the overall trend has been downward.

Figure 4.7 shows some of the evidence concerning an even more important recent political change: a cross-national trend toward a rising participant potential. Here, we are dealing with a battery of questions concerning one's readiness to take part in four forms of unconventional political action: boycotts, demonstrations, unofficial strikes, and occupying buildings. The text of the questions used to measure this behavior appears beneath Figure 4.7.

These questions are derived from *Political Action*, the study carried out by Barnes et al. (1979). They are designed to test the hypothesis that intergenerational changes in values and skill levels are giving rise to a more activist public that is readier to intervene directly in political decision-making rather than limiting itself to participation by voting, in which the public periodically authorizes one or another elite group to make all important political decisions for the next several years. This form of unconventional participation is much more intrusive than voting

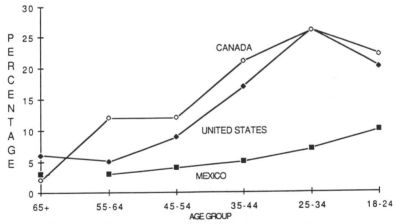

Figure 4.7. Unconventional political action potential, by age group. Respondents were asked whether they had done, or might do any of the following things: (a) joining in boycotts, (b) attending lawful demonstrations, (c) joining in unofficial strikes, or (d) occupying buildings or factories. Shown above are the percentages, with an average score of 2 lower, when 1 = "have actually done it," 2 = "might do it," and 3 = "would never, under any circumstances, do it." The value in Mexico's 65+ group is missing because the Mexican sample contains fewer than 30 cases over 65 years of age. *Source:* 1981 World Values Survey.

and is usually designed to influence specific decisions, often at a particular time and place.

As Figure 4.7 demonstrates, in all three countries the younger respondents are much readier to engage in unconventional political action than are the older ones. The differences between younger and older cohorts are remarkably large, with the youngest group being at least three times as likely to engage in unconventional political action as the oldest group. Similar findings were made concerning the U.S. public in the earlier study by Barnes et al. (which did not include either Canada or Mexico).

Like Barnes et al., we also find strong correlations between unconventional political action potential and materialist/postmaterialist values. In both Canada and Mexico, postmaterialists are more than twice as likely to rank high on unconventional political action as are materialists; in the United States, postmaterialists are nearly *three* times as likely to show high levels of unconventional political action potential. Despite a great deal of journalistic writing about growing political apathy in the contemporary United States, we find strong and consistent indications of an intergenerational shift toward higher levels of potential for unconventional political participation. Do the changes over time confirm this interpretation?

As Figure 4.8 demonstrates, the answer is yes. We find significant increases in mass potential for unconventional participation in all three countries. Though the increase is impressive in both the United States and Canada, it is truly remarkable in Mexico, which from a position far behind both of its northern neighbors in 1981, ranks almost as high in 1990. This phenomenon seems linked with the surge of political activism that has called the one-party domination of Mexican politics by the PRI increasingly into question in recent years. The Mexican public has become more involved in both conventional and unconventional action during the past decade. In the 1988 presidential elections, there was an unprecedented surge of opposition activity that transformed the PRI's usual overwhelming victory into a relatively narrow one.

Is this increase in mass politicization a cause or an effect of the rise of opposition movements in Mexico? It probably works both ways. On one hand, an awareness that the results of the 1988 election might not be a forgone conclusion undoubtedly stirred greater mass interest in politics than in the past. On the other hand, this development seems to be a deep-rooted one: it was already strongly foreshadowed in the 1981 data, which showed large intergenerational differences in the potential for mass participation. There seems to be a long-term component of these changes, as well as short-term situational factors—and the gradual rise in participant potential probably contributed to the emergence of unprecedentedly effective opposition forces in Mexico. This was one rea-

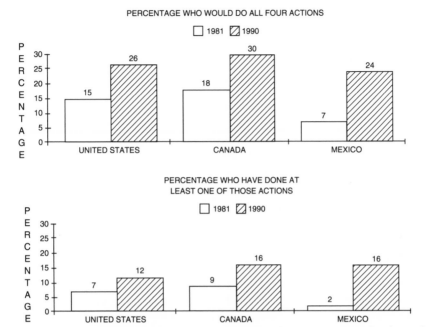

Figure 4.8. Unconventional political action potential, 1981 vs. 1990. (See legend to Figure 4.7.) *Source:* 1981 and 1990 World Values Surveys.

son why results of the 1988 election (and, probably, subsequent ones) *were* no longer a forgone conclusion. These developments on the Mexican scene seem to parallel processes that have recently emerged even more dramatically in Eastern Europe.

DEMOCRATIZATION AND ECONOMIC DEVELOPMENT IN MEXICAN POLITICS

The rise of unconventional political participation had already begun to impact on politics in the United States and Canada in the 1960s, when it was associated with protest against the war in Vietnam and other forms of student protest. Though student protest had some echo in Mexico at that time, it was relatively limited in both time (1968) and space (Mexico City). Mexico now seems to be catching up with its northern neighbors in political activism. If so, this may be a major factor in helping transform Mexican politics into a more open and pluralist system.

The revolution of 1910 left a lasting imprint on Mexican political life. On one hand, it broke the power of the traditional landowning oligarchy, led to land redistribution, and put a new generation of politicians in power who, rhetorically at least, represented the interests of labor. But in the long run, it gave rise to an authoritarian regime dominated by a new group organized in one party, the Institutional Revolutionary Party or PRI, which took permanent control of the federal government and virtually all state governments.

Like the Communist oligarchies of Eastern Europe, the Mexican ruling elite has strengthened its monopoly of power through control over key sectors of the economy. Government control of the economy dates back to the 1920s, but it was extended by nationalization of the oil industry in 1938 and electricity in 1959 and culminated in the nationalization of the banking system in 1982. By that time, the Mexican government was spending 42 percent of the country's gross domestic product.

The decline of the oligarchy based on the PRI during the late 1980s partly reflected long-term structural changes such as urbanization, industrialization, rising educational levels, and changing values. However, they interacted with short-term factors such as a drop in real salaries, and a stagnation of economic growth and employment.

The oil crash of 1981 exacerbated the problems implicit in Mexico's nearly $100 billion external debt and suddenly halted the grandiose dreams of the Mexican government. In very similar fashion, the collapse of the peso in December 1994 was a replay of this drama. In 1982, Mexico faced difficult economic times. They reflected the inflexibility of economic policy, falling oil prices, rising interest rates, an excessive public deficit, widespread capital flight, inflation, and a decline in GNP. These events shaped the closing years of Lopez Portillo's presidency (1976–1982) and led to his decision to nationalize the banking system in 1982. This marked the high-water level of government intervention in the economy.

The election of President de la Madrid in 1982, just after the bank nationalization, began a reversal of this trend. Facing growing evidence of the inefficiency of the public sector, de la Madrid cut state subsidies and began privatizing state enterprises.

The unsettling presidential succession process, in which each president chooses his successor, has negative effects on the economy. It helped contribute to a 1987 stock market crash. Economic decline and political dissatisfaction led to a split within the PRI in late 1987, bringing the most strongly contested elections in the last fifty years. As a result, the administration of President Salinas (1988–1994) started an intense modernization program, for both the economy and politics. The promotion of NAFTA is part of an attempt to bring about economic modernization. Unfortunately, Salinas did not find the path to modernize politics as well, and the whole attempt started collapsing. In January 1994 the

Chiapas rebellion took place. Three months later the PRI's presidential candidate was assassinated, and in September there was another assassination of a top figure (that of the secretary of the ruling party). The basic political consensus was broken. Although kept under control, the economy reflected the effects of those events on the stock and capital markets. Finally, by December 1994 the dollar's exchange rate against the peso was no longer sustainable and during 1995 it almost tripled. Inflation rose from 7 to 50 percent in the same period. Unemployment rocketed. The economy collapsed.

Were these events unforeseeable? And were they unavoidable? They should not have come as a surprise. To some extent, they were foreseen (Basañez 1993); and they were by no means unavoidable. What happened was a political miscalculation. The Mexican government underestimated the potential disruptive power of the forces it was trying to exclude from the political arena. Some elements within the PRI had suggested that the administration should build up a new social base among the conservative forces in the Mexican society, in order to enhance the political viability of its free-market-oriented economic program. This group urged Salinas to pursue *perestroika* without *glasnost*, in order to avoid the mistakes Gorbachev had made by simultaneously pursuing both political and economic reform. What they overlooked was the fact that Mexico was well ahead of the Soviet Union in business practices, profit and price structures, trained people, and legal framework. They also underestimated the extent to which the Mexican Left would by then have endorsed these economic policies in order to share political power.

Salinas took some major steps toward political reform, but he did so on a highly selective basis, by changing three key principles of the political system:

1.   He re-established diplomatic relations with the Vatican as part of a broader move toward reconciliation between the PRI and practicing Catholics. This had historically been an important goal for much of the Mexican population.

2.   He ended the *ejido* structure (the collective tenure system of rural land among the peasant population), which had been one of the key symbols of the 1910 revolution. In so doing, he was responding to a conservative demand.

3.   Most important of all, he moved toward allowing genuine electoral competition by opposition parties—but only for one side of the political spectrum. The center-right PAN began to receive fairer treatment, but this was denied to the center-left PRD. The crisis cycle was set for its fifth repetition.

Mexico is experiencing many changes. An excellent recent journalistic summary concludes that "there is a new fluidity about Mexican politics. It could become a stable system with two parties alternating in power; or it could turn into a mafia-ridden narco-state" (*Economist* 1995). As the evidence examined in this chapter demonstrates, Mexico—like the United States and Canada—seems to be undergoing a deep-rooted shift in the nature of mass orientations toward government.

The authority of governments to tell their people what to do is in gradual but long-term decline. Conversely, the public is becoming increasingly adept at telling governments what to do—and increasingly likely to intervene directly in political decision-making. Will the government be able to stop the long-term changes that our data show are occurring at the societal level?

We suspect that the answer to these questions is no: although there is no one-to-one linkage between economic and political reform, it will be difficult to decentralize and modernize the economy without yielding to growing pressures for a more open political system.

5

In Search of a New Balance between State and Economy, Individual and Society

In his celebrated analysis of American society, David Riesman (1950) argued that individualism (emphasized as a distinctive American trait by a long line of observers going back to Alexis de Tocqueville) was disappearing. An "inner-directed" personality type was gradually being replaced by "other-directed" people. Another landmark study of the 1950s, William Whyte's (1956) *The Organization Man*, reached similar conclusions: the Protestant ethic of hard work, thrift, and competition as the route to individual salvation was giving way to a belief in "belongingness" as the ultimate goal. Both Riesman and Whyte had grave misgivings about what they saw as the decline of individualism in America.

In contrast with these diagnoses, numerous more recent journalistic accounts have described the 1980s in the United States as a decade characterized by an explosion of individual greed and the abdication of collective responsibility. An insightful study by Bellah, Madsen, Sullivan, Swidler, and Tipton (1985) concludes that the central problem of American life today is that individualism has grown cancerous; they seek to rediscover cultural traditions that can limit and restrain the destructive side of individualism.

These diagnoses seem contradictory: do we have too little individualism or too much? Examined more closely, however, they turn out to be compatible. They deal with different aspects of a complex change that is taking place in the relationship between the individual and society—a process of change that is not uniquely American, though it may be particularly acute there.

These changes may seem contradictory because they are complex. On one hand, we are witnessing a decline in the degree to which the individual is subordinated to society. We have seen evidence of this in the two preceding chapters, which demonstrated the declining strength of traditional cultural norms that helped maintain the family and ensure the reproduction of society, and the declining acceptance of the authority of hierarchical institutions, both political and nonpolitical. Related changes are taking place in the public's motivations to work and in its orientations toward the control of business and industry, as we will see in this chapter. Here, we find a pervasive trend toward weakening hierarchical controls over the individual.

At the same time, however, we find indications of a *rising* emphasis on society's responsibilities *to* the individual, and a tendency to blame society, rather than the individual, for social problems such as poverty. In other words, there has been a rising emphasis on individual *rights* and entitlements, coupled with a declining emphasis on individual *responsibility*.

The latter trend may be approaching its limits, however, in face of a growing awareness that giving the state responsibility for individual well-being may be beneficial in some areas, but tends to become oppressive and unworkable when applied on a comprehensive scale. An awareness of these limits has emerged most acutely and most dramatically in the ex-Communist societies of Central and Eastern Europe, but to some extent it has affected prevailing worldviews throughout industrial society.

Wildavsky (1987) and his associates (Thompson, Ellis, and Wildavsky 1990) hold that the degree to which the individual is subordinated to the society is one of the two crucial dimensions on which cultures vary. They argue that there is a limited range of variation on this dimension because both extremes tend to be fatal: a viable society must maintain an equilibrium between the conflicting demands of individual freedom and conformity to societal norms. We agree with their basic point. One of the major developments in the rise of industrial society has been a long-term shift from social control toward individual freedom, and this shift is still progressing. Nevertheless, there are limits to how far this or any other cultural change can move. Industrial society may currently be at a historical turning point at which it is testing the limits to how much farther this long-term shift can move.

The most important political event of recent years has been the collapse of Communism. Though it was unexpected by most observers, it reflects underlying long-term forces that are common to all industrial societies. One such common factor has been a gradual decline in public support for state ownership and control of the economy. Already in 1981, this core element of the Marxist prescription for the good society had lost most of its mass appeal; by 1990, with the increasingly evident failure of Marxist societies, public support for state intervention fell still farther.

But the global movement away from communism is not a move back to traditional capitalism. Though most advanced industrial societies have been moving away from Marxism, the trend is *not* back toward the laissez-faire capitalism that prevailed sixty or ninety years ago. Indeed, one reason why capitalism is thriving today is the fact that it had already made a series of incremental but cumulatively massive reforms, which brought about some much needed governmental regulation of the economy and society, and developed extensive welfare state institutions through successive waves of change in the 1930s, the postwar era, and into the 1960s and early 1970s. Today "capitalism" is a misnomer for the welfare states of Western advanced industrial society, in which state expenditures range from a third to well over half of a given country's gross national product.

Clearly, the trend in these societies is not toward increasing the state hold on the economy; more often, it is toward privatization of functions carried out by a state that is now widely perceived as having grown too big. The idea that small is beautiful was novel when it first emerged in the 1970s. It has gradually come to seem almost self-evident—and the beauty of smallness has been applied to government as well as to private organizations. Increasingly, big government is coming to be viewed with suspicion. Nevertheless, in some very important ways, Western publics are still moving *away* from the traditional capitalist model, toward reducing the authority of owners. In other words, the wave of the future is *neither* communism *nor* traditional capitalism; both types of societies are groping toward an optimal balance between state and society. It has gradually become evident that neither laissez-faire capitalism nor a state-run society works very well. The optimal model for industrial society cannot be defined a priori by some ideology. Finding it is a pragmatic empirical process; but a common model does seem to be emerging with a tendency toward convergence from both extremes. This global process can be seen taking place within the North American context.

Figure 5.1 shows the responses of our three publics to a question about who should own and manage business and industry. Four options were offered, ranging from the traditional capitalist position ("the owners should run their business or appoint the managers") to the classic Marxist position ("the state should be the owner and appoint the managers"), plus two other options, one giving employees a voice in selecting the managers, and the other giving employees full ownership and control.

Already in 1981, public support for the Marxist option was almost nonexistent in the United States and Canada, and was backed by only a small minority in Mexico. During the 1980s, its support eroded even further, approaching the vanishing point in all three countries.

In both the United States and Canada, clear majorities of the public supported the classic capitalist option. This did *not* hold true in Mexico,

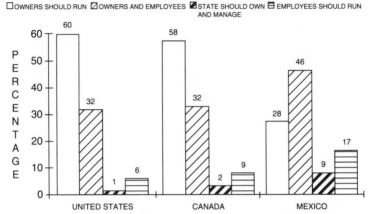

Figure 5.1. Attitudes toward private vs. public vs. employee management of business and industry in three nations. Question: There is a lot of discussion about how business and industry should be managed. Which of these four statements comes closest to your opinion (percentage choosing each option)?

1. The owners should run their business or appoint the managers.
2. The owners and employees should participate in the selection of managers.
3. The state should be the owner and appoint the managers.
4. The employees should own the business and elect the managers.

The value in Mexico's 65+ group is missing because the Mexican sample contains fewer than 30 cases over 65 years of age. *Source:* 1981 World Values Survey.

where only 28 percent of the public wanted to leave control in the hands of the owners. In keeping with the Mexican revolutionary tradition, which brought the expropriation of large landowners and the nationalization of large foreign holdings, the Mexican public was much more supportive of all three noncapitalist options than were the Canadians or Americans.

Needless to say, this sharp contrast in attitudes toward private ownership and control of business and industry constitutes a major ideological difference between the Mexicans and their two northern neighbors. The fact that most North Americans are committed to control by the owners, while most Mexicans favor some alternative form of organization, could present an almost insurmountable stumbling block to full economic integration in a North American common market. But the question arises, Is this a permanent feature of the political landscape? We argue that it is not. The evidence indicates that both sides are changing, and that the overall tendency is toward convergence.

First, let us examine changes in support for the Marxist alternative from 1981 to 1990. As Figure 5.2 demonstrates, support for state ownership and control, already low in 1981, dwindled to almost nothing by 1990. Among the U.S. public, support for a command economy could scarcely fall any farther: in both 1981 and 1990 it was supported by barely 1 percent. In Canada, support for state ownership fell from 2 percent in 1981 to 1 percent in 1990. And in Mexico, the only country in which the Marxist alternative commanded at least modest public support, the figure fell from 9 percent in 1981 to 3 percent in 1990.

For many years, the conventional wisdom had held that youth naturally gravitated toward Marxism: "If my son were not a socialist at the age of 20, I would disown him; if he is still a socialist when he is 40, I will disown him then," as Clemenceau put it. This may have been true in the past, but our 1990 data provide no indication that it is true today. The differences associated with age and value type are extremely small in both the United States and Canada, with only a faint trace of greater support for public ownership among the young than the old in those two countries: among the youngest age group, state ownership is backed by about 2 percent of the respondents, while among older groups the figure is about 1 percent. In Mexico, we find a reversal of

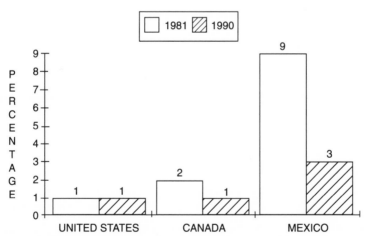

Figure 5.2. Support for state ownership and management of business and industry in 1981 and 1990 (percentage choosing third option). (See legend to Figure 5.1.) The value in Mexico's 65+ group is missing because the Mexican sample contains fewer than 30 cases over 65 years of age. *Source:* 1981 and 1990 World Values Surveys.

relationships: state ownership is *less* likely to be supported by the young than by the old, with support being strongest among Mexicans aged fifty-five and older.

We find a similar reversal of relationships in the Mexican data when we cross-tabulate this attitude by materialist/postmaterialist values. As the previous two chapters have demonstrated, postmaterialists tend to support the conventional left position on most social issues. They do *not* do so here. In both the United States and Canada, there is practically no relationship between materialist/postmaterialist values and support for state ownership of business and industry, and in Mexico, we find that postmaterialists are *less* likely to support state ownership than are those with materialist values. This does not seem to be a fluke. It parallels the situation in Eastern Europe. Though in most Western countries, post-materialists still tend to be slightly more favorable to state ownership of industry than do materialists, in the formerly socialist countries the young, the better educated, and the postmaterialists tend to be *less* favorable to state ownership than do the old, the less educated, and the materialists.

There is no reason why postmaterialism should automatically be linked with support for state ownership. Traditionally, this was viewed as the progressive or leftist position; and probably for this reason, when postmaterialists first appeared in significant numbers in Western Europe during the 1960s, they tended to think of themselves as Marxists. But this tendency weakened during the 1970s, and by the late 1980s it had all but vanished (Inglehart 1990). In the East European context, this relationship has now actually reversed itself: their experience with the deadening repression of the socialist regimes under which they have grown up has led Polish postmaterialists to see state ownership and control as incompatible with the individual autonomy and self-expression that they value so highly (Inglehart and Siemienska 1988). For them, expansion of state authority does not appear to be a progressive policy, but a repressive one. Their outlook has parallels in Mexico. Though never dominated by Marxist governments, Mexico's experience with state-run industries has been rather similar to that of Eastern Europe.

Neither efficient nor responsive to the people, most of Mexico's state-run industries have become monstrously inefficient fiefs held by members of the PRI, and grossly overstaffed in order to provide jobs for the bosses' adherents. The Mexican oil monopoly PEMEX is an extreme example. It was estimated in 1968 that its 250,000 employees produced no more than 15,000 employees would in Texas (Sanders 1989:67). PEMEX became incredibly corrupt and out of control by the government. When President Salinas decided to try to clean up PEMEX in 1989, he was able to remove the union leader who had dominated it for decades only by sending in the Mexican army to arrest him. In the light of such experiences, it is not surprising that the young and the post-materialists in Mexican society no longer see state ownership and control of industry as a desirable solution to their country's economic problems.

This illustrates an important point: postmaterialists do *not* automatically adopt whatever happens to be the conventional left position. On many issues, they gravitate toward the Left. But the rise of postmaterialism has brought a new perspective into play, one that sometimes runs against established political orthodoxy; it is reshaping the meaning of left and right.

The ongoing cultural shift does not fit easily into conventional models of left and right. Though we find evidence of a deep-rooted trend away from the Marxist model for society, it is not simply a move back to orthodox capitalism, as Figure 5.3 illustrates. In all three societies, the young are markedly more favorable to giving the employees a role in choosing management than are the old. The differences are quite sizable. In the United States, for example, among the oldest group, only 25 percent endorse either option 2 or option 4, both of which would give employees a stronger voice. This figure rises as we move to younger groups, and among the youngest group, employee participation is supported by fully 48 percent of the public. We find an almost identical

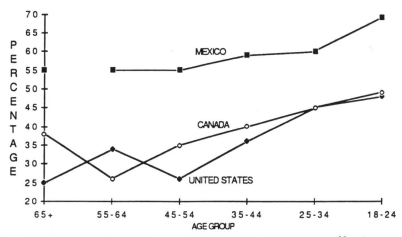

Figure 5.3. Support for employee participation in management of business and industry, by age group (percentage choosing second or fourth option). (See legend to Figure 5.1.) The value in Mexico's 65+ group is missing because the Mexican sample contains fewer than 30 cases over 65 years of age. *Source:* 1981 World Values Survey.

figure among the youngest group in Canada: in two societies that are citadels of the traditional capitalist viewpoint, almost half of the youngest age group favors a major shift of authority away from the owners.

By themselves, these differences between the views of old and young might be attributed to a simple life cycle effect: being at the start of their careers and relatively unlikely to hold power, the young are naturally favorable to sharing authority in business and industry. However, the evidence in Figure 5.4 undermines this interpretation, for it shows that in both the United States and Canada, postmaterialists are more favorable to increased employee participation than are materialists. Here too, the differences are pronounced: in the United States, only 27 percent of the materialists favor giving employees a stronger voice, while 50 percent of the postmaterialists take this position. Given the fact that emphasis on autonomy and self-expression are core elements of the postmaterialist syndrome, this finding is not surprising. However, it is not automatic, for Mexico does *not* show this pattern: postmaterialists there are no more favorable to employee participation than are materialists. But in both the United States and Canada, we find that attitudes toward employee participation show the now-familiar pattern of coherent correlations with both age and value type, in which the old are to the young as the materialists are to the postmaterialists.

We interpret this pattern as meaning that the age differences are *not* due to life cycle effects, but reflect historical shifts, based on the distinc-

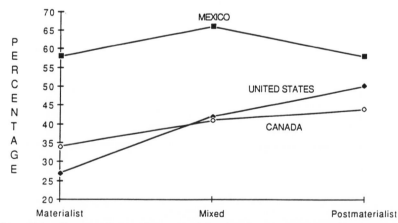

Figure 5.4. Support for employee participation in management of business and industry, by value type (percentage choosing second or fourth option). (See legend to Figure 5.1.) Because these values were not measured in the 1981 U.S. Survey, we show the 1990 results for that country. *Source:* 1981 World Values Survey.

tive formative experiences of the respective birth cohorts. Consequently, these patterns in the 1981 data lead us to predict that levels of support for employee participation should rise from 1981 to 1990 in both the United States and Canada (but not in Mexico).

This is exactly what we do find, as Figure 5.5 demonstrates. From 1981 to 1990, there was a significant rise in support for employee participation in management of business and industry among both the Canadian and U.S. publics. In Mexico, on the other hand (where postmaterialism was *not* linked with employee participation), support for this option declined. This reversal of patterns between what happened in Mexico and what happened in its two northern neighbors is a further reflection of fundamental differences in the historic situations of the respective countries. In Mexican history, both state-owned industries and state-sponsored cooperatives have played major roles; and the Mexican public was originally far more favorable to state ownership, shared employee-owner participation, and employee ownership than were the Canadians or Americans. In recent years, however, the dismal performance of Mexican state-owned industries and the dwindling away of its cooperative sector have given rise to a growing acceptance of classic capitalist principles.

From a Mexican perspective, the idea of turning authority over to independent ownership may seem a healthy corrective to slow strangulation by an overcentralized state. It may even seem more compatible with human liberty than an economy dominated directly or indirectly by state authority. Consequently, we find another contrast between the

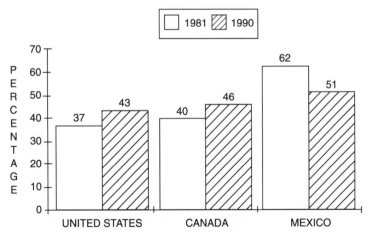

Figure 5.5. Support for employee participation in management of business and industry in 1981 and 1990 (percentage choosing second or fourth option). (See legend to Figure 5.1.) *Source:* 1981 and 1990 World Values Surveys.

outlook of Mexican postmaterialists and their counterparts in the United States and Canada: while postmaterialists in the two latter countries are markedly less favorable to the proposition "Owners should run their business" than are materialists, in Mexico there is scarcely any difference between materialists and postmaterialists on this question. Both the United States and Canada show the familiar configuration in which the young and the postmaterialists tend to reject untrammeled control by owners. In Mexico, the young tend to reject this formula, but there is virtually no correlation with value type.

Quite possibly the postmaterialists in Mexico tend to assume that increased employee participation could only come about if it were enforced by state authority. In fact, this is occurring naturally in the information sector of advanced industrial societies, simply because such changes are increasingly essential to the effective functioning of enterprises that depend on creativity and individual judgment. But this trend is not yet very visible in the Mexican economy. In the United States, the information sector now employs a majority of the work force. It is still a small segment of the Mexican economy. Once again, we have clear indications of an intergenerational shift in the United States and Canada, but not in Mexico.

Figure 5.6 shows the changes that occurred from 1981 to 1990 in the three countries. In both the United States and Canada, we find the decline in emphasis on owners' authority that is predicted by our two indicators of intergenerational change. In Mexico, we find change mov-

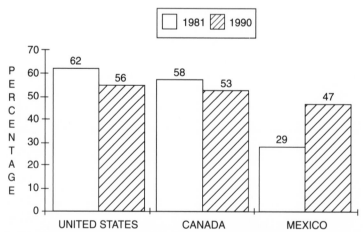

Figure 5.6. Support for owners having sole authority in management of business and industry in 1981 and 1990 (percentage choosing first option). (See legend to Figure 5.1.) *Source:* 1981 and 1990 World Values Surveys.

ing in the *reverse* direction, with a strong increase in acceptance of owners' authority. Clearly, the latter shift does *not* reflect intergenerational change. It seems to reflect a powerful procapitalist period effect.

Paradoxically, though contrasting changes are taking place in Mexico, on one hand, and the United States and Canada, on the other hand, the net result has been to make the prevailing economic ideology in these countries more similar. Starting from a tradition that combined a strong, highly centralized state with widespread suspicion of individual entrepreneurs, the Mexican public has been moving toward growing acceptance of classic capitalist principles. Starting with strongly procapitalist traditions, the publics of the United States and Canada continue to reject state ownership and control, but are moving toward a more egalitarian version of private enterprise. The young and the postmaterialists do not automatically support limiting the authority of owners. It depends on the context. In capitalist settings, it has for decades seemed self-evident that a progressive position favors increasing state regulation and control of the economy, shifting authority from owners to government. But in settings like Poland or Mexico, where the state seems to be strangling society, giving entrepreneurs a freer hand makes sense in terms of postmaterialist values, and may appeal to that constituency. Progress does not consist in mechanically following a fixed formula, but in moving toward an optimal balance between state and society.

So far in this chapter, we have analyzed the responses to one revealing question, but other evidence from the 1981 and 1990 World Values Surveys is equally illuminating. For example, let us examine the responses to a question about whether one should follow the instructions of one's superior at work, even if one does not agree with them. As Figure 5.7 demonstrates, in all three countries, the young are less likely to support this idea than are the old. It would not be difficult to think up an explanation for this finding, based on life cycle effects: the young are less likely to *be* in positions of authority, so they are less likely to endorse it than are the old. But it would be equally plausible to see this pattern as reflecting a historic decline in emphasis on unquestioning obedience to authority, linked with rising educational levels, changes in the nature of work, and intergenerational value shifts that place greater emphasis on individual autonomy. The data from Figure 5.7 alone are simply not adequate to tell us *why* we find these differences across age groups.

Figure 5.8 provides important supplementary information. It tells us that in both the United States and Canada, the age-related differences are paralleled by a consistent set of value differences in which postmaterialists contrast with materialists in the same way that the young contrast with the old. But here again, Mexico does not conform to the pattern: though we find differences across age groups that are similar to

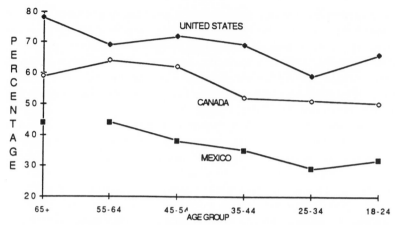

Figure 5.7. Attitudes toward authority at work, by age group (percentage saying "should follow instructions"). Question: People have different ideas
about following instructions at work, some say that one should follow the
instructions of one's superiors even when one does not fully agree with
them; others say one should follow one's superior's instructions only when
one is convinced that they are right. With which of those two opinions do
you agree? The value in Mexico's 65+ group is missing because the Mexican
sample contains fewer than 30 cases over 65 years of age. *Source:* 1981 World
Values Survey.

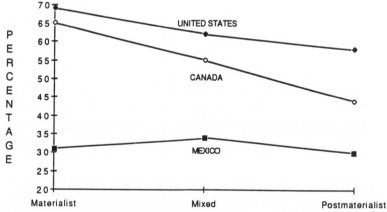

Figure 5.8. Attitudes toward authority at work, by value type (percentage saying "should follow instructions"). (See legend to Figure 5.7.) Because these
values were not measured in the 1981 U.S. Survey, we show the 1990 results
for that country. *Source:* 1981 World Values Survey.

those found in the United States and Canada, we do *not* find a parallel decline in emphasis on authority across the three value types.

Once again, when we examine the changes that took place from 1981 to 1990, we find a shift in the direction that the intergenerational change model predicts, among both the U.S. and Canadian publics—and a shift in the *reverse* direction in Mexico. As Figure 5.9 shows, starting from a considerably lower base than its northern neighbors, the Mexican public became *more* supportive of following the instructions of one's superiors in the workplace. Note that this trend applies specifically to following instructions *at work*. The Mexicans are not becoming more authoritarian in general—the overall trend is in the opposite direction. But acceptance of entrepreneurial authority has been growing. Even after this shift, the Mexicans remain less committed to following instructions than the Canadians or Americans, but they have moved toward acceptance of traditional capitalist norms. Thus, in North America, the work force of a newly industrializing nation is becoming more disciplined, while the publics of two postindustrial societies are shifting toward the norms of an information society. The Mexican results, both here and in the findings cited earlier, illustrate the fact that age differences alone do not provide a reliable prediction of the direction (if any) in which social change is moving. Only when age differences are complemented by coherent value differences is prediction possible.

In Mexico—a society having an average per capita income about one-seventh as high as its northern neighbors and an economy that is still in the early stages of industrialization—the prevailing shift is toward a

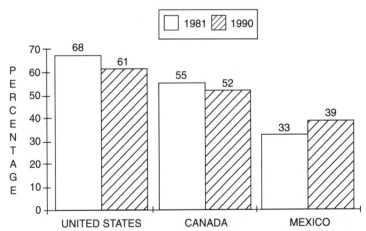

Figure 5.9. Attitudes toward authority at work 1981 vs. 1990 (percentage saying "should follow instructions"). (See legend to Figure 5.7.) *Source:* 1981 and 1990 World Values Surveys.

more disciplined work force. In both the United States and Canada, we find an intergenerational shift toward more egalitarian relations between employer and employees. The main thrust of this intergenerational change concerns authority relations, rather than ownership of property. Though state ownership has been increasingly discredited in all three societies during the past decade, this seems to reflect current events more than intergenerational change.

Figure 5.10 shows the distribution of attitudes toward public versus private ownership in each of the three North American countries in 1990. Though we do not have time series data for this variable, the results are interesting. The responses of the U.S. and Canadian publics are very similar: in both countries, an overwhelming majority (70 percent or more) favor moving toward more privatization; only one-tenth or less of these publics favor more public ownership: increased privatiza-

□ FAVOR MORE PRIVATE OWNERSHIP ▨ STATUS QUO OR NEUTRAL ▥ FAVOR MORE PUBLIC OWNERSHIP

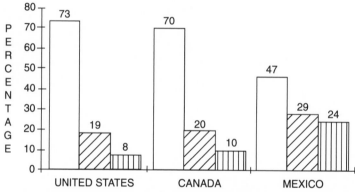

Figure 5.10. Support for public vs. private ownership, by nation. Question: For each pair of contrasting issues, 1 means you agree completely with the statement on the left; 10 means you agree completely with the statement on the right; or you can choose any number in between. How would you place your views on this scale?

1 2 3 4 5 6 7 8 9 10

Private ownership of	Government ownership of
business and industry	business and industry
should be increased.	should be increased.

Favor more private ownership (choose 1, 2, 3, or 4).
Status quo or neutral (choose 5 or 6).
Favor more public ownership (choose 7, 8, 9, or 10).
Source: 1990 World Values Survey.

tion prevails over nationalization of industry by a ratio of at least seven to one.

In Mexico, support for increasing public ownership is far stronger, reflecting Mexico's distinctive historical tradition. But in 1990, even there support for privatization outweighed support for more public ownership by a two-to-one margin. We suspect that a decade ago, responses would have been more favorable to government ownership of business and industry—especially in Mexico. There is no obvious evidence of intergenerational change with this orientation, however. Support for increased public ownership is relatively flat across the various age groups: in the United States, there is a slight rise in support among the very youngest group; in Canada, there are bulges of support among the youngest *and* oldest groups; and in Mexico, there is a drop among the oldest group. On the whole, the correlation with age is negligible.

Much the same holds true of the correlation with value types. In the United States and Canada, there is slightly weaker support for public ownership among the materialists than among the mixed types and postmaterialists, but the differences are well within the range of normal sampling error. In Mexico, there is no difference whatsoever between the position of materialists and postmaterialists on this issue.

These might seem to be dull findings: they do not give any indication of intergenerational change at any rate. But this nonfinding, like Sherlock Holmes's dog that did not bark in the night, is significant: it reflects a major historical shift. For decades, nationalization of industry constituted the cornerstone of the policy program of the Left, and for decades, throughout industrial society, the young tended to be much more supportive of left policies than were the old—to such an extent that it seemed a self-evident truism. This was not an illusion: the available evidence indicates that it generally held true until the 1970s.

Today, it does not hold true for this issue in any of the three societies examined here—and we suspect it does not hold true in most other countries. The young (and the postmaterialists) no longer support this core policy of the Left. In other words, one of the most significant generational changes of recent years has been the *vanishing* of longstanding intergenerational differences concerning increasing government controls over economy and society. By the early 1980s (long before the collapse of Communism in Eastern Europe), this age differential had disappeared (Inglehart 1990). The wave of the future halted—and in some countries actually reversed its direction.

Orthodox leftist ideologues have lamented the fact that the young have abandoned the statist programs of the Left, interpreting this as proof that the young have become selfish, narcissistic, and conservative. This diagnosis is profoundly mistaken. As the evidence presented in this book demonstrates, the young are anything but conservative on a wide range of issues. More and more, however, they have come to the conclusion that further increases in government control and management of society are dangerous and unlikely to provide effective solutions. This constitutes sufficient grounds for excommunicating them from the Left, in the view of the orthodox. But on many other issues—for example, workers' participation, the rights of women and sexual minorities, and protection of the environment—the young are far more open to new ideas than are the old. Today, these newer issues are at the cutting edge of social change and increasingly define where the Left really is.

IS THE WORK ETHIC DECLINING?

There has been a great deal of discussion about the decline of the "work ethic" in the United States and other advanced industrial societies. The citizens of these countries have come to take a comfortable life for granted, it is argued, and no longer feel the need to scramble for a living. The peoples of less prosperous countries (especially those in East Asia) are still hungry, it is said—and still eager to put in long hours of diligent effort for the sake of economic achievement.

Our evidence on this score shows a more complex pattern than the above suggests. These *are* some indications of an intergenerational shift in which the young and the postmaterialists in North America are de-emphasizing competition and hard work, and increasingly attributing poverty to social injustice rather than to a failure of individual effort. This suggests a shift away from the traditional emphasis on individual achievement, but the pattern is complex: These attitudes correlate clearly with *either* age *or* values, but not with both. Moreover, along with this we find evidence of a *rising* sense of pride in one's work.

We suspect that these mixed results reflect ongoing changes in both the nature of work and in the values that people bring to work. Nevertheless, the *kind* of work people do is shifting from work that requires sweat and dogged determination to work that requires judgment and creativity. Furthermore, it is not that postmaterialists are lazier than materialists, but that they are motivated by different concerns. In looking for a job, materialists are mainly concerned with getting a job that pays a good salary and has little risk of unemployment; postmaterialists are most interested in finding interesting and congenial work.

This is not just a matter of lip service. Controlling for the fact that they start with higher levels of education, postmaterialists tend to be economic underachievers, choosing jobs that pay less but have higher prestige (and are more interesting) than those chosen by materialists (Inglehart 1990:169–76). In other words, materialists tend to maximize income, while postmaterialists maximize the *quality* of their work life. Since the postmaterialists have grown up with a relatively secure sense that their economic needs will be met, this seems like a rational shift in goals, to maximize utilities that are not yet adequately fulfilled.

Figure 5.11 shows the age differences associated with an index of emphasis on individual achievement. This index sums up how strongly one believes in (1) individual responsibility, (2) competition, and (3) the effectiveness of hard work. These are among the crucial values associated with the rise of capitalism and individual economic achievement. As Figure 5.11 demonstrates, the old emphasize these values more strongly than the young; this is true in all three countries, but the differences are greatest in the United States and Canada. Mexico, which starts

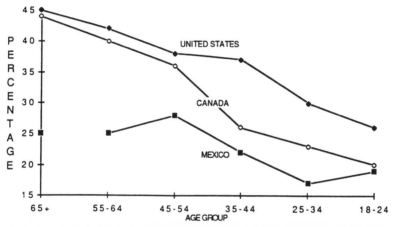

Figure 5.11. Emphasis on individual achievement, by age group. Percentage who gave relatively strong support (above the mean on a ten-point scale) to the first of the two alternatives, in response to all three questions:

1. Individuals should take more responsibility for themselves . . .
. . . The state should do more to see that everyone is provided for.
2. Competition is good, it stimulates people to work . . .
. . . Competition is bad, it brings out the worst in people.
3. Hard work usually bring about a better life . . .
. . . Hard work does not bring success, it is more a matter of luck and connections.

The value in Mexico's 65+ group is missing because the Mexican sample contains fewer than 30 cases over 65 years of age. *Source:* 1990 World Values Survey.

at a lower level, shows less decline as one moves from old to young—with the result that the youngest Mexicans emphasize these values as much as the younger Canadians and nearly as much as the younger Americans.

Postmaterialists emphasize individual achievement less than materialists do—but the differences are small except in Mexico (see Figure 5.12). These results hint at an intergenerational shift away from individual achievement, but the linkage with materialist/postmaterialist values is so faint that we are left in doubt—particularly in view of the fact that in previous cases when the correlation with age and materialist/ postmaterialist values was inconsistent, it was *values* that proved the better predictor. Why is the relationship with postmaterialism so weak? One possible reason is that the postmaterialists tend to be recruited from the upper socioeconomic strata (their relative economic security is one reason why they *are* postmaterialists). Accordingly, they grew up in a milieu that emphasized individual responsibility, competition, and hard work (one reason why their parents or grandparents *became* relatively prosperous). Though their personal life experiences lead them to downplay the importance of these attributes, the postmaterialists started from a relatively high level: hence, the modest net size of the differences in their attitudes toward economic achievement.

To test this interpretation we would need data on these attitudes from at least two, and preferably three, generations of respondents, so we must leave the question undecided. We do not have such data; this battery was asked only in the 1990 surveys. The available evidence suggests intergenerational change, but the signals are not clear.

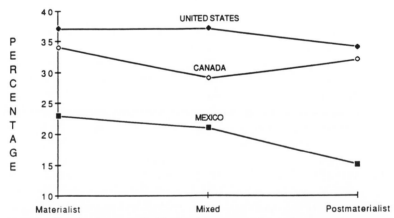

Figure 5.12. Emphasis on individual achievement, by value type (percentage placing relatively strong emphasis on individual responsibility, competition and hard work). *Source:* 1990 World Values Survey.

Now let us turn to a set of attitudes that shows the converse pattern: the correlations with age are weak (and curvilinear), but there is a strong correlation with materialist/postmaterialist values. These attitudes respond to the question:

> Why are there people in this country who live in need? Here are four possible reasons. Which one do you consider to be most important?
> 1. Because they are unlucky.
> 2. Because of laziness and lack of will power.
> 3. Because there is injustice in our society.
> 4. It is an inevitable part of modern progress.

Reality, of course, is more complex than any of these explanations. In given cases, poverty can be traced to random events, such as accidents or illness; to individual motivational factors; to racial or sexual discrimination; to structural unemployment; or to the interaction of two or more such factors. But it is clear that some people tend to see poverty as due to one of these factors, above all, while others attribute it mainly to other causes.

The second of these choices is particularly interesting, because it places responsibility squarely on individuals: they could escape poverty if they were willing to work. The third alternative, on the other hand, places the blame on society: poverty is due to social injustice.

The former choice attributes poverty to internal causes, while the latter choice attributes it to external causes. Social-psychological research indicates that internal attribution is linked with greater effort and higher rates of academic achievement than is external attribution. This finding is logical: if one considers the causes of success or failure to be outside one's control, there is no point in putting forth extra effort. Thus, the responses to these questions may tell us something about one's achievement orientations.

First, let us examine the responses of those who attribute poverty to individual laziness. As Figure 5.13 indicates, the young are slightly less apt to make this attribution than are the old, but the differences are not very large: for both the United States and Canada, the most striking feature of the relationship with age is its curvilinearity. In both countries, the oldest group tends to attribute poverty to individual laziness (in the United States, fully half of the group makes this their first choice, out of four alternatives). The proportion making this choice falls steeply among those aged thirty-five to sixty-four, but then shows a resurgence among the two youngest groups. Could this curvilinear pattern reflect the recent reversal of a historic trend? Or does it reflect a life cycle effect? One might posit, for example, that those who are in their prime earning years are less likely to attribute poverty to laziness than those who are

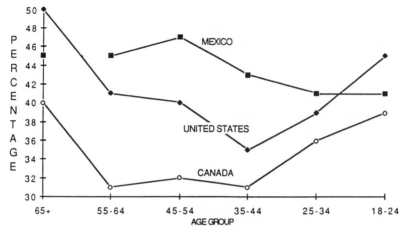

Figure 5.13. Poverty attributed to individual laziness, by age group. Question: Why are there needy people in this country? The following are four possible reasons, which *one* reason do you consider to be most important?

1. Because they are unlucky
2. Because of laziness and lack of will power
3. Because there is injustice in our society
4. It is an inevitable part of modern progress.

The value in Mexico's 65+ group is missing because the Mexican sample contains fewer than 30 cases over 65 years of age. *Source:* 1981 World Values Survey.

retired or just at the start of their careers. This life cycle explanation seems somewhat counterintuitive, however: it makes those with the lowest incomes *most* likely to attribute poverty to laziness. This is particularly implausible for the retired, for whom poverty *is* largely beyond their control. It seems more plausible to assume that the oldest group tends to attribute poverty to laziness because of persisting attitudes from earlier life, rather than because they themselves are now old. Again, we would need data from a long time series in order to determine exactly what is at work here, and we do not have it: these questions were first asked in the 1990 surveys.

However, we do have some supplementary evidence in Figure 5.14, which shows the linkage between this response and material-ist/postmaterialist values. Here, by contrast with Figure 5.13, the pattern is unambiguous. In all three countries, the postmaterialists are less likely to attribute poverty to laziness than are the materialists. The tendency is moderate in Mexico and strong in the United States and Canada. This is an interesting finding. Postmaterialists were only a little less likely than

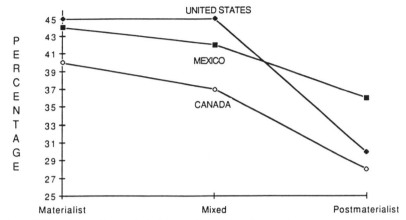

Figure 5.14. Poverty attributed to individual laziness, by value type. Question: Why are there needy people in this country? The following are four possible reasons, which *one* reason do you consider to be most important?

1. Because they are unlucky
2. Because of laziness and lack of will power
3. Because there is injustice in our society
4. It is an inevitable part of modern progress.

Source: 1990 World Values Survey.

materialists to emphasize individual responsibility, competition, and hard work (see Figure 5.11), but they are a good deal less likely to attribute poverty to laziness. Why?

Probably because the former items are framed in terms that apply to oneself and one's own view of achievement, while the latter question refers specifically to people who live in poverty. Coming from middle-class backgrounds, postmaterialists are themselves almost as achievement oriented as anyone else. But having experienced economic security throughout their formative years, postmaterialists tend to take it for granted: for anyone to be impoverished seems abnormal, an indication that something must be wrong with the system.

Figure 5.15 shows an age breakdown for the percentage of respondents who chose the leading alternative, which attributes poverty to social injustice. The pattern is a mirror image of Figure 5.13: it too is curvilinear, but here the middle-aged groups are *most* likely to choose this alternative. Overall, the young are more likely to choose this explanation than the old, but the pattern is weak: its most striking feature, again, is its curvilinearity. Figure 5.16 completes the picture, demonstrating that while the age relationship may be ambiguous, the relation-

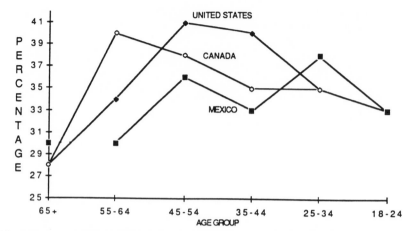

Figure 5.15. Poverty attributed to social injustice, by age group. (See legend to Figure 5.14.) The value in Mexico's 65+ group is missing because the Mexican sample contains fewer than 30 cases over 65 years of age. *Source:* 1990 World Values Survey.

ship with materialist/postmaterialist values is not: postmaterialists are a good deal likelier to attribute poverty to social injustice than are materialists, in all three countries.

The two variables show complementary patterns. When examining explanations for poverty, we find a pattern in which analyses by value type suggest an intergenerational shift from attributing poverty to internal factors, toward attributing it to external causes. This would tend to relocate one's focus from individual efforts at achievement, toward placing the responsibility on society. While the age and value differences linked with these attitudes are consistent (with the young deviating in the same direction as the postmaterialists), the age correlation is weak, and a marked curvilinearity is present, which *could* be an indication that the intergenerational shift has reversed direction in recent years.

The evidence concerning emphasis on individual achievement is a mirror image of the above: here we found a clear tendency for the young to endorse individual responsibility, competition, and hard work less strongly than the old—but the differences across value types were faint. Overall, the evidence suggests an intergenerational shift, but we cannot be sure.

Finally, let us examine another type of work-related attitude: the degree to which one takes pride in one's work. Here, too, the signals given by our two indicators are mixed. In this case, however, we *do* have time series data, and they show a trend that is consistent across all three nations.

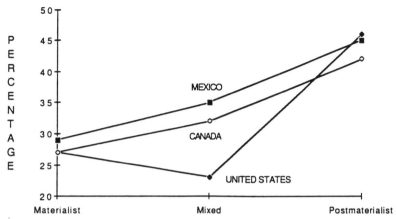

Figure 5.16. Poverty attributed to social injustice, by value type. (See legend to Figure 5.14.) *Source:* 1990 World Values Survey.

The young tend to take less pride in their work than do the older respondents. The differences are not large, but they appear in all three nations. This might well reflect a life cycle phenomenon: in both the United States and Canada, the difference is mainly due to a drop among the eighteen- to twenty-four-year-old cohort, many of whom are not yet engaged in long-term occupations, so they would not be likely to take much pride in their occupation (if any).

Our values indicator, on the other hand, shows that postmaterialists take *more* pride in their work than do materialists. The differences are modest, but in all three countries they point in the opposite direction from the (rather weak) age group differences. Our experience so far has been that, when age and materialist/postmaterialist values give contradictory indicators, *value type* has proven to be the more accurate predictor of subsequent changes. Given the presence of a highly plausible life cycle explanation for the age relationship found here, we might expect changes to move toward increased pride in one's work.

Figure 5.17 compares responses to this item in 1981 and in 1990. In all three countries, we find at least a modest *increase* in the percentage saying they take "a lot" of pride in their work. Once again, when the age differences contradict the differences across materialist/postmaterialist value types, we observe changes that move in the direction of postmaterialist values.

Taken together, these findings do not support the notion that the work ethic is declining in any simple fashion. Instead, the data suggest that emphasis on individual responsibility, hard work, and competition may be declining, together with a shift from internal to external attribu-

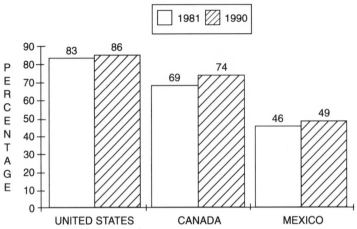

Figure 5.17. Percentage who take "a lot" of pride in their work 1981 vs. 1990. *Source:* 1981 and 1990 World Values Surveys.

tion of the causes of poverty—*but*, at the same time, people are coming to take more pride in their work. The kind of work that most people are doing has been undergoing relatively rapid change in the past decade, moving in a direction where people are likelier to identify with it and take pride in it. At the same time, they may be downplaying the importance of individual achievement. These questions refer to different aspects of one's orientation toward work, and they could be moving in different directions. Our findings indicate that what is happening is not simply a decline in the work ethic, but a shift in what motivates people.

PREDICTING SOCIAL CHANGE: A SUMMARY OF RESULTS

In the last three chapters, we have analyzed indicators of intergenerational change in social, political, and economic attitudes. When significant differences exist across both age groups and value types and when they point in a consistent direction, our theory predicts that change should occur and specifies the direction in which it should move. For most of these attitudes, we have data from both 1981 and 1990 that enable us to test these predictions. Table 5.1 sums up the overall success and failure of these predictions.

The evidence examined in Chapters 3, 4, and 5 generated a total of thirty-four predictions for which time series data are now available. The changes actually observed from 1981 to 1990 conformed to our predictions in thirty-one out of these thirty-four cases. In three instances, changes took place that ran counter to our predictions. In one of these

Table 5.1. Changes Predicted from 1981 Data and Changes Observed, 1981–1990

Variable	Does this variable show consistent correlations with both age and value type (i.e., old : young = materialist : postmaterialist)	Do the responses to this variable shift in the predicted direction from 1981 to 1990[a]
A. Sexual restrictiveness		
U.S.	Yes	Yes
Canada	Yes	Yes
Mexico	Yes	Yes
B. Emphasize independence, imagination, overobedience, good manners for children		
U.S.	Yes	Yes
Canada	Yes	Yes
Mexico	Yes	Yes
C. Favor greater respect for authority		
U.S.	Yes	Yes
Canada	Yes	Yes
Mexico	Yes	Yes
D. Religious outlook		
U.S.	Yes	(Yes)
Canada	Yes	Yes
Mexico	Yes	Yes
E. Church attendance		
U.S.	Yes	(Yes)
Canada	Yes	Yes
Mexico	Yes	Yes
F. Civil permissiveness		
U.S.	No	—
Canada	Yes	Yes
Mexico	No	—
G. Emphasis on family duty		
U.S.	Yes	No
Canada	Yes	No
Mexico	Yes	Yes
H. Confidence in govt. institutions		
U.S.	Yes	Yes
Canada	Yes	Yes
Mexico	No	—
I. Confidence in nongovt. institutions		
U.S.	Yes	Yes
Canada	Yes	Yes
Mexico	Yes	(No)
J. National pride		
U.S.	Yes	Yes
Canada	Yes	Yes
Mexico	Yes	Yes

(continued)

Table 5.1. (*Continued*)

Variable	Does this variable show consistent correlations with both age and value type (i.e., old : young = materialist : postmaterialist)	Do the responses to this variable shift in the predicted direction from 1981 to 1990[a]
K. Unconventional political participation		
U.S.	Yes	Yes
Canada	Yes	Yes
Mexico	Yes	Yes
L. Support for employee participation in business		
U.S.	Yes	Yes
Canada	Yes	Yes
Mexico	No	—
M. Following instructions at work		
U.S.	Yes	Yes
Canada	Yes	Yes
Mexico	No	—
Total number of cases that generate predictions	34	
Correct predictions	31	(91%)
Incorrect predictions	3	(9%)

Source: 1981 and 1990 World Values Surveys.
[a] Parentheses indicate weak relationship, dash indicates no prediction.

three cases (levels of confidence in nongovernmental institutions among the Mexican public), the disconfirmation was very weak (a shift of one percentage point in the wrong direction).

But with one set of attitudes (emphasis on family duty), our predictions were dead wrong. In two of the three countries, substantial changes took place that moved in the opposite direction from the one we predicted. These changes are too large to be attributed to sampling error. There is convincing evidence that the Canadian and U.S. publics really did shift toward placing greater emphasis on parents' obligations toward their children and children's obligations toward their parents. This seems to be a significant phenomenon, and it demonstrates once again that intergenerational change is not the *only* factor at work in social change.

In this book we have focused mainly on those aspects of social change that reflect intergenerational value shifts. We have done so because this type of change is particularly interesting: it is a component of change that can be predicted. But no sensible person would assume that generational differences *alone* determine what happens. As Figure 3.2 demonstrated, even when strong and enduring intergenerational value dif-ferences are present, the responses at any given time are *also* influenced by conditions in the current socioeconomic environment.

Both in 1981 and in 1990, the young placed less emphasis on family duty than did the old; and postmaterialists emphasized them less heavi-ly than did materialists. The Mexican data show the trend predicted by these facts, but in both the United States and Canada, our prediction is resoundingly refuted: from 1981 to 1990, both publics shifted toward placing *more* emphasis on family duty. Any explanation we could offer for this period effect would be ad hoc: we did not expect it, but it clearly did occur. It seems likely that enduring intergenerational differences *do* exist with this variable, but that from 1981 to 1990 the effects of inter-generational population replacement were swamped by a strong period effect favoring family duty. This might even represent the beginning of a new intergenerational shift in the opposite direction, though we find no evidence of such a reversal so far: even in 1990, the youngest group still placed least emphasis on family duty in all three countries. In any case, these findings illustrate an important point: our predictions do not al-ways come true. They are based on evidence of intergenerational differ-ences, and intergenerational population replacement is never the only factor involved. Over short periods of time, its effects are usually rather modest. They can easily be swamped by period effects. But over the long term, fluctuations due to current events tend to cancel themselves out—whereas generational differences may persist over several decades, in which case their cumulative impact can be massive.

Despite these disclaimers about the importance of period effects, thir-ty-one of our thirty-four predictions *did* come true: in these cases, signifi-cant changes did occur from 1981 to 1990—and they moved in the predicted direction. This is a remarkable record, vastly better than one would attain by chance. It is encouraging to those who believe that with a sufficient investment of time and resources, social science can develop into a predictive science. Moreover, the number of successful predic-tions is actually a good deal larger than thirty-one, for most of the vari-ables dealt with in Table 5.1 are actually compound indices, based on the responses to several questions. The largest battery of questions in both the 1981 and 1990 World Values Surveys concerns religion: more than forty items have significant loadings on the factor that generates our index of religious outlook. Most of these items show correlations with age and materialist/postmaterialist values that are similar to those shown for this index—and most of them show changes in the predicted direction from 1981 to 1990. If we analyzed each of these items sepa-rately, we would bore the reader to death, but we would greatly increase the number of successful predictions. To be fair, we would also need to perform separate analyses on each of the four items that make up our index of family duty, which would increase the number of incorrect predictions—but on the whole, our batting average would improve.

Correct prediction on thirty-one out of thirty-four topics is remarkable, and to be frank it is better than we expected. Knowing that intergenerational population replacement is not the only factor involved, we were most confident of finding confirmation on those variables that showed relatively strong value differences and strong age group differences in 1981, and less confident that the other variables would move in the expected direction. In fact, 91 percent of the predictions that we could test held up.

One reason for this is the fact that the period from 1981 to 1990 was a time of rising prosperity—at least for the United States and Canada. This was not true of Mexico, where the 1980s were a decade of economic stagnation and high unemployment. But for two of our three countries, our time series spans a period of economic expansion, which should be conducive to the spread of postmaterialist values and other orientations favored by conditions of economic security. Thus, for the United States and Canada, the period effects were working in the same direction as the prevailing intergenerational changes. In an era of economic decline, period effects would tend to work *against* population replacement effects, and would be likelier to neutralize or reverse them. Not all period effects are linked with economic conditions, of course: the forces that brought about a resurgence of emphasis on family duty seem to be a case in point. But by and large, we would expect our predictions to hold up better during periods of rising prosperity than during periods of decline.

For the period from 1981 to 1990, however, we were able to make correct forecasts of mass attitude changes in thirty-one out of the thirty-four cases in which the indicators gave consistent signals. We should note that these were not "predictions" of the type in which one set of variables is used to explain another set of variables within the same survey. These were genuine predictions, published long before the data used to test them were collected. Analyzing the 1981 surveys, Inglehart (1986, 1988, 1990) found a pattern of consistent correlations with age and value types and interpreted their evidence as pointing to a pervasive cultural shift in advanced industrial societies—one that went far beyond the materialist/postmaterialist shift noted earlier, and encompassing changing religious, sexual, economic, social, and political norms.

The 1990 surveys carried out in the United States, Canada, and Mexico clearly confirm these predictions. Comparable surveys were carried out from 1990 to 1993 in over forty-three societies around the world. It remains to be seen to what degree the data from these surveys indicate that a pervasive but coherent process of cultural change is reshaping advanced industrial societies (these data are analyzed in Inglehart, forthcoming). The data from three North American countries, at least, give convincing evidence that these societies are undergoing profound changes—and on the whole, they are converging toward a common set of goals. What they are moving toward is *not* Americanization: the United States is changing like other societies. They are moving toward something new, something that in the long run may provide a global cultural consensus within which a wide variety of cultures can coexist harmoniously.

6

Political Integration in North America?

North America may be on the verge of becoming something more than a geographical expression. The United States, Canada, and Mexico are moving toward continental free trade to avoid isolation in a world that is increasingly organized into regional trading networks, and to exploit the advantages that come from stable access to large markets. In some respects, continental free trade might be viewed as window dressing, a formal regularization of de facto economic integration that has been welding the three economies together since the 1950s. However, that perspective obscures the fact that comprehensive continental free trade represents a substantial policy shift for each of the three partners. For the United States, the North American Free Trade Agreement (NAFTA) signifies a historic departure from a long-standing commitment to the multilateralism that governed American international economic thinking throughout most of the postwar period. For Canadians and Mexicans, whose policies throughout this century were designed to resist continental economic integration, the decisions to embrace comprehensive North American free trade amount to even more momentous policy shifts. Like other small states that rely heavily on trade with a single market, both Canadian and Mexican governments sought to diversify export opportunities in order to dilute dependence on a single trading partner. For both countries, a comprehensive continental trade agreement closes that chapter; it means that the search for a "third way" has been abandoned.

Continental economic integration sparks vigorous domestic debates in the three North American countries for at least two reasons. First, economic motives are central for both Canada and Mexico. For the United States, which already is a large economic unit, political concerns may be paramount: the greatest benefit of North American free trade may be its role in helping establish a stable and prosperous Mexico, to its south. Nevertheless, opening trade realigns the comparative advantages of the economic sectors within domestic economies and brings new winners and losers. Thus public attitudes to free trade in each country are related to where individual citizens sit in their domestic economies.

135

Second, free trade brings into sharp focus long-standing political, social, and cultural dilemmas, which are particularly acute for Canada and Mexico; within Canada these dilemmas have had a profound impact on the Quebecois. They involve national and individual autonomy, cultural identity, and prosperity; they concern powerful economic incentives and collective values. The central problem has been, How can Canadians and Mexicans control their own fate when both countries are locked into such asymmetrical economic relations with the United States? Even in the United States, many people express anxiety about whether they will be able to preserve their traditional way of life in the face of large-scale immigration, much of which is Hispanic.

Because these dilemmas stem both from evaluations of economic interests *and* from judgments about what impact economic integration has on national cultures and autonomy, we would expect public attitudes toward freer trade to reflect value differences within the three national publics. Our evidence indicates that they do. Postmaterialists tend to be more concerned with cultural issues than do materialists. Freer trade poses much less of a threat to American national culture than it does to its continental neighbors and, as Figure 6.1 shows, public support for closer economic ties with Canada and Mexico is as high among postmaterialists as it is among materialists in the United States. In Canada, however, the postmaterialists are far less enthusiastic about closer economic ties with the United States than are materialists, and this same pattern emerges in Mexico. When it comes to closer economic ties with *Mexico*, however, in both the United States and Canada it is the postmaterialists who support closer ties. Our interpretation is simple: when their society's cultural autonomy does not seem threatened, postmaterialists are even more supportive of international ties than are materialists; when cultural autonomy *does* seem threatened, by incorporation into a more massive entity, postmaterialists are wary. Hence, both the Canadian and Mexican publics support NAFTA mainly for economic reasons.

There is little question that global change has eroded the importance of national borders. States are less autonomous than they once were and a variety of economic transformations have contributed to this trend. Increasingly, international capital and multinational corporations are indifferent to national boundaries. They locate where the balance between risk and return on investment is most favorable (Keohane and Ooms 1975). Postwar tariff reductions resulted in massive increases in cross-border transactions and simultaneously reduced the relative significance of domestic markets. Free trade advances this process one step further. As free traders argue, political borders artificially distort markets and introduce inefficiencies by imposing unnecessary transfer costs. Noneconomic factors, notably revolutionary advances in technology and information, have also hastened globalization and made political

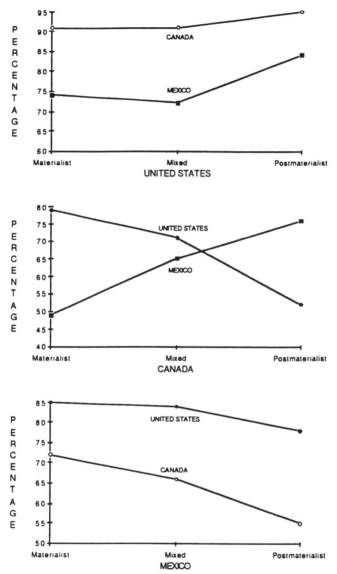

Figure 6.1. Support for "closer economic ties" by value type. *Source:* 1990 World Values Survey.

borders more porous. Information is transmitted instantly around the globe. Publics are more aware of and more knowledgeable about world events. Publics have become less parochial and more cosmopolitan and the world is a smaller place psychologically. Freer trade makes national economies more vulnerable to world events, and these other transformations made national communities more open to global trends in ideas and values.

Political boundaries, of course, may still provide environments in which national publics can exercise unique collective choices even though freer trade may encourage policy harmonization and constrain the range of choices available to publics within those boundaries. Conventional wisdom holds that national boundaries in North America are important because they delimit communities with different collective values. The key assumption is that national values *are* different. Generalizations about national values usually rely upon inferences drawn from indirect evidence. But the clear conclusion emerging from our analysis of direct evidence is that substantial value changes have taken place in each of the three North American countries in the course of the last decade. Significantly, the evidence indicates that national values are not as distinct, or unique, as they once were. National differences still prevail and these differences may indeed reflect the residues of founding circumstances. But when it comes to the "main values" that Deutsch (1968) argues are crucial to integration, our central finding is that values are converging between the three societies. If North Americans increasingly want similar things for themselves and for their children, if the kinds of public choices they want to make have become more similar with the passage of time, then fundamental questions arise: What purposes do national borders serve in *contemporary* North America? Is political union a logical extension of economic union? Is there any public support for the idea of abolishing the borders between these three countries?

The idea that Canadians or Mexicans would seriously consider doing away with the borders between their country and the United States is a radical one. It amounts to a flat contradiction of the founding rationales of both countries and it flies in the face of long-standing national policy efforts to resist the economic, political, social, and cultural influences of their powerful American neighbor. If we simply relied upon conventional assumptions and projected past history into the present, it would be surprising if *any* Canadian or Mexican nationals supported political integration with the United States. However, as we have seen, values change, and we need not assume that national loyalties have necessarily retained the salience they once had. Indeed, evidence presented in Chapter 4 indicates that they have *not*.

SUPPORT FOR POLITICAL UNION

To probe the prospects for North American political union, respondents in each of the three North American countries were asked a simple "bottom line" question: "All things considered do you think we should do away with the border between the United States and Canada?" In Mexico, the wording was "between Mexico and the United States."

Needless to say, this question goes far beyond any proposal that is currently being discussed by the governments of these countries. But the levels of support for political union that we find are much higher than a projection based on past history would predict, especially in Canada and Mexico. As Table 6.2 shows, about one in four Canadians (24 percent) and Mexicans (25 percent) support such a radical change as doing away with the border with the United States, and nearly half of all American respondents (46 percent) favor abolishing the U.S.-Canadian border.

As would be expected, support for continental political union varies not only across publics but also within publics and it does so in ways that echo national distributions in support for free trade. For example, American support for union with Canada is strongest among those in big business. By contrast, those working for big business in Canada and Mexico—those whose jobs are more likely to depend on long-standing protectionist policies behind which domestic branch plant economic sectors grew—are among the most strident opponents of political union. Following the same logic, it is reasonable to suppose that those Canadians and Mexicans with the most to gain—low-income groups and unskilled labor—would be most likely to favor political union. The clearest support for these expectations is found in the Canadian evidence. Of all occupational groups, unskilled labor is among the most likely to support doing away with the border, and the relationship between income level and continental union is consistent and strong in the predicted direction: the lower the income level, the higher the support for political union.

Systematic regional variations also come into play. Americans who live farthest away from the Canadian border, for example, are least likely to support union with that country. A similar pattern emerges in Mexico; opposition to political union increases as distance from the American border increases. In Canada, one in three Quebecois favors eliminating the border with the United States, as compared to one in five Canadians from other regions—a finding that reflects the weaker Quebecois attachments to the Canadian state. Partisanship and patriotism also shape attitudes to political union in predictable ways. Supporters of those parties that have been most critical of "foreign influences" on domestic economies and cultures—the Republicans in the United States, the New Democratic party in Canada, and the PRD in Mexico—are the staunchest opponents of political union. Predictably also, those respondents who express the most national pride are least likely to favor continental union.

No previous national surveys have ever asked the three North American publics about abolishing the borders, so we cannot measure how these attitudes toward political union may have changed over time. But our analysis in the preceding chapters has shown that many value changes are consistently linked to two indicators: age and the rise of postmaterialism. We have demonstrated, for example, that national pride is declining in each of the three countries and that the erosion of national pride is significantly related to both age and postmaterialism; in all three countries it is the young and postmaterialists who score lowest on our patriotism index. Are age and value type related to support for political union? The evidence is mixed but intriguing. As Figure 6.2 shows, young Americans and Mexicans are most likely to support political union. Age effects are most consistent among our American respondents and they are present but weaker in Mexico. However, no such pattern emerges among Canadians; in that setting it is the forty-five- to fifty-four-year-old age group that most favors political union. When we turn to consider how different value types react to abolishing borders, the evidence is striking. As Figure 6.3 demonstrates, in both Mexico and Canada, political union appeals to materialists, who are primarily concerned with potential economic gains. By contrast, the postmaterialists are more concerned about potential losses of autonomy and cultural

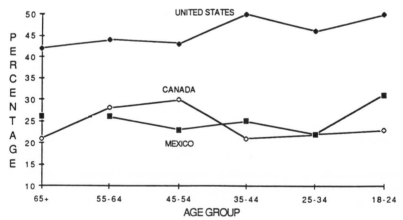

Figure 6.2. Support for abolishing the border, by age group. The question reads: All things considered, do you think we should do away with the border between the United States and Canada (U.S.)/Canada and the United States (Canada)/Mexico and the United States (Mexico)? (percentage in favor of abolishing the border). The value in Mexico's 65+ group is missing because the Mexican sample contains fewer than 30 cases over 65 years of age. *Source:* 1990 World Values Survey.

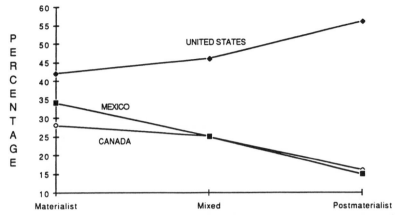

Figure 6.3. Support for abolishing the border, by value type. (See legend to Figure 6.2.) *Source:* 1990 World Values Survey.

independence, and are much more likely to oppose political union. Given the fact that the United States has nearly 70 percent of the population of the three North American countries, political union does not pose the same threat to American cultural identity that it seems to represent to many Canadians and Mexicans. On the other hand, the material gains from union would also be considerably smaller for the United States: the size of its market will increase only marginally. Thus American support for political union consistently conforms to precisely the opposite pattern: support is lower among materialists and highest among the more cosmopolitan postmaterialists.

ADVANTAGES AND DISADVANTAGES

Doing away with the border implies trade-offs and the three publics are plainly divided on the issue. What kinds of concerns underpin these different positions? Respondents in each of the three countries were asked two open-ended questions. The first probed for perceived advantages: "What do you think would be the main advantages of the United States and Canada forming one country?" (This was the formulation used in the United States and Canada; the Mexican survey asked about Mexico and the United States.) The second question asked: "And what do you think would be the main disadvantages?" (The same question was used in all three surveys.)

Open-ended questions are a useful tool for probing such novel and unexplored issues as political union. Because open-ended questions encourage publics to formulate their answers in their own words and without any cues, these responses enable us to check our assumptions and may provide further insights. We have assumed that these publics would support union for economic reasons and oppose it for the kinds of cultural reasons that historians have speculated about. But is that really the case? Do citizens in each of the three countries see it that way? And do other considerations enter public calculations about what kinds of benefits and losses political union might bring? Table 6.1 summarizes a great deal of evidence, but several common themes emerge from the data. The central finding confirms the assumption that publics do see economic factors as the primary and overwhelming advantage of political integration. At the same time, respondents see other advantages as well. A significant proportion of the American public (17 percent), for example, sees political advantages in doing away with the U.S.-Canadian border. "A bigger country" and such strategic considerations as "a better defense" were the most frequently cited reasons. Equally intriguing is the discovery that about one in ten Canadians (three times the proportion of their Mexican counterparts) also see political advantages to that arrangement and they offer very similar reasons for doing so: "more military protection" and "being part of a superpower." Some express a preference for the American system of government. Predictably though, few Canadians or Mexicans see *any* social/cultural advantages to forming one country. The most revealing finding is that the publics in each of the three countries are about evenly divided between

Table 6.1.   Abolishing Borders: Advantages and Disadvantages[a]

	U.S. with Canada (%)	Canada with U.S. (%)	Mexico with U.S. (%)
Advantages			
Economic	33	42	41
Political	17	11	3
Social/cultural relations	9	3	7
General/other	9	4	18
No advantages	32	41	32
Disadvantages			
Economic	10	11	5
Political	28	10	5
Social/cultural relations	34	60	52
General/other	—	6	30
No disadvantages	28	13	7

Source: 1990 World Values Survey.
[a] See text for questions asked

those who see "no advantages at all" to doing away with borders and those who focus on expected economic payoffs.

The tension between economic advantages and sociocultural disadvantages comes into full view when we contrast distributions in the top half of Table 6.1 with the distributions in the bottom half of the table. More than half of all Canadians and Mexicans, and over a third of Americans, cite a variety of sociocultural objections to the idea of forming one country. When the broad sociocultural category is examined more closely, we can see wide but predictable national variations in the kinds of concerns publics raised. Overall, the American responses are relatively diffuse; they are scattered across a variety of issues. Some think that "language differences" or "differences in customs" would become a problem if the border with Canada were erased. Others respond "we can't take care of ourselves," or more generally suggested that Americans and Canadians are "just too different" and "wouldn't get along." These diffuse and general views stand in sharp contrast to the tight clusterings found in the Canadian and Mexican responses. Nearly half of all Canadians harmonized on the same single theme: "the loss of Canadian identity." The Mexicans' responses are about evenly divided between two concerns: the "loss of national identity" and "discrimination against Mexicans." In both cases though, social/cultural concerns are obviously paramount and political or economic disadvantages come a very distant second and third.

The tensions between economic advantages and social/cultural disadvantages are also evident *within* national publics and these tensions too are distributed in predictable ways. There are striking differences, for example, between how Anglophones and Francophones in Canada view the prospects of political union with the United States. French Canadians are more likely than their Anglophone counterparts to see economic advantages to political union, but they are also much less concerned about social/cultural disadvantages that union might bring. Above all, they are much less likely to view "loss of Canadian identity" as a drawback.

The answers volunteered by postmaterialists and materialists are also quite different. In each national setting, materialists are more likely than postmaterialists to stress the economic advantages of union while postmaterialists in Canada and Mexico are more likely to express reservations about the social and cultural consequences of political integration. Regardless of whether we rely on the detailed responses or on the broader cross-national configurations of responses, the message emerging from our data is the same: the primary areas of concern reflect the same central dilemma, the tension between the expected economic benefits and the social/cultural costs of integration.

VIEWS ABOUT POLITICAL INTEGRATION:
HOW ROBUST ARE THEY?

So far, our examination of support for and opposition to North American political integration has focused upon how the three publics responded to the bottom line question: "All things considered do you think that we should do away with borders?" But the responses to this question provide no information about how firm or soft public attitudes toward political integration are. Undoubtedly, for some, doing away with the border is an unthinkable prospect under any circumstances. Responses to the open-ended questions indicate that only a minority of the public in each country (Americans, 32 percent; Canadians, 41 percent; and Mexicans, 32 percent) sees no advantage whatsoever in abolishing the borders. Similarly, only a minority of the public in each country supports the idea of abolishing borders (Americans, 46 percent; Canadians, 24 percent; and Mexicans, 25 percent). Taken together, these findings suggest that a significant proportion of all three publics occupy a middle ground; they are neither deeply committed nor opposed to political integration. Figure 6.4 shows how these attitudes are distributed. The pattern suggests that under the right conditions, a majority of publics in all three countries might be persuaded to support a single North American political unit. The critical question is: Just how flexible is public opinion about political union? Can we identify the "right conditions" that would be required to produce majority support for political union in each country?

One way to test the flexibility of public opinion is to see whether, and how much, public attitudes shift in response to various political union scenarios. The publics in all three countries were presented with seven scenarios, each of which spelled out different conditions for political integration. Specifically, they were asked whether they would support the idea of the United States and Canada (or Mexico and the United States in the Mexican survey) forming one country:

- if it meant that you would enjoy a higher standard of living?
- if it meant having a large French-speaking minority [American survey]/losing Canada's cultural identity [Canadian survey]?
- if it meant that we could deal more effectively with environmental issues like acid rain and pollution?
- if it meant that Canada would form 12 new states in the United States? [American and Canadian surveys]/that Mexico would form 32 new states in the United States [Mexican survey]?
- if it meant a better quality of life?
- if it meant having a government funded (rather than private) health-care system [American survey]/a privately funded rather than a government-funded health-care system [Canadian survey]/better public health care [Mexican survey]?

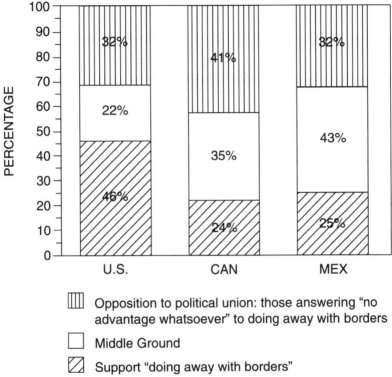

Opposition to political union: those answering "no advantage whatsoever" to doing away with borders

Middle Ground

Support "doing away with borders"

Figure 6.4. Views about political integration: How robust are they? *Source:* 1990 World Values Surveys.

As it turns out, these scenarios correspond almost precisely to the issues that our respondents had volunteered to open-ended questions that tapped views about the advantages and disadvantages of political union.

Do these scenarios have any impact on views about political union? The answer is an unequivocal yes. Table 6.2 summarizes the national responses to the seven scenario questions. The results are striking, for they suggest that public support for political union is remarkably fluid. They show that a clear majority of the publics in all three countries would support political union under either of two conditions: (1) "if it meant a better quality of life"; or (2) "if it meant that we could deal more effectively with environmental issues." Plainly, political integration is *not* an unthinkable prospect for most North Americans.

Discovering that North Americans would support forming one country if it meant a better quality of life is not entirely surprising. After all, a better quality of life can mean different things to different people and it seems likely that almost everyone would want it. More remarkable are

Table 6.2. Political Union Scenarios: National Responses

	U.S. with Canada (% favor)	Canada with U.S. (% favor)	Mexico with U.S. (% favor)
Better quality of life	81	50	64
Environmental issues	79	56	53
Higher std. of living	72	38	61
Public/private health care	67	12	51
12 new Canadian states	60	18	24
Less tax/services	45	17	37
Cultural identity	43	11	16
Abolish border	46	24	25

Source: 1990 World Values Survey.

the responses to the environmental scenario, for it captures a much more specific set of concerns. This finding underscores how central ecological issues have become to contemporary North Americans. In Mexico, the prospect of a higher standard of living is also a powerful incentive for political union; it raises support for political integration from 25 to 61 percent.

Responses to the health-care scenario are also striking in both the United States and Mexico. Health care has become an increasingly salient and controversial policy issue in the United States for a combination of at least two reasons: Medical costs have spiraled dramatically in the last decade. At the same time, some thirty million Americans have no access to the health-care system. That controversy revolves around the merits of a private versus a public health-care system. Our survey asked American respondents if they would support political union if it meant having a publicly funded health-care system, and the answers show that there is considerable enthusiasm for such a system: Canadians have had a publicly funded health-care system for a long time and they clearly like it. When asked, "What makes you most proud of Canada?" one in three Canadians volunteered, "Our health-care system." When asked a reversed version of the American health-care scenario, "Would you support political union if it meant a *private* health-care system?" the reply was a resounding *no*: support for political integration with the United States slumps. Mexicans also have a publicly funded health-care system but it is not generally thought to function well. Mexicans were asked, "Would you support political union if it meant a more efficient public health-care system?" As Table 6.2 shows, adding that condition boosts Mexican support for political integration.

One scenario dramatically decreases support for political union in all three publics, the scenario that relates to culture. We have already shown that concerns for national cultural identity underpin both Canadian and Mexican opposition to continental political union. A comparison of how publics react to the higher standard of living and cultural identity scenarios graphically illustrates once more the fundamental dilemmas between the prospects of economic gains and the threat to collective values that political union implies. Canadian national identity is fragile and has become more so during the last ten years. To the French and English founding peoples have been added waves of immigrants who claim neither English nor French ancestry. Further, the rights of new groups to retain their ethnic identities have been constitutionally protected and fostered by a variety of policies that work to foster multiculturalism. Increased cultural heterogeneity together with the policy of multiculturalism combine to project a weak image of Canadian national culture. At the same time, that culture absorbs powerful and unified national images from the United States. From a distance, the differences between Canadian and American values may not be obvious but Canadian-American cultural value differences seem significant to many Canadians, and they value these differences. Compared to the Canadian case, the Mexican cultural identity projects a much sharper image. Mexico is culturally more homogeneous than Canada, it has a population three times the size of Canada's, and the fact that relatively few Mexicans are fluent in English tends to weaken the impact of American cultural exports on Mexico. Even so, the perceived threat of cultural assimilation also stands as the major barrier to political integration between Mexico and the United States.

Historically, the United States has demonstrated a remarkable capacity to absorb immigrants and to forge a single, powerful national culture out of diverse peoples. Nonetheless, cultural concerns, such as concerns about Canada's Francophones, also have the effect of depressing American enthusiasm for political union with Canada. America's capacity to culturally integrate new groups may have been stretched to the limit by the relatively recent and growing influx of a Hispanic community of some twenty million, 63 percent of whom come from Mexico. Despite the fact that the United States has a long and successful record of integrating Francophones of Canadian origin in Louisiana and Maine, we might also anticipate that different cultural groups in both the United States and Canada may well have different attitudes toward political union between the two countries. They do. There are significant subcultural differences in attitudes toward the bottom line question, abolishing the border, and to most of the seven scenarios. White Americans are most likely to support doing away with the border and American Hispanics are the least likely to support it. The cultural differences within the Canadian population are even more striking. French Canadians are 50 percent more likely than their English Canadian counterparts to support doing away with the border. They are more likely to support political union if it means a better quality of life or solving environmental problems, and a near majority (49 percent) supports it if it means a higher standard of living. French Canadians evidently are much less concerned than English Canadians about cultural identity—or, at any rate, they are less concerned with preserving *Canadian* cultural identity. American Hispanics are less enthusiastic than American whites or blacks about political union with Canada, but the prospect of embracing a French minority has little impact on that opinion. There is virtually no difference between white and black Americans when it comes to the bottom line question about political union, but different scenarios do have different effects on the attitudes of the two groups. The environmental scenario has a much bigger impact on white Americans than it does on the other groups. For black Americans, public health care is a powerful incentive as is the higher standard of living scenario. Blacks are less likely than whites to receive prenatal care and black infant mortality rates are significantly higher. Understandably, economic and social welfare issues carry greater weight in that segment of the American population that is overrepresented in the underclass.

In the absence of time series data, we cannot be sure whether support for political integration is increasing or decreasing over time. But as before, two variables—age and postmaterialism—may provide some indications about the likely future direction of value change. When we examine national responses to the seven scenarios and pay particular attention to age effects and to the distribution of materialist and post-materialist values, a number of trends emerge. First, age is powerfully and consistently related to responses to the higher standard of living scenario and its impact is the same in all three national settings. The youngest groups are far more likely than older ones to support political union if union were to produce economic benefits. Three-quarters of the American public under forty-five years of age favors union while two-thirds of those over forty-five do so. Nearly 50 percent of young Canadians support union with the United States, compared to less than 30 percent of the oldest group. And in Mexico about 68 percent of the young and less than 60 percent of the oldest support union with the United States. The age effects operate in the same direction and produce even more emphatic results when the quality of life and environmental scenarios are considered. Age is unrelated to the health-care scenario in both Canada and Mexico but its impact on the American public is striking, and in one sense the findings are counterintuitive. Objectively, it is the older age groups who stand to gain most by public rather than private health care and consequently we might anticipate that the old would find public health care most attractive. The evidence suggests the opposite: it is the *young*, not the old, who are most likely to support public health care in the United States.

POLITICAL UNION, VALUE CHANGE, AND POLICY CONVERGENCE

We began exploring the prospects for continental political union by reviewing responses to a question about support for abolishing borders and by delving into public perceptions of the advantages and disadvantages of political union. These findings point to a seemingly straightforward conclusion. Most citizens recognize that political union would bring economic gains, but on balance these publics see cultural and other costs as outweighing those economic gains. When presented with a simple option, a majority of citizens in each country opposes the idea of political union.

However, when public attitudes are probed in greater detail, the evidence points to rather different conclusions. Opposition to political union is far less rigid than one might expect—indeed, it is remarkably fluid. Political union could only become a reality if the idea appealed to a majority of publics in each country. Under what conditions could majorities be forged? And are circumstances changing to make those conditions more likely?

To answer these questions, we must consider the various national perspectives. For the American public, support for continental political union is relatively high. A majority of postmaterialists there support political union under all seven of the scenarios considered. If, as we have also shown, the proportion of postmaterialists is growing with the passage of time, then we would expect continental political union to become more appealing to Americans as long as their country continues along this trajectory of value change. Postmaterialist values have the opposite effect on the Canadian and Mexican public: they depress support for political union. In the Mexican case the materialist-postmaterialist value divide is a much weaker cleavage for reasons we have already discussed, and support for political union is higher in Mexico than in Canada. Indeed, a majority of Mexicans support political union under four of the seven scenarios. By these indications it is Canadians who are the staunchest opponents of political union.

Opponents of free trade in both Canada and Mexico voice the fear that free trade would erode unique and treasured national policies. For that reason Canadians sought assurance that cultural industries and key social programs, such as the national public health system, would not be a part of the bargain. For very similar reasons, Mexicans seek a social contract as a part of a wide free-trade arrangement. The conventional wisdom assumes that policy convergence means that Canadian and Mexican domestic policies would be brought into line with American standards. Our evidence suggests that North American public opinion moves in precisely the opposite direction: A majority of Americans and Mexicans support political union if it means publicly funded health care (American survey) or a better public health system (Mexican survey). Conversely, Canadians are much less likely to support political union if it means a privately funded health-care system. The evidence is intriguing for two reasons: First, it contradicts the view that policy convergence is an unpopular by-product of integration or that it necessarily feeds opposition to greater integration. Second, it also challenges the assumption that the *direction* of policy convergence will be harmonization on American standards.

If the evidence of public attitudes to health care is instructive, then the evidence of public attitudes toward environmental issues is truly remarkable. The most striking finding clearly is that a majority of publics in all three countries support political union "if it means that we could deal more effectively with environmental issues like acid rain or environmental pollution." The implications of that finding are far-reaching in several respects. Not only do they indicate that environmental concerns override the staunchest Canadian opposition to political union, but they also illustrate the significance of North American convergence on yet another policy domain. In North America as elsewhere, pollution ignores national borders. It has been estimated that in 1985 alone some 3.8 million tons of sulfur dioxide blew into Canada from the United States, while some 1.8 million tons of the toxic gas drifted the other way. Half of all the acid rain falling on Canada originates in the United States and a quarter of the acid rain falling on the American northeast comes from Canada. Atmospheric and water-borne pollution has acidified thousands of lakes, corroded buildings, degraded crops and livestock, and toxic waste from industrial plants is directly linked to rising levels of respiratory diseases, particularly in children.

Although Mexico is far less industrialized than the United States or Canada, atmospheric pollution in Mexico City is as severe as in any metropolitan area on earth. The pollution crisis along the Mexican-U.S. border is of more recent vintage. Few Mexican border towns have the capacity to treat raw sewage, and environmental degradation has reached staggering proportions. On the Arizona side of the border, the incidence of hepatitis is twenty times the national average.

Differences in pollution standards create comparative economic advantages in exactly the same way that the price of labor or other factors of production do. In effect, lax environmental standards amount to a subsidy for polluting industries; they reap substantial economic gains by relocating to areas like the Mexican border towns, where labor costs are low and where environmental regulations and enforcement are less stringent. Mexico's Secretariat of Urban Development and Ecology reports that over one thousand American-owned plants on the Mexican side of the U.S.-Mexican border generate hazardous waste. Only 30 percent of these comply with Mexican regulations requiring them to file information on how they dispose of these wastes, and only 19 percent could demonstrate that they comply with Mexican environmental regulations. More than most issues, pollution is a transborder policy problem; it generates continental alliances and conflict that are played out in continental and national settings.

Public concern about the environment has increased dramatically in the last decade particularly in advanced industrial states, and environmentalism has been linked to the broad value changes that we have already described in the North American setting. The future implications for continental political union are clear. If public concern about the environment increases, then public support for political union is also likely to increase. Is there any evidence that environmentalism is on the rise?

Our 1991 surveys asked all three publics a battery of questions about environmental issues, questions that were quite separate from the political union scenarios. Do our two predictors of value change—age and postmaterialism—seem to have any impact on environmental concern? They do, although they work somewhat differently in the three national settings. Younger North Americans are more concerned about the environment than their older counterparts, but these age effects are stronger in Mexico than in the United States or Canada. Postmaterialism has a very significant impact on environmental attitudes in the American and Canadian publics, but little effect in Mexico. Only for the United States do both indicators predict rising emphasis on environmental protection, but there is partial support for this prediction in each of the other countries. We suspect that environmentalism *will* increase with the passage of time, and if it does, opposition to political union will tend to wane.

ECONOMIC AND POLITICAL INTEGRATION: THE CONNECTIONS

We began our investigation by suggesting that the European experience may contain important lessons for North Americans as the United States, Canada, and Mexico pursue free trade. At the outset, the original six members of the European Community were preoccupied with the tasks of lowering tariffs, increasing the mobility of labor and capital, and through cooperative efforts maximizing their competitive positions in a world in which prosperity increasingly depended on trade. This motive remains significant. But after thirty years and with an expanded membership, the European Community pursues greater political integration because making its combined strength effective requires policy coordination. Formal political integration, of course, does not inevitably proceed from greater economic integration but the lesson from the European experience is that economic and political forces cannot be easily disentangled.

A variety of integration theorists have concluded that similarity of values is conducive to integration (Etzioni 1965; Haas 1971; Nye 1968; Schmitter 1971; Puchala 1971). Indeed, according to Deutsch, mutual compatibility of values is an essential condition for integration (1968:126). The weight of our analysis in the last three chapters shows that North American values *have* been changing in the last decade, and the direction of those changes indicates that value convergence has taken place. Table 6.3 summarizes much of the evidence presented earlier, showing the trajectories and direction of change in fifteen value domains for each of the three countries. Here we are primarily concerned with those value domains that are of particular relevance to our theory of value change.

With many of the variables included in these surveys, there is no reason why we would expect to find significant changes, and most of them show none. They are not included here. But many of the value domains reported in Table 6.3 are based on responses to multiple items, so it sums up a large body of evidence. The pattern is a remarkably consistent one. In most cases, the values of all three publics are moving in the *same* direction. In the long term, this is likely to result in convergence: no trend can continue forever, and eventually the societies that have advanced farthest on a given dimension will begin to slow down as they approach the limits to that trend, and other societies will begin to catch up with them. This is already happening in a number of cases: though all three societies are moving in the same direction, Mexico is changing more rapidly than the United States or Canada.

In some cases, such as the question about how business and industry should be managed, the Mexicans have been moving in the *opposite* direction from that of the Canadian and American publics. As we have already noted, one major difference between traditional Mexican values and the values of the other two North American countries is the emphasis that Mexican society has historically placed on state intervention. In this domain, as in many others, value change in Mexico has been rapid.

Table 6.3.   Converging Values in North America

Variable	Trajectory
Materialist/postmaterialist values	All moving in same direction
Sexual restrictiveness	All moving in same direction
Emphasize autonomy over obedience for children	All moving in same direction
Favor greater respect for authority	All moving in same direction
Emphasis on family duty	Mexico moving in opposite direction from U.S. and Canada but *converging*
Civil permissiveness	All moving in same direction
Religiosity	All moving in same direction
Church attendance	All moving in same direction
Confidence in government institutions	All moving in same direction
Confidence in nongovernment institutions	Mexico moving in opposite direction from U.S. and Canada and *diverging*
National pride	All moving in same direction
Conventional political participation	All moving in same direction
Unconventional political participation	All moving in same direction
Support for state ownership of industry	All moving in same direction
Support for employee participation in management	Mexico moving in opposite direction from U.S. and Canada but *converging*
Following instructions at work	Mexico moving in opposite direction from U.S. and Canada but *converging*

Source: 1981 and 1990 World Values Surveys.

Between 1981 and 1990, Mexicans became far more favorably inclined toward the classic principles of the capitalist economy. During the same period, Americans and Canadians continued to reject state ownership but their support for the classic capitalist model became more nuanced; they attached increasing importance to employee participation in making decisions. Thus, by 1990 all three publics had moved closer to support for a regulated market economy; North American values in this domain converged.

Of all the value domains considered in Table 6.3, we discover only *one* instance in which the three publics were neither converging nor moving along the same trajectory. That case concerns confidence in nongovernmental institutions. In both the United States and Canada, confidence in nongovernmental institutions declined from 1981 to 1990, while in Mexico it rose (though only very slightly). The net result is that on this dimension, the three societies were less similar in 1990 than they were in 1981. This was a very exceptional finding, however. For the most part, the three societies were moving on a common trajectory.

Not all values have an equally important impact on the prospects for political integration. Following Deutsch (1968), we distinguish between main and peripheral values. For Deutsch, two kinds of main values are particularly crucial for successful integration: (1) those concerning the *political regime*—the key question being whether or not the norms essential to liberal democracy prevail over authoritarian norms; and (2) those concerning the *economic* regime—here, the emerging consensus seems to be moving toward a regulated market economy, with a significant but not unlimited welfare state. From this perspective we would expect consensus on governmental institutions to be more important than consensus on nongovernmental institutions. The distinction between main and peripheral values is important because it implies that successful integration does not hinge upon the publics in various countries holding similar values on all matters. For example, the fact that all three of these societies are moving toward more permissive sexual norms may be important. But from the standpoint of integration theory, these particular values are relevant only insofar as they are linked to main values concerning the political regime or the economic system. Under some circumstances, each of the three societies could have different norms and laws concerning marriage, abortion, prostitution, and other aspects of sexual life without undermining the prospects for successful integration.

The conclusion that American, Canadian, and Mexican values have converged in the last decade is important from the perspective of integration theory: If there was greater main values compatibility in 1990 than in 1981, the prospects for successful North American integration have improved in the last decade. Greater value compatibility, according to Deutsch (1968), is conducive to successful integration because it creates the expectations that others will behave in the same way in similar situations; it encourages mutual trust (1968:57). Mutual trust, in turn, is conducive to greater support for integration.

We have already shown that levels of mutual trust are asymmetrical in the North American setting (Table 1.1). Americans and Canadians have relatively high levels of mutual trust whereas Mexicans are more likely to distrust Americans than to trust them. Once again, though, the European evidence is instructive; it shows that trust between nations can and does change. As we noted previously, Merritt and Puchala (1968) found that in the 1950s, after generations of conflict, the French and German publics distrusted each other deeply. But by 1980, after decades of working together within common European institutions, the French regarded West Germans as the nationality they trusted most (Inglehart 1991).

We do not have the data that would be needed to analyze changing levels of trust between the three North American peoples, since questions about trusting different nationalities were not asked in the 1981 surveys. However, there is little reason to suppose that the dynamics driving levels of cross-national trust in the European setting work differently in North America. We can examine one central hypothesis emerging from integration theory, namely, that mutual trust is related to support for closer economic integration. As Figure 6.5 illustrates, levels of mutual trust *are* systematically related to support for closer economic ties in North America. The strength of the relationships varies somewhat: it is strongest between Canada and Mexico and between Mexico and the United States, but all of the relationships are fairly strong, and they all operate in the direction predicted by integration theory (Deutsch 1968).

In the United States, for example, among those who do not trust the Mexicans, only slightly more than one-third are in favor of closer economic ties with that country. Among those who trust them either "a little" or "completely," solid majorities (over 70 percent) favor closer economic ties. The U.S. public shows significantly higher levels of support for closer economic ties with Canada, but the trend parallels the one found in the Mexican case: among those who do not trust the Canadians, only half are in favor of closer economic ties; among those who trust them "a little" or "completely," over 90 percent favor closer economic ties. Similar strong relationships between trust and support for closer economic ties exist in both Mexico and Canada.

In both Canada and Mexico, the opponents of free trade argue that it will unleash forces that will severely constrain the ability of these governments to make independent choices (Smiley 1988). The fear is that, as happened in the European Community, once the three countries embark on the course set by free trade, Canada and Mexico will be drawn into a single political community—and that it will be dominated by the United States. That fear is not new—it has shaped Canadian and Mexican policies toward the United States for generations. At the same time, it is based on the idea that political and economic forces are closely connected. Free trade and political integration may be clearly linked in the minds of scholars and of some politicians, but are these themes linked in the minds of the three national publics? Our evidence indicates that they are. As Figure 6.6 shows, public support for closer economic ties is closely linked to opinions about political union in all three countries. In Figure 6.6, the curve rises more steeply in Canada and Mexico than in the United States: as we would expect, these ideas are more powerfully linked in Canada and Mexico than in the United States. But in each

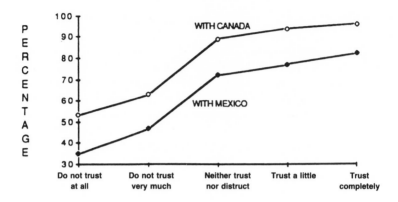

ATTITUDES OF UNITED STATES PUBLIC

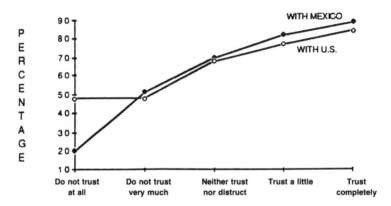

ATTITUDES OF CANADIAN PUBLIC

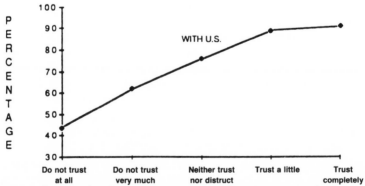

ATTITUDES OF MEXICAN PUBLIC

Figure 6.5. Support for closer economic ties with a given nation by trust in that nationality (percentage in favor of "much closer" or "somewhat closer" economic ties). *Source:* 1990 World Values Survey.

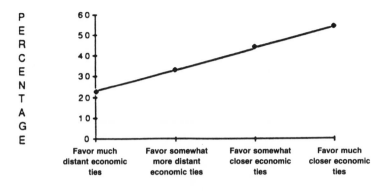

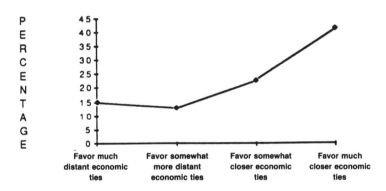

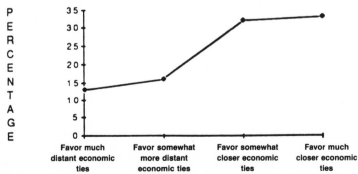

Figure 6.6. Support for political integration by support for closer economic ties.
Source: 1990 World Values Survey.

setting the pattern is clear: those favoring closer economic ties are twice as likely as those opposing them to support doing away with borders. Spillover from economic to political integration *does* seem to exist among the general public.

Attitudes toward political union are not entirely driven by how a respondent stands on free trade, of course. Noneconomic factors such as nationalism also help shape opinions about free trade and political union. To refer back to an attitude already examined in Chapter 4, we would expect those with strong feelings of pride in their country to be relatively likely to reject political union with another state. The evidence confirms this expectation. In all three countries, those who express relatively strong national pride *are* less likely to support political union than are those who are less nationalistic. This linkage is relatively weak among the U.S. public: since the United States is by far the largest of the three countries in both population and economic capacity, North American political union is not perceived as very threatening to American cultural identity or national independence. In both Canada and Mexico, however, those with a strong sense of national pride are markedly less favorable to political union than are the rest of their compatriots.

As we saw in Chapter 4, feelings of nationalism seem to be on a downward trajectory in all three countries. National pride is considerably weaker among the young and the postmaterialists than among the old and the materialists. Our model of intergenerational change implies that this configuration predicts a decline in feelings of national pride—and, as we saw, from 1981 to 1990 there actually *was* a substantial decline in national pride in all three countries.

This is not an isolated finding. It seems to be part of a broader shift from a parochial sense of identity toward an increasingly cosmopolitan outlook. In both the 1981 and the 1990 surveys, the publics of these three countries were asked:[1]

> To which of these geographical groups would you say you belong, first of all? . . . And what would come next?
> 1. The locality or town where you live.
> 2. The state (province) or region of the country in which you live.
> 3. Your country as a whole.
> 4. North America as a whole.
> 5. The world as a whole.

Responses to this question tap an underlying parochial/cosmopolitan dimension: Those whose first choice is for the town or state in which they live tend to choose one of these immediate localities as their second choice as well. Those who feel they belong to their country as a whole, or even North America or the world as a whole, are much likelier to choose one of these broader geographical units as their second choice as well. For example, in the United States, among those whose first choice was their town, only 16 percent said they belonged to "the world as a whole" for their second choice. But among those whose first choice was "North America," 36 percent said they belonged to "the world as a whole" as second choice. In Canada, the corresponding figures were 7 and 26 percent; in Mexico they were 10 and 25 percent.

Figure 6.7 shows the percentages who felt they belonged to each of

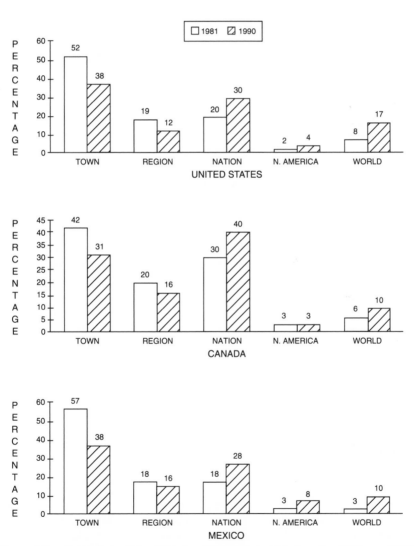

Figure 6.7. Percentage belonging to given geographical units: 1981 vs. 1990. *Source:* 1981 and 1990 World Values Surveys.

the respective groups first of all, in each of the two surveys. The changes from 1981 to 1990 are impressive, and they show a consistent pattern: in all three countries, there was a substantial shift from emphasis on the town in which one lives (or one's state or province) toward the broader geographical units. What we observe is a pervasive shift from a parochial to a more cosmopolitan focus of identity. In 1981, about half of the respondents in all three countries felt they belonged to the town in which they lived, first of all. By 1990, identification with one's town had eroded considerably. All three of the larger geographical groups gained strength, from 1981 to 1990, with one important shift being from the city, state, or region in which one lived, to the nation. But the increases were even greater, proportionally, for the two broadest groups, "North America" and "the world as a whole." In 1981, only small minorities said that they belonged to either of these groups, first of all: a total of 10 percent in the United States, 9 percent in Canada, and 6 percent in Mexico made one of the two supranational options their first choice. But by 1990, the proportions whose identity went beyond the nation had doubled to 21 percent in the United States, increased to 13 percent in Canada, and *tripled* in Mexico, rising to 18 percent of the total.

Here again, these changes are predicted by our model. In the 1981 surveys, the young and the postmaterialists were likelier to feel they belonged to one of the more cosmopolitan geographic units than were the old and the materialists. And this tendency was even stronger in the 1990 surveys, as Figures 6.8 and 6.9 demonstrate.

Across the three nations, those in the eighteen- to twenty-four-year-

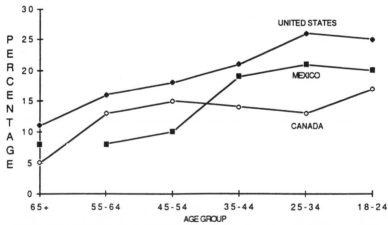

Figure 6.8. Percentage belonging to "North America" or "world as a whole," by age group. The value in Mexico's 65+ group is missing because the Mexican sample contains fewer than 30 cases over 65 years of age. *Source:* 1981 World Values Survey.

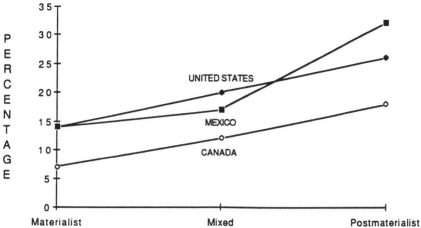

Figure 6.9.   Percentage belonging to "North America" or "world as a whole," by value type. Because these values were not measured in the 1981 U.S. Survey, we show the 1990 results for that country. *Source:* 1981 World Values Survey.

old group were two and one-half to three times as likely to say they belonged to North America or to the world as a whole as were those in the oldest group. Among the old, even in 1990 a sense of supranational identity remained very unusual; but among the youngest group, it was chosen by as much as one-fifth to one-fourth of the public.

The analysis by value type, shown in Figure 6.9, also points to an intergenerational shift. In all three countries, postmaterialists are two or three times as likely as materialists to have a cosmopolitan sense of identity. In view of the pronounced differences across both age groups and across value types in 1990, our model predicts a shift toward a more cosmopolitan sense of identity in all three countries during the next decade or two. This forecast is certainly plausible, since a substantial shift in that direction has already been observed from 1981 to 1990.

If there is a secular trend from a relatively parochial outlook toward a sense of belonging to broader geographic units, this bodes well for a potential North American political community, or even broader forms of integration. We should not overinterpret the data, however. Across the three nations, feelings of belonging to some geographical unit larger than the nation rose from an average figure of 9 percent in 1981 to 17 percent in 1990—but the latter figure is still a small minority.

Forecasts over such long periods are hazardous, but at this rate of growth a supranational outlook would not become the majority outlook until the year 2031. In all three countries the trend seems to be moving toward a more cosmopolitan sense of identity—but these changes are occurring gradually. In the long run, political union is possible, but clearly it would take a long time to gain general acceptance.

The experience of the European Community seems instructive in this respect. More than a third of a century has passed since the Treaty of Rome established the European Common Market. At that time, it was still taken for granted that the Germans and French were hereditary enemies who naturally hated each other and were doomed to fight a major war every few decades. After more than three decades of working together, these feelings of antagonism have gradually disappeared. This is an immensely important change in the political landscape of Western Europe, though one that has largely escaped attention because it has taken place so gradually. Some observers still accept the old stereotype of Franco-German hostility as a permanent fact. They are wrong: things have changed. After decades of increasingly close cooperation, the peoples of the European Community are now beginning to undertake measures that imply significant political integration: a common European Community passport is already a reality, a common currency seems likely, and a common foreign policy and perhaps even a common defense system are now under serious discussion. Sometime in the early twenty-first century, a politically integrated European Community may become a reality. The European case suggests that economic integration *can* lead to eventual political integration—but the European experience also indicates that there is likely to be a considerable time lag. One reason for this time lag is the fact that the process depends partly on intergenerational changes in basic orientations toward the political community—and intergenerational change is inherently slow.

As we have seen, one of the major sources of opposition to the economic integration of North America has been grounded in the fear that it would erode the distinctive cultures of given nations. This fear is not wholly unfounded—there *is* evidence that in many respects the basic values of Canadians, Mexicans, and Americans have been gradually converging, as Chapters 3, 4, and 5 of this book demonstrate. But these changes had been taking place even before the free-trade agreements and would probably have continued in any event, and they do *not* seem to reflect the Americanization of Canada and Mexico (though that is how they are often perceived). Instead, they derive from the fact that all three societies are modernizing, in response to technological and economic changes that impinge on them all; adaptation to these forces brings cultural changes that are, to some extent, predictable and similar. It is not that they are all being remade in the image of the United States (in some ways, Canada leads the United States, as we have seen) but that they are moving on a common trajectory.

Does this mean that the distinctive cultural heritage of each nation is doomed? By no means. These technological and economic changes require adaptation in some but not all sectors of a given culture. Thus, although Japan is one of the *most* modern of all advanced industrial societies, its culture remains highly distinctive. This book has focused mainly on sectors that *do* tend to respond to the forces of global modernization. Other spheres, such as art and cuisine, may be affected much less.

One should not underestimate the degree to which different peoples can live under common economic and political institutions and still retain a high degree of cultural diversity. The Swiss, for example, have lived under common political and economic institutions for centuries, yet one sees pronounced cultural differences as one moves from the French-speaking to the German-speaking or Italian-speaking regions of Switzerland. The Swiss have assimilated a common set of political (and economic) norms that enable them to live together in harmony, while remaining different in many other ways. The Quebecois have been living under common political and economic institutions with other Canadians for generations, and they want autonomy to protect their culture. But that does not mean that they want to opt out of North America (Nevitte 1996). The various peoples of the European Community, having lived under common institutions for only a matter of decades, remain even more distinctive. Some convergence will almost inevitably take place in North America, whether North American free trade becomes a reality or not; the fear that the peoples of North America will become one dull, homogeneous mass is unrealistic.

Another image that North American free trade sometimes evokes is that it will lead to massive Hispanic immigration into the United States: ultimately, the English-speaking culture and perhaps even the democratic political institutions of the United States will be swept away by a Hispanic flood. Since a very sizable flow of Hispanic immigration into the United States already exists, this idea seems plausible, but is it realistic? Let us start with some basic parameters: the United States has a population three times as large as that of Mexico; even if the entire population of Mexico moved to the United States, the English-speaking population would still constitute a solid majority. But the idea of the entire nation moving north is wildly unrealistic. In the *long* run, North American free trade is likely to increase economic opportunities in Mexico and will almost certainly result in *less* Mexican immigration to the United States than would have occurred without it.

Again, the experience of the European Community provides a relevant illustration. In the aftermath of World War II, West Germany staged an economic miracle that brought a rapidly rising standard of living, full employment, and a sizable labor shortage which drew in massive immigration of workers from Southern Europe. The establishment of the European Common Market in the late 1950s accelerated this process somewhat. By the early 1960s, there were millions of foreign workers living in West Germany, most of them Italians.

However, precisely because a barrier-free common market existed, investment flowed into Italy—the region of the Common Market with the lowest labor costs. Italy began to experience its own economic miracle. By 1980, the exodus of Italian labor had not only ended, but most Italian workers had returned to the sunnier and (for them) culturally more inviting climate of Italy. Today, there is still considerable immigration into Northern Europe, but by no coincidence it comes mainly from *outside* the European Community, from regions that have not experienced the developmental stimulus of membership in the Community.

Whether one fears change or is eager for it, all three North American countries are inevitably going to experience change during the next few decades. Technological and economic developments will continue to reshape these societies whether NAFTA succeeds or not. The question is not whether one accepts change or excludes it: the question is *how* one adapts to change. On the whole, developing a North American free-trade area seems likely to give the peoples of these countries more control over their destiny, and more resources to help cope with change, than they would have otherwise.

NOTE

1.   In the United States and Canada, there was a change in the format of this question from 1981 to 1990. In 1981, the "region in which you live" was offered as a separate alternative, immediately after "the state (province) in which you live," instead of being combined with it as in 1990. For the sake of cross-national standardization (since all other countries including Mexico had only five alternatives), state and region were combined in 1990. Conceivably, this might contribute to the slight reduction in the total number choosing state or region in 1990: the two separate options might attract more choices than the one combined option. But if the shifts were simply an artifact of this type, we would expect the exodus to flow toward *both* of the neighboring options, resulting in increased numbers choosing "the town where you live" as well as "your country as a whole." Nothing of the kind occurred. Instead, there was a massive shift *away* from "the town where you live" toward *all three* of the larger geographical units (the nation, North America, and the world as a whole). This does not look like an artifactual finding caused by combining the state with the region; it looks like a systematic shift from a parochial to a more cosmopolitan sense of identity. The fact that we observe exactly the same pattern of shifts in Mexico (where no change of format took place) as in the United States and Canada helps confirm this interpretation.

7

Conclusions

The basic goals and values of the peoples of the United States, Canada, and Mexico are converging in a number of crucial respects. They are moving toward consensus concerning both the political regime and the type of economic system they support; more gradually, they seem to be moving toward a broader but looser type of political community.

The three peoples are converging toward increasingly participant and liberal democratic political systems. The most striking changes are taking place in Mexico, which seems to be moving from a highly centralized polity permanently dominated by one party, toward a more pluralistic political system. The one-party state is still in place, but underlying changes are occurring among the Mexican public that are eroding its long-term viability. Political change is less obvious in the United States and Canada, but evidence examined here indicates that they, too, are changing—and moving toward higher levels of public participation that is more finely targeted on specific issues than the elite-mobilized participation that has prevailed thus far.

The three peoples are moving toward consensus on marketization as well as democratization. Here, too, change is most noticeable in Mexico, but it is occurring in all three countries, with Mexico withdrawing from an overcentralized state-dominated economy, while the United States and Canada continue their long-standing patterns of making incremental adjustments to their economic systems.

Both the political and economic compatibility of these societies tend to be enhanced by the fact that they are moving on a similar trajectory with a wide range of other basic norms, concerning family, religion, and sexual behavior.

Finally, all three societies seem to be groping toward a new formula concerning how much power is concentrated in the existing nation-state. While no one today is discussing supranational political integration, the ongoing economic integration of the three nations has far-reaching implications that to some extent inevitably entail increased coordination of important aspects of policymaking. The term *globalization* is used frequently in this connection. As we have suggested, the real long-term trend may actually be moving in two directions, toward broader but also looser forms of political community.

Historically, international trade policy has usually been decided by political elites, but the coordinated maneuvers toward a North American continental trade agreement in the last five years have given rise to public involvement on a very different scale. Like the European publics facing an increasingly integrated European Union, North American publics have entered the fray, and in the process public disputes have moved well beyond the confines of economic theory.

Global changes have introduced new dynamics for states searching for economic competitiveness in the twenty-first century. These new imperatives have forced states to consider strategies they would not have taken seriously only twenty-five years ago. Expanding trade environments create new opportunities, and free-trade advocates accept the fact that this means that some producers will deploy capital and labor more efficiently by relocating. This reshuffling is necessary for long-term prosperity. Predictably, opposition to free trade sprang from the immediate potential victims of short-term dislocations. Organized labor in Canada resisted the Canada - U.S. free-trade agreement from the start, and when talks expanded to include Mexico, American-organized labor took a similar position. The Mexican response to these concerns has been short and to the point: if Mexico cannot export its goods it will export its people.

Much of the North American free-trade debate can be understood from an economic perspective. Those who stand to gain are for it, and the potential losers oppose it. But that is only the beginning. Free trade began to attract widespread public interest not because the general public suddenly developed a new appreciation for the intricacies of comparative economic advantage but because free trade galvanized public concern for a much wider set of issues, such as cultural integrity, the future of the environment, health, education policies, and national identity. The free-trade debate involved an increasingly large share of the public in all three countries because it raised fundamental issues relating to public values.

This book has broadened the analysis of free trade beyond purely economic considerations by explicitly examining the linkages between trade and values in North America. Not limiting ourselves to the perspective of economic theory or the viewpoint of elites, we have begun to explore the perspectives of the three national publics, drawing on a unique body of evidence to systematically examine:

1. the basic value similarities and differences between the American, Canadian, and Mexican publics;

2. the extent to which these publics are becoming more dissimilar or more alike;

3. how these values are linked to orientations toward free trade and possible political integration.

KEY FINDINGS

The most basic finding from this study is that in all three countries fundamental values are undergoing pervasive changes. These changes are gradual but they are rooted in long-term generational differences; consequently, they will probably endure, and their cumulative effects are likely to be massive. Moreover, most of these changes tend to diminish the differences on key values between the three publics of North America. Among the value domains dealt with in Table 6.3, the Mexican, Canadian, and American peoples were moving in the same direction in twelve of the sixteen cases. In three more cases, the Mexicans were moving in the opposite direction from the U.S. and Canadian publics, but were doing so in a manner that brought about convergence. In only one case were they diverging.

The publics of the United States and Canada are ahead of the Mexican public on most of these trends, but the Mexicans are generally on the same trajectory; frequently, we find that Mexican society has been changing more rapidly than that of the United States or Canada, producing a tendency toward gradual convergence of basic norms. More often than not, the Canadians are leading the Americans on these trends, not the other way around: culturally, what is happening is not the Americanization of North America, but a common response to global forces. This process is frequently misperceived as Americanization simply because the United States is the mass media center of the world, and the symptoms of change are often seen first in the United States. In reality, the three societies seem to be converging toward a model that none of them has yet attained.

One central element of this cultural change is a shift from materialist to postmaterialist values—which reflects the change from a world in which most people are absorbed in the tasks of sheer survival, to a world in which concern for the quality of life is becoming increasingly important. As one might expect, the peoples of Canada and the United States are well ahead of the Mexican public on this dimension, but during the 1980s all three publics showed substantial shifts toward increasing emphasis on postmaterialist concerns.

This is only one component of a much broader cultural change, however. We find similar shifts toward broader acceptance of divorce, abortion, homosexuality, and other forms of sexual behavior. We also see a trend toward encouraging independence, imagination, and determination, rather than obedience and good manners, in the child-rearing goals of all three societies; and a broad trend toward more emphasis on individual autonomy, rather than acceptance of elite authority.

In the economic realm, we find two opposite trends, which result in growing compatibility. The United States and Canada both start from strongly capitalist heritages. Mexico, on the other hand, has a statist tradition that has emphasized centralized control and ownership of large parts of the economy. The publics of all three countries now show very little support for state ownership (and what support there is seems to be declining). But at the same time, the publics of the United States and Canada show growing support for employee participation in management of business and industry, together with diminishing support for conforming to authority in the workplace, regardless of whether one agrees with it. The Mexican public, on the other hand, shows a shift toward greater acceptance of managerial authority and toward giving entrepreneurs a free hand in managing their businesses. Here, we have an exceptional case in which cross-national comparisons show trends that are moving in opposite directions. However, because the Mexican public started from a position so far away from the traditional capitalist position, the result is that prevailing norms in Mexico and in its two northern neighbors are gradually converging.

In the political domain, the main trends tend to make life more difficult for those in power. We find pervasive tendencies in all three countries toward:

1.   less confidence in governmental institutions, such as parliament, the civil service, the armed forces, and the police; and to a lesser degree declining confidence in churches, schools, the legal system and mass media;
2.   less willingness to accept elite authority;
3.   but at the same time, an increasing likelihood that these publics participate in politics.

Along conventional lines, the publics in all three countries are becoming more interested in politics, likelier to discuss politics, and likelier to sign petitions. Even more dramatically, they are increasingly likely to take part in demonstrations, boycotts, or occupations of buildings— intervening directly, in order to influence specific decisions. These findings run counter to the conventional wisdom, which depicts the public (at least in the United States and Canada) as passive and uninvolved. This impression is based largely on the fact that voting turnout has declined. But voting turnout has always been largely mobilized by elite-directed party machines, which are able to produce massive turnout even when no real issue is being decided. Electoral participation rates have been declining precisely because the established parties and political machines have been losing their grip. At the same time, other more active and more issue-oriented forms of participation have been rising sharply. This combination of diminishing confidence in elites and established institutions, together with the emergence of a more articulate, better educated, and more participant public, may make the task of governing more complex—but it also is inherently conducive to democracy. Indeed, we believe that similar processes have been taking place gradually in all industrial societies, and that they have contributed to global democratization.

The last major set of changes may be directly conducive to the development of a North American free-trade zone (and, in the long run, to closer political ties): in all three publics, we find evidence of a decline of nationalism and the gradual emergence of a more cosmopolitan sense of identity.

One very interesting aspect of these changes is that they can, to a certain degree, be predicted. Among the data in the 1981 survey, thirty-four variables showed a coherent pattern of linkages with both age and materialist/postmaterialist values. With these variables, we predicted that changes would take place in a specific direction: and in thirty-one out of the thirty-four cases, we actually observed changes from 1981 to 1990 that moved in the predicted direction.

This is a surprisingly high success rate; quite frankly, we did not expect our predictions to come true this often. Our predictions are based on intergenerational population replacement effects. This component of change is relatively predictable, but it was not the only factor influencing shifts in outlook from 1981 to 1990: any number of additional economic, political, or social events might also influence attitudinal changes, and their effects might well swamp those of population replacement over short periods of time. Our model enables us to estimate the size of population replacement effects for each variable, and the expected size of these effects is generally no larger than 5 or 6 percentage points. The impact of a major current event could easily be larger than this, but as it turned out, this usually did not happen. During the period from 1981 to 1990, period effects did not overwhelm the effects of intergenerational change; in most cases, they added to them. As a result, we generally found that our predictions were not only confirmed, but that there was even more change in the predicted direction than intergenerational population replacement alone would produce. One reason why period effects generally went with, rather than against, population replacement effects was the fact that most of the intergenerational changes examined here are linked with the long-term effects of security; for both the United States and Canada (though not for Mexico), the years from 1981 to 1990 were a period of rising economic security: thus short-term effects were reinforcing cohort replacement effects.

Our model only predicts the effects of intergenerational population replacement. For short periods of time, its effects are relatively small and could easily be swamped by short-term fluctuations or period effects. But these short-term fluctuations can move in either direction and in the long run they are likely to cancel each other out. The effects of intergenerational population replacement, on the other hand, tend to be cumulative: for most of the variables examined here, it seems likely that they will move in the same direction for several decades at least. In the long run, their direction may have a major impact—and one that seems to be relatively predictable.

THE OUTLOOK FOR NORTH AMERICAN INTEGRATION

North American publics want closer economic ties with each other, but our investigation also demonstrates that important value changes are taking place. North Americans are becoming more alike in important respects; they are responding to the kinds of value changes that are also reshaping the political cultures of other countries. These changes do not mean that Canadians or Mexicans are becoming Americanized; instead, the evidence indicates that all three publics are being reshaped by similar forces. These value changes, we have shown, have similar predictable consequences for how North Americans view social phenomena, for how they view the workplace, for the kinds of values parents want future generations to have, and for the kinds of political behavior they are likely to undertake. For a variety of reasons, national political boundaries have become far more porous than ever before and the quickening pace of cross-border transactions—commercial, informational, and personal travel—is powerfully felt in contiguous countries on the same continent. At the same time, public horizons and identities have become more expansive. North Americans are less parochial than before; they are becoming more cosmopolitan.

One provocative implication that flows from these findings is that the traditional, historically entrenched rationale for the existence of political borders separating the three North American countries seems to be eroding. History, of course, provides many examples of the fact that political borders do change, and the transformations now taking place in the countries of the European Union seem likely to provide another contemporary example. But the idea that a significant proportion of Canadians or Mexicans are prepared to do away with the borders separating them from the United States is a remarkable finding. It is remarkable because some of the most powerful themes in the domestic history and politics of both Mexico and Canada have focused on resisting the powerful cultural, political, and economic presence of the United States.

One assumption advanced by Canadian and Mexican opponents of continental free trade is that a North American free-trade area is a slippery slope and that with free trade the ability of those national communities to exert meaningful independence will be lost. Reaching a consensus on what meaningful independence entails would be a difficult task, but there is little evidence to suggest that doing away with borders means that cultural differences will disappear. Powerful cultural differences have persisted within many nations, from Switzerland to Canada and the Soviet Union, long after those different cultures have been brought under common institutions. Another assumption is that comprehensive free trade will result in the standardization of public policies, bringing Canadian and Mexican conformity to American standards in such areas as health care. Our evidence suggests that this will not necessarily happen. Our findings indicate, for example, that clear majorities of the citizens in all three countries want a public health insurance system. In this instance one would expect policy harmonization *away* from current American standards, if public preferences carry any weight—and the evidence indicates that this factor is becoming increasingly important.

A third assumption advanced by opponents of free trade is that a continental economy would be ecologically damaging because the Mexican public is prepared to sacrifice environmental standards for material prosperity. Our evidence points in the opposite direction. It shows that the Mexican public does not lag behind the Canadians and Americans when it comes to caring about the environment. This does not automatically translate into public policy, but it is a significant factor. More than twenty American, Canadian, and Mexican environmental groups have joined forces to demand that enforceable environmental regulations be made an explicit part of NAFTA.

We do not suggest that political union is imminent, but our evidence does indicate that the reasons for maintaining political borders are not as strong as they once were. The historical logic that kept these countries apart does not apply to contemporary circumstances for significant proportions of these publics. Indeed, given the right conditions, it does not apply to a majority of citizens in *any* of these states. North America may be closer to economic union than most people imagine. In the more distant future, even political union may be on the agenda.

Appendix

The Value Systems of Forty-Four Societies in Comparative Perspective

Figure 1.3 showed the relative positions of forty-four societies on two broad dimensions of cross-cultural variation. Figure A.1 (reproduced from Inglehart 1997) shows the results of the principal components factor analysis underlying that figure. This analysis is based on the data from representative national surveys in the forty-four societies included in the 1990–1991 World Values Survey. The responses to each of the variables used here are boiled down to a mean score for each country; using the society as the unit of analysis, we examine cross-cultural variation in evaluations of a wide range of important topics.

Figure A.1 sums up an immense amount of information. It presents a broad overview of findings from the World Values Surveys, showing the relationships between scores of items. Other chapters in the book probe more deeply into the causal relationships between key variables, and examine changes over time. This figure is based on the responses to scores of questions, given by more than sixty thousand respondents in forty-four societies. Space constraints do not allow us to provide the full text of each question used here. A short phrase (such as **Abortion OK**) is used to convey the gist of each item on Figure A.1; the full text is given below. The forty-seven variables used here reflect a considerably larger number of questions, since some of them are based on responses to whole batteries of questions. **Affect balance**, for example, sums up each respondent's answers to the ten questions in the Bradburn Affect Balance Scale. Similarly, **Postmaterialist values** sums up the responses to a series of questions through which each respondent ranks a set of twelve basic goals.

Furthermore, these variables were chosen to reflect an even larger number of related items that show a similar pattern. **God is important**, for example, taps a cluster of more than thirty items that measure the extent to which religion is or is not an important part of the respondent's life. Similarly, **Life satisfaction**, **Affect balance**, and **Not happy** reflect a larger cluster of items that tap subjective well-being. To avoid redundan-

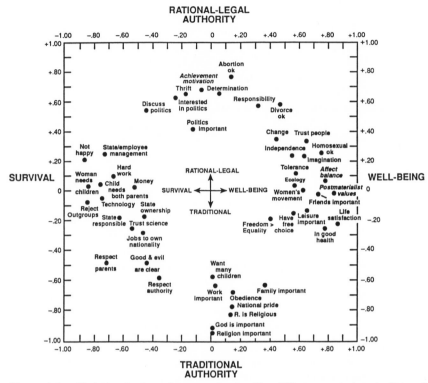

Figure A.1. Variation in the values emphasized by different societies: traditional authority vs. rational-legal authority and survival values vs. well-being values. This figure shows the first and second principal components emerging from a factor analysis of data from representative national surveys of 40 societies, aggregated to the national level. The scales on the margins show each item's loadings on the two respective dimensions. The items in italics are multi-item indices. *Source:* 1990–1991 World Values Survey.

cy, and to limit Figure A.1 to a readable size, we have only included the most sensitive indicators of each cluster. Figure A.1 depicts the structure underlying responses to more than 100 questions dealing with many aspects of life in forty-four societies, providing an overview of basic cultural patterns.

Our first major finding is that there is a great deal of constraint among cultural systems. The pattern found here is anything but random. The first two dimensions that emerge from the principal components factor analysis depicted in Figure A.1 account for fully 51 percent of the cross-national variation among these forty-seven variables! Additional dimensions explain relatively small amounts of variance, and these dimensions are robust, showing little change if we drop some of the items, even high-loading ones. The vertical axis reflects the polarization between traditional authority and rational-legal authority; the horizontal axis depicts the polarization between a cluster of items labeled Survival and another cluster labeled Well-being. The scales on the borders of Figure A.1 indicate each item's loadings on these two dimensions.

The answer to the question, "Do societies that place relatively strong emphasis on religion also tend to favor large families?" is an unequivocal yes, as the proximity of **Religion important** and **Want many children** near the bottom of Figure A.1 suggests: the correlation between these two items is $r = .51$ (significant at the .001 level). Moreover, societies characterized by an emphasis on religion also tend to place relatively strong emphasis on work, as the proximity between **Work important** and **Religion important** suggests (here, $r = .62$, significant at the .0000 level). These same societies also tend to stress **Obedience** as an important quality to teach a child ($r = .58$), to view the family as relatively important (**Family important**, $r = .56$), and to express a strong sense of **National pride** (the correlation with **Religion important** is .74, significant at the .0000 level). And, as one would expect, those societies in which the public considers **Religion important** also tend to be those in which the public believe that **God is important**, and describe themselves as religious people, rather than agnostics or atheists (**R. is Religious**): these are almost 1 : 1 relationships ($r = .95$ and $r = .87$, respectively). The last two linkages are obvious; the others, though intuitively plausible, are far from obvious. All of these items have high loadings on the second principal component, labeled Traditional Authority vs. Rational-Legal State Authority.

As these findings demonstrate, high levels of constraint exist between various cultural attributes. For example, if we know that a society ranks high on national pride, we can pretty accurately predict its position on child-rearing practices, religiosity, and a number of other important attributes. But the pattern extends even farther. Societies that emphasize the importance of religion tend to attach *low* importance to politics, as the relatively distant locations of **Religion important** and **Politics important** on the vertical dimension suggests: the correlation between the two is .39. These societies show an even stronger tendency to place *low* emphasis on **Thrift** and **Determination** as important qualities to teach a child ($r = .57$ and .59, respectively). As we see in Chapter 5, emphasis on these values is strongly linked with the economic growth rates of given societies. Not surprisingly, these societies also tend to reject abortion (the correlation with **Abortion OK** is .71).

So far, we have been discussing items with high loadings on the *second* principal component, labeled Traditional Authority vs. Rational-

Legal Authority. This dimension reflects the modernization process, in which authority moves away from a traditional (usually religious) basis, toward increasing emphasis on impersonal bureaucratic authority. This is an important dimension, accounting for 21 percent of the variance among these forty-seven variables. But it is overshadowed by the *first* principal component, which accounts for 30 percent of the total variance. This dimension taps Survival vs. Well-being. A key item on this dimension is **Postmaterialist values** (located near the right-hand pole of the horizontal axis on Figure A.1). This is a central element in a much broader cultural configuration.

Societies with large numbers of postmaterialists tend to be characterized by a relatively strong sense of subjective well-being. Their publics tend to express high levels of satisfaction with their lives as a whole (**Postmaterialist values** has a .68 correlation with **Life satisfaction**). Moreover, they report relatively high levels of positive affect (saying that within the past few days they felt interested in something, or proud, or pleased about having accomplished something) rather than negative affect (reporting that they were so restless that they couldn't sit long in a chair, or felt lonely, or upset because someone criticized them), which produces high scores on the Bradburn **Affect Balance** scale. Furthermore, the publics of societies with high levels of postmaterialism are likely to rate their themselves as **In good health** ($r = .58$) and are *not* likely to describe themselves as **Not happy** (the correlation with **Postmaterialist values** is .71).

Space does not permit us to discuss the rich and complex array of findings underlying this analysis; but the full text of each item included in Figure A.1 appears in Table A.1. A fuller discussion of this analysis appears in Inglehart (1997).

Table A.1.   Values Systems of 44 Societies: Items Used in Factor Analysis (Short Labels Shown on Figure A.1 Appear in **Bold**)

Please say, for each of the following, how important it is in your life:

		Very important	Quite important	Not very important	Not at all important
Work important	A) Work	1	2	3	4
Family important	B) Family	1	2	3	4
Friends important	C) Friends, acquaintances	1	2	3	4
Leisure important	D) Leisure time	1	2	3	4
Politics important	E) Politics	1	2	3	4
Religion important	F) Religion	1	2	3	4

(*continued*)

Table A.1. (*Continued*)

___

Discuss politics
When you get together with your friends, would you say you discuss political matters frequently, occasionally or never?

1 Frequently
2 Occasionally
3 Never

Not happy
Taking all things together, would you say you are . . .

1 Very happy
2 Quite happy
3 Not very happy
4 Not at all happy

Reject outgroups [*scores on this index range from 0 to 3, depending on how many of the following groups are mentioned*].
On this list are various groups of people. Could you please sort out any that you would *not* like to have as neighbors?

		Mentioned	Not mentioned
I)	Immigrants/foreign workers	1	2
J)	People who have AIDS	1	2
L)	Homosexuals	1	2

In good health
All in all, how would you describe your state of health these days? Would you say it is . . .

1 Very good
2 Good
3 Fair
4 Poor
5 Very poor

Affect balance [*scores on the Bradburn Affect Balance Scale are the number of mentions of items A, C, E, G, and I minus the sum of items B, D, F, H and J: in short, the number of positive feelings reported minus the number of negative feelings reported*].
We are interested in the way people are feeling these days. During the past few weeks, did you ever feel . . .

		YES	NO
A)	Particularly excited or interested in something	1	2
B)	So restless you couldn't sit long in a chair	1	2
C)	Proud because someone had complimented you on something you had done	1	2
D)	Very lonely or remote from other people	1	2

(*continued*)

Table A.1.   (*Continued*)

		YES	NO
E)	Pleased about having accomplished something	1	2
F)	Bored	1	2
G)	On top of the world/feeling that life is wonderful	1	2
H)	Depressed or very unhappy	1	2
I)	That things were going your way	1	2
J)	Upset because somebody criticized you	1	2

Trust people
Generally speaking, would you say that most people can be trusted or that you can't be too careful in dealing with people?

1 Most people can be trusted
2 Can't be too careful

Have free choice
Some people feel they have completely free choice and control over their lives, and other people feel that what they do has no real effect on what happens to them. Please use the scale to indicate how much freedom of choice and control you feel you have over the way your life turns out.

1   2   3   4   5   6   7   8   9   10
None at all   A great deal

Life satisfaction
All things considered, how satisfied are you with your life as a whole these days? Please use this card to help with your answer.

1   2   3   4   5   6   7   8   9   10
Dissatisfied   Satisfied

State/employee management
There is a lot of discussion about how business and industry should be managed. Which of these four statements comes closest to your opinion?

1 The owners should run their business or appoint the managers
2 The owners and the employees should participate in the selection of managers
3 The government should be the owner and appoint the managers
4 The employees should own the business and should elect the managers

Jobs to own nationality
Do you agree or disagree with the following?

C)	When jobs are scarce, employers should give priority to [American] people over immigrants [*outside U.S.: substitute own nationality*]	1	2	3

(continued)

Table A.1. (*Continued*)

Good and evil are clear
Here are two statements which people sometimes make when discussing good
and evil. Which one comes closest to your own point of view?

    A. There are absolutely clear guidelines about what is good and evil.
        These always apply to everyone, whatever the circumstances.
    B. There can never be absolutely clear guidelines about what is good and evil.
        What is good and evil depends entirely upon the circumstances at the time.
    1 Agree with statement A
    2 Disagree with both
    3 Agree with statement B

R. is religious
Independently of whether you go to church or not, would you say you are . . .

    1 A religious person
    2 Not a religious person
    3 A convinced atheist

God is important
And how important is God in your life? Please use this card to indicate—10
means very important and 1 means not at all important.

    1   2   3   4   5   6   7   8   9   10
    Not at all   Very

Want many children
What do you think is the ideal size of the family—how many children, if any?

    0 None
    1 1 child
    2 2 children
    3 3 children
    4 4 children
    5 5 children
    6 6 children
    7 7 children
    8 8 children
    9 9 children
   10 10 or more

Child needs both parents
If someone says a child needs a home with both a father and a mother to grow up
happily, would you tend to agree or disagree?

    1 Tend to agree
    2 Tend to disagree

(*continued*)

Table A.1.   (Continued)

Woman needs children
Do you think that a woman has to have children in order to be fulfilled or is this
not necessary?

1 Needs children
2 Not necessary

Respect parents
With which of these two statements do you tend to agree?

A. Regardless of what the qualities and faults of one's parents are, one must
always love and respect them
B. One does not have the duty to respect and love parents who have not
earned it by their behavior and attitudes

1 Tend to agree with statement A
2 Tend to agree with statement B

Here is a list of qualities which children can be encouraged to learn at home.
Which, if any, do you consider to be especially important?

			IMPORTANT
Independence	B)	Independence	1
Hard work	C)	Hard work	1
Responsibility	D)	Feeling of responsibility	1
Imagination	E)	Imagination	1
Tolerance	F)	Tolerance and respect for other people	1
Thrift	G)	Thrift, saving money and things	1
Determination	H)	Determination, perseverance	1
Obedience	K)	Obedience	1

Interested in politics
How interested would you say you are in politics?

1 Very interested
2 Somewhat interested
3 Not very interested
4 Not at all interested

Freedom > Equality
Which of these two statements comes closest to your own opinion?

A. I find that both freedom and equality are important. But if I were to choose
one or the other, I would consider personal freedom more important, that
is, everyone can live in freedom and develop without hindrance.
B. Certainly both freedom and equality are important. But if I were to choose
one or the other, I would consider equality more important, that is, that
nobody is underprivileged and that social class differences are not so strong.

1 Agree with statement A
2 Neither
3 Agree with statement B

(continued)

Table A.1. (*Continued*)

Now I'd like you to tell me your views on various issues. How would you place your views on this scale? 1 means you agree completely with the statement on the left, 10 means you agree completely with the statement on the right, or you can choose any number in between.

State ownership

B   Private ownership of   Government ownership of
    business and industry should   business and industry should be
    be increased   increased

    1   2   3   4   5   6   7   8   9   10

State responsible

C   Individuals should take more   The state should take more
    responsibility for providing   responsibility to ensure that
    for themselves   everyone is provided for

    1   2 · 3   4   5   6   7   8   9   10

Postmaterialist values [*scores on this index range from 0 to 5, depending on how many of items C, F, H, J, and K are chosen as either first or second priority in their group*]
There is a lot of talk these days about what the aims of this country should be for the next ten years. On this card are listed some of the goals which different people would give top priority. Would you please say which one of these you, yourself, consider the most important?

And which would be the next most important?

		First choice	Second choice
A.	Maintaining a high level of economic growth	1	1
B.	Making sure this country has strong defence forces	2	2
C.	Seeing that people have more to say about how things are done at their jobs and in their communities	3	3
D.	Trying to make our cities and countryside more beautiful	4	4

If you had to choose, which one of the things on this card would you say is most important?

And which would be the next most important?

		First choice	Second choice
E.	Maintaining order in the nation	1	1
F.	Giving people more say in important government decisions	2	2
G.	Fighting rising prices	3	3
H.	Protecting freedom of speech	4	4

(*continued*)

Table A.1. (*Continued*)

Here is another list. In your opinion, which one of these is most important?

And what would be the next most important?

		First choice	Second choice
I.	A stable economy	1	1
J.	Progress toward a less impersonal and more humane society	2	2
K.	Progress toward a society in which ideas count more than money	3	3
L.	The fight against crime	4	4

Here is a list of various changes in our way of life that might take place in the near future. Please tell me for each one, if it were to happen whether you think it would be a good thing, a bad thing, or don't you mind?

			Good	Don't care	Bad
Money	A	Less emphasis on money and material possessions	1	2	3
Technology	C	More emphasis on the development of technology	1	2	3
Respect authority	E	Greater respect for authority	1	2	3

Trust science

In the long run, do you think the scientific advances we are making will help or harm mankind?

1 Will help
2 Some of each
3 Will harm

There are a number of groups and movements looking for public support. For each of the following movements, which I read out, can you tell me whether you approve or disapprove of this movement?

			Approve		Disapprove	
			Strongly	Somewhat	Somewhat	Strongly
Ecology	A	Ecology movement or nature protection	1	2	3	4
Women's Movement	E	Women's movement	1	2	3	4

Please tell me for each of the following statements whether you think it can always be justified, never be justified, or something in between, using this card.

(*continued*)

Table A.1. (*Continued*)

			Never justified			In between				Always justified	
Homosexual ok	L	Homosexuality	1	2	3	4	5	6	7	8	9	10
Abortion ok	N	Abortion	1	2	3	4	5	6	7	8	9	10
Divorce ok	O	Divorce	1	2	3	4	5	6	7	8	9	10

National pride
How proud are you to be [French] ? *[outside France: substitute own nationality]*

1 Very proud
2 Quite proud
3 Not very proud
4 Not at all proud

Change
Now I want to ask you some questions about your outlook on life. Using this scale, could you tell me where you would place your own view? 1 means you agree completely with the statement on the left, 10 means you agree completely with the statement on the right, or you can choose any number in between.

         1   2   3   4   5   6   7   8   9   10
One should be cautious about   You will never achieve much
making major changes in life   unless you act boldly

References

Abramson, Paul. 1979. "Developing Party Identification: A Further Examination of Life Cycle, Generational and Period Effects." *American Journal of Political Science* 23:78–96.

Abramson, Paul and Ronald Inglehart. 1995. *Value Change in Global Perspective.* Ann Arbor: University of Michigan Press.

Alduncin, Enrique. 1986. *Los Valores de los Mexicanos.* Mexico City: Fomento Cultural Banamex.

Almond, Gabriel and Sidney Verba. 1963. *The Civic Culture.* Princeton, NJ: Princeton University Press.

Alwin, Duane. 1986. "Religion and Parental Child-Rearing Orientations: Evidence of a Catholic-Protestant Convergence." *American Journal of Sociology* 92:412–40.

Axelrod, Robert. 1984. *The Evolution of Cooperation.* New York: Basic Books.

Baer, Doug, Edward Grabb, and William A. Johnston. 1990. "The Values of Canadians and Americans: A Critical Analysis and Reassessment." *Social Forces* 68(3):693–713.

Basañez, Miguel. 1993a. "Is Mexico Headed Toward Its Fifth Crisis?" Pp. 95–115 in *Political and Economic Liberalization in Mexico*, edited by Roett Riordan. Boulder, CO: Lynne Rienner.

Basañez, Miguel. 1993b. "Protestant and Catholic Ethics: An Empirical Comparison." Paper presented at conference on *Changing Social and Political Values: A Global Perspective*, Complutense University, Madrid, September 27–October 1.

Ball, George. 1968. *The Discipline of Power.* Boston: Little, Brown.

Banfield, Edward. 1958. *The Moral Basis of a Backward Society.* Chicago: Free Press.

Barnes, Samuel, Max Kaase, Klaus R. Allerbeck, Barbara G. Farah, Felix Heunks, Ronald Inglehart, M. Kent Jennings, Hans D. Klingemann, Alan Marsh, Leopold Rosenmayr (eds.). 1979. *Political Action: Mass Participation in Five Western Democracies.* Beverly Hills: Sage.

Bell, Daniel. 1976. *The Cultural Contradictions of Capitalism.* New York: Basic Books.

Bell, David and Lorne Tepperman. 1979. *The Roots of Disunity.* Toronto: McClelland and Stewart.

Bellah, Robert N., Richard Madsen, William M. Sullivan, Ann Swidler, and Steven M. Tipton. 1985. *Habits of the Heart: Individualism and Commitment in American Life.* New York: Harpers.

Bergsten, C. Fred. 1982. "The United States in the World Economy." *Annals* 460:11–20.

Boorstin, Daniel J. 1953. *The Genius of American Politics*. Chicago: University of Chicago Press.

Cardoso, Fernando Henrique and Enzo Faletto. 1979. *Dependency and Development in Latin America*. Berkeley: University of California Press.

Clark, S.D. 1976. *Canadian Society in Historical Perspective*. Toronto: McGraw-Hill Ryerson.

Cohen, Benjamin J. 1990. "The Political Economy of International Trade." *International Organization* 44(2):261–81.

Coleman, Kenneth M. and Charles L. Davis. 1988. *Politics and Culture in Mexico*. Ann Arbor, MI: Institute for Social Research.

Cornelius, Wayne A. 1986. "Political Liberalization in an Authoritarian Regime: Mexico 1976–1985." Pp. 15–39 in *Mexican Politics in Transition*, edited by Judith Gentleman. Boulder CO: Westview.

Craig, Ann L. and Wayne Cornelius. 1980. "Political Culture in Mexico: Continuities and Revisionist Interpretations." Pp. 325–93 in *The Civic Culture Revisited*, edited by Gabriel A. Almond and Sidney Verba. Boston: Little Brown.

Dealy, Glen. 1977. *The Public Man: An Interpretation of Latin American and Other Catholic Countries*. Amherst: University of Massachusetts Press.

Deutsch, Karl W. 1952. *Nationalism and Social Communication*. Cambridge, MA: MIT Press.

Deutsch, Karl W. 1963. *The Nerves of Government*. New York: Free Press.

Deutsch, Karl W. 1968. *Political Community and the North Atlantic Area*. Garden City, NY: Doubleday.

Deutsch, Karl W., Sidney A. Burrell, Robert A. Kann, Maurice Lee, Jr., Martin Lichterman, Raymond E. Lindgren, Francis L. Loewenheim, and Richard W. Van Wagenen. 1957. *Political Community and the North Atlantic Area*. Princeton, NJ: Princeton University Press.

Diebold, William (ed.). 1988. *Bilateralism, Multilateralism and Canada in U.S. Trade Policy*. Washington, DC: Council on Foreign Relations.

Dominguez, Jorge de la Vega. 1992. "Mexico and the Commercial Integration of North America." Pp. 13–20 in *North America Without Borders: Integrating Canada, the United States and Mexico*, edited by Stephen J. Randall. Calgary: University of Calgary Press.

Easton, David. 1966. *A Systems Analysis of Political Life*. New York: Wiley.

Economist. 1995. *A Survey of Mexico*, October 28.

Etzioni, Amitai. 1965. *Political Unification: A Comparative Study of Leaders and Forces*. New York: Holt, Rinehart and Winston.

Etzioni, Amitai. 1968. *The Active Society: A Theory of Societal and Political Processes*. New York: Free Press.

Fry, Earl H. 1980. *The Financial Invasion of the USA: A Threat to American Society?* McGraw-Hill: New York.

Fuentes, Carlos. 1991. "Nacionalismo e integracion." *Este Pais* 1(1):10–16.

Gibbins, Roger and Neil Nevitte. 1985. "Canadian Political Ideology: A Comparative Analysis." *Canadian Journal of Political Science* 18(3):577–98.

Gilpin, Robert. 1974. "Integration and Disintegration on the North American Continent." *International Organization* 4:28(Autumn):851–74.

Gourevitch, Peter. 1986. *Politics in Hard Times: Comparative Responses to International Economic Crises*. Ithaca, NY: Cornell University Press.

Granato, James, Ronald Inglehart, and David Leblang. 1996. "The Effect of Culture on Economic Development: Theory, Hypotheses and Some Empirical Tests." *American Journal of Political Science* (August).

Greeley, Andrew. 1972. *Unsecular Man: The Persistence of Religion*. New York: Shocken.

Hart, Vivien. 1973. *Distrust and Democracy*. Cambridge: Cambridge University Press.

Harvard Business Review. 1991. The Boundaries of Business: World Leadership Survey. Cambridge, MA: Harvard Business School.

Haas, Ernst. 1958. *The Uniting of Europe*. Stanford, CA: Stanford University Press.

Haas, Ernst. 1971. "The Study of Regional Integration." Pp. 3–42 in *Regional Integration: Theory and Research*, edited by Leon N. Lindberg and Stuart A. Scheingold. Cambridge, MA: Harvard University Press.

Hartz, Louis. 1964. *The Founding of New Societies*. New York: Harcourt Brace.

Hill, David B. 1981. "Attitude Generalization and the Measurement of Trust." *Political Behavior* 133:257–70.

Horowitz, Gad. 1966. "Conservatism, Liberalism and Socialism in Canada: An Interpretation." *Canadian Journal of Economics and Political Science* 32:143–70.

Horowitz, Gad. 1978. "Notes on 'Conservatism, Liberalism and Socialism in Canada.'" *Canadian Journal of Political Science* 11:383–400.

Inglehart, Marita R., Daniel McIntosh, and Rose Pacini. 1990. "Postmaterialism and Religiosity: An Empirical Investigation." Paper presented at 13th annual meeting of the International Society of Political Psychology, Washington, D.C., July.

Inglehart, Ronald. 1971. "The Silent Revolution in Europe: Intergenerational Change in Post-Industrial Societies." *American Political Science Review* 65(4, December):991–1017.

Inglehart, Ronald. 1977. *The Silent Revolution: Changing Values and Political Styles among Western Publics*. Princeton, NJ: Princeton University Press.

Inglehart, Ronald. 1986. "Intergenerational Changes in Politics and Culture: The Shift from Materialist to Postmaterialist Values." Pp. 81–105 in *Research in Political Sociology*, vol. 2, edited by Richard Braungart. Greenwich, CT: JAI.

Inglehart, Ronald. 1988. "Cultural Change in Advanced Industrial Societies: Postmaterialist Values and Their Consequences." *International Review of Sociology* (3):77–100.

Inglehart, Ronald. 1990. *Culture Shift in Advanced Industrial Society*. Princeton, NJ: Princeton University Press.

Inglehart, Ronald. 1991. "Trust between Nations: Primordial Ties, Societal Learning and Economic Development." Pp.145–86 in *Euro-Barometer: The Dynamics of European Public Opinion*, edited by Ronald Inglehart and Karlheinz Reif. London: Macmillan.

Inglehart, Ronald. 1997. Modernization and Postmodernization: Cultural, Economic and Political Change in 43 Societies. Princeton, NJ: Princeton University Press.

Inglehart, Ronald, Sue Ellis, James Granato, and David Leblang. 1996. "Economic Development, Political Culture and Democracy: Bringing the People Back In." Paper presented at the annual meeting of the Midwest Political Science Association, Chicago, April.

Inglehart, Ronald and Renata Siemienska. 1988. "Political Values and Dissatisfaction in Poland and the West." Government and Opposition 23(2):440–57.

Inkeles, Alex and Larry Diamond. 1980. "Personal Qualities as a Reflection of National Development." In Comparative Studies in Quality of Life, edited by Frank Andrews and Alexander Szalai. London: Sage.

Jacob, Philip E. 1964. "The Influence of Values in Political Integration." Pp. 209–46 in The Integration of Political Communities, edited by Philip E. Jacob and James V. Toscano. Philadelphia: Lippincott.

Johnson, Harry G. 1965. "An Economic Theory of Protectionism, Tariff Bargaining and the Formation of Customs Unions." Journal of Political Economy 73:256–83.

Katzenstein, Peter J. (ed.). 1978. Between Power and Plenty: Foreign Economic Policies of Advanced Industrial States. Madison: University of Wisconsin Press.

Katzenstein, Peter J. 1988. Small States in World Markets: Industrial Policy in Europe. Ithaca, NY: Cornell University Press.

Keohane, Robert O. 1986. "Reciprocity in International Relations." International Organization 40, 1:1–28.

Keohane, Robert O. and Joseph S. Nye. 1977. Power and Interdependence: World Politics in Transition. Boston: Little, Brown.

Keohane, Robert O. and Van Doorn Ooms. 1975. "The Multinational Firm and International Regulation." Pp. 169–209 in World Politics and International Economics, edited by C. Fred Bergsten and Lawrence B. Krause. Washington, DC: Brookings Institution.

Kotejin, B. A. 1988. "Separating the Seekers from the Doubters." Paper presented at annual meeting of the Society for the Scientific Study of Religion, Chicago, October.

Krasner, Stephen. 1978. Defending the National Interest. Princeton, NJ: Princeton University Press.

Levitt, Kari. 1970. Silent Surrender: The Multinational Corporation in Canada. Toronto: Macmillan.

Lindberg, Leon N. and Scheingold, Stuart A. 1970. Europe's Would-be Polity: Patterns of Change in the European Community. Englewood Cliffs, NJ: Prentice-Hall.

Lipset, Seymour Martin. 1963. Political Man. Garden City, NY: Doubleday.

Lipset, Seymour Martin. 1990. Continental Divide: The Values and Institutions of the United States and Canada. Toronto and Washington: C.D. Howe Institutes and National Planning Association.

Luhmann, Niklas. 1979. Power and Trust. Chichester and New York: Wiley.

Maira, Luis. 1983. "Prospects and Options for United States Society." Pp. 83–108 in *U.S.–Mexico Relations: Economic and Social Aspects,* edited by Clark W. Reynolds and Carlos Tello. Stanford, CA: Stanford University Press.

Merritt, Richard L. and Donald J. Puchala. 1968. *Western European Perspectives on International Affairs.* New York: Praeger.

Milbrath, Lester and M. Goel. 1977. *Political Participation,* 2nd ed. Chicago: Rand McNally.

Miller, Arthur. 1974. "Political Issues and Trust in Government: 1964–1970." *American Political Science Review* 71:67–84.

Milner, Helen V. 1988. *Resisting Protectionism: Global Industries and the Politics of International Trade.* Princeton, NJ: Princeton University Press.

Milner, Helen V. and David B. Yoffie. 1989. "Between Free Trade and Protectionism: Strategic Trade Policy and a Theory of Corporate Trade Demands." *International Organization* 43(2)239–72.

Miyake, Ichiro. 1982. "Trust in Government and Political Cleavages: A Cross-National Comparison." *Doshisha Law Review* (171, 172).

Moran, Theodore H. 1974. *Multinational Corporations and the Politics of Dependence: Copper in Chile.* Princeton, NJ: Princeton University Press.

Morse, Robert. 1964. "The Heritage of Latin America." Pp. 123–77 in *The Founding of New Societies,* edited by Louis Hartz. New York: Harcourt Brace.

Nevitte, Neil. 1991. *New Politics, The Charter and Political Participation.* Ottawa: Report to the Royal Commission on Electoral Reform and Party Financing.

Nevitte, Neil. 1996. *The Decline of Deference.* Toronto: Broadview.

Nevitte, Neil and Roger Gibbins. 1990. *New Elites in Old States: Ideologies in the Anglo-American Democracies.* Toronto and New York: Oxford University Press.

Nie, Norman, Sidney Verba, and John Petrocik. 1979. *The Changing American Voter.* Cambridge, MA: Harvard University Press.

Nincic, Miroslav and Bruce Russett. 1979. "The Effect of Similarity and Interest on Attitudes Toward Foreign Countries." *Public Opinion Quarterly* 43(1, Spring):68–78.

Nye, Joseph S., Jr. 1968. "Comparative Regional Integration: Concept and Measurement." *International Organization* 22(4):855–80.

Nye, Joseph S. Jr. 1976. "Transnational Relations and Interstate Conflicts: An Empirical Analysis." Pp. 367–402 in *Canada and the United States: Transnational and Transgovernmental Relations,* edited by Annette Baker Fox, Alfred O. Hero, Jr., and Joseph S. Nye. New York: Columbia University Press.

Nye, Joseph S., Jr. 1988. "Neorealism and Neoliberalism." *World Politics* 40:238–39.

Ostry, Sylvia. 1992. "The NAFTA: Its International Economic Background." Pp. 21–30 in *North America Without Borders: Integrating Canada, the United States and Mexico,* edited by Stephen J. Randall. Calgary: University of Calgary Press.

Pomper, Gerald. 1975. *The Voter's Choice: Varieties of American Electoral Behavior.* New York: Dodd, Mead.

Pruitt, Dean G. 1965. "Definition of the Situation as a Determinant of International Action." Pp. 391–432 in *International Behavior: A Social-Psychological*

Analysis, edited by Herbert C. Kelman. New York: Holt, Rinehart and Winston.

Puchala, Donald J. 1968. "The Pattern of Contemporary Regional Integration." *International Studies Quarterly* 12:38–64.

Puchala, Donald J. 1971. "International Transactions and Regional Integration." Pp. 128–59 in *Regional Integration: Theory and Research*, edited by Leon N. Lindberg and Stuart A. Scheingold. Cambridge, MA: Harvard University Press.

Purcell, Susan Kaufman. 1975. *The Mexican Profit Sharing Decision: Politics in an Authoritarian Regime*. Berkeley and Los Angeles: University of California Press.

Putnam, Robert D. 1988. "Diplomacy and Domestic Politics: The Logic of Two-Level Games." *International Organization* 42(3):427–60.

Redekop, John H. 1978. "Continentalism: The Key to Canadian Politics." In *Approaches to Canadian Politics*, edited by John H. Redekop. Scarborough, Ontario: Prentice-Hall of Canada.

Reynolds, Clark, Leonard Wanesman, and Gerardo Bueno. 1991. *The Dynamics of North American Trade and Investment*. Stanford, CA: Stanford University Press.

Rhodes, Carolyn. 1989. "Reciprocity in Trade: The Utility of a Bargaining Strategy." *International Organization* 43(2):273–99.

Riesman, David. 1950. *The Lonely Crowd*. New Haven, CT: Yale University Press.

Rogowski, Ronald. 1989. *Commerce and Coalitions: How Trade Affects Domestic Political Alignments*. Princeton, NJ: Princeton University Press.

Rugman, Alan M. 1987. *Outward Bound: Canadian Direct Investment in the United States*. Toronto: Canadian-American Committee.

Sanders, Sol. 1989. *Mexico: Chaos on Our Doorstep*. Lanham, MD: Madison.

Scheingold, Stuart A. 1971. "Domestic and International Consequences of Regional Integration." Pp. 374–98 in *Regional Integration: Theory and Research*, edited by Leon N. Lindberg and Stuart A. Scheingold. Cambridge, MA: Harvard University Press.

Schmitter, Philippe C. 1971. "A Revised Theory of Regional Integration." Pp. 232–64 in *Regional Integration: Theory and Research*, edited by Leon N. Lindberg and Stuart A. Scheingold. Cambridge, MA: Harvard University Press.

Schott, Jeffrey J. and Murray G. Smith. 1988. "Services and Investment." Pp. 137–50 in *The Canada–United States Free Trade Agreement: The Global Impact*, edited by Jeffrey J. Schott and Murray G. Smith. Washington: Institute for International Economics and the Institute for Research and Public Policy.

Sigler, John H. and Dennis Goresky. 1976. "Public Opinion on United States–Canadian Relations." Pp. 44–75 in *Canada and the United States: Transnational and Transgovernmental Relations*, edited by Annette Baker Fox, Alfred O. Hero, Jr., and Joseph S. Nye. New York: Columbia University Press.

Smiley, Donald V. 1988. "A Note on Canadian-American Free Trade and Canadian Policy Autonomy." Pp. 442–53 in *The Trade-offs on Free Trade: The Canada–U.S. Free Trade Agreement*, edited by Marc Gold and David Leyton-Brown. Toronto: Arswell.

Smith, Murray G. 1988. "The Free Trade Agreement in Contest: A Canadian Perspective." Pp. 37–64 in *The Canada–U.S. Free Trade Agreement: The Global Impact*, edited by Jeffrey J. Schott and Murray G. Smith. Washington: Institute for International Economics and Institute for Research on Public Policy.

Stairs, Dennis and Gilbert R. Winham (eds.). 1985. *The Politics of Canada's Economic Relationship with the United States*, vol. 29, *Studies of the Royal Commission on the Economic Union and Prospects for Canada*. Toronto: University of Toronto Press.

Statistics Canada. 1991. *An International Business Comparison*. Ottawa: Canada Communication Group.

Stern, Robert (ed.). 1989. *Trade and Investment Relations Among the United States, Canada and Japan*. Chicago and London: University of Chicago Press.

Stewart, Michael. 1984. *The Age of Interdependence: Economic Policy in a Shrinking World*. Cambridge, MA: MIT Press.

Thompson, Michael, Richard Ellis, and Aaron Wildavsky. 1990. *Cultural Theory: Foundations of Socio-Cultural Variability*. Boulder, CO: Westview.

Tocqueville, Alexis de. [1830] 1955. *Democracy in America*. New York: Vintage.

Verba, Sidney, Norman Nie, and Jae-on Kim. 1978. *Participation and Political Equality*. Cambridge and New York: Cambridge University Press.

Vernon, Raymond. 1977. *Storm over the Multinationals: The Real Issues*. Cambridge, MA: Harvard University Press.

Wagner, R. Harrison. 1988. "Interdependence, Bargaining Power and Political Influence." *International Organization* 42(3):461–83.

Weber, Max. [1904–1905] 1958. *The Protestant Ethic and the Spirit of Capitalism*. New York: Scribner's.

Weintraub, Sidney. 1990. *A Marriage of Convenience: Relations Between Mexico and the United States*. New York: Oxford University Press.

Whyte, William H. 1956. *The Organization Man*. New York: Simon and Schuster.

Wildavsky, Aaron. 1987. "Choosing Preferences by Constructing Institutions." *American Political Science Review* 81:3–21.

Wylie, Laurence. 1957. *Village in the Vaucluse*. Cambridge, MA: Harvard University Press.

Yarborough, Beth V. and Robert Yarborough. 1986. "Reciprocity, Bilateralism and Economic 'Hostages': Self-Enforcing Agreements in International Trade." *International Organization* 30:7–21.

Index

Absolute norms, 60
Achievement, individual, 15–17
Activism, political
  age-related differences in, 95–101
  in Canada, 87, 100
  conventional, 83–87, 94–99, 168
  education and, 86
  elite-directing mode of, 85–87
  in late nineteenth and early twen-
    tieth centuries, 85
  materialist/postmaterialist values
    and, 96–97, 100
  in Mexico, 87, 100–101
  rise in, 83, 86, 94–101, 169
  unconventional, 99–101, 168
  in United States, 87, 100
  voting, 85–86, 95, 98, 168–169
Age-related differences
  activism, political, 95–101
  business management attitudes,
    109–115
  child-rearing attitudes, 68, 70–71
  civil permissiveness, 75–77
  confidence in governmental institu-
    tions, 88–94
  decrease in, 56–57
  health care scenario of political in-
    tegration, 148–149
  materialist/postmaterialist values,
    50–51, 55, 63, 66–67
  parent-child ties, 71–75
  parochial/cosmopolitan outlooks,
    160–162
  political integration support, 140–
    141
  religious norms, 77–81
  respect for authority, 70–71
  reversal of trends in, 72–75

sexual norms, 61–63, 66
social norms, 66
United States, 56
value changes, 49–52, 167
voting, 95
work authority attitudes, 115–119
Agricultural sector, 42–43
Authority
  child-rearing attitudes and, 68, 70–
    71
  political, 83–84, 91
  respect for, age-related differences
    in, 70–71
  shifts in patterns of, 36
  social value changes in, 68, 70–71
  traditional vs. rational-legal, 18–21
  work, 115–119
Autonomy, individual, 36, 68

Branch plant economies, 32
Business management attitudes, 107–
  115, 119

Canada
  activism in, political, 87, 100
  bilateral trade agreement (1989)
    with United States, 2
  business management attitudes in,
    107, 114–115, 119
  confidence in government institu-
    tions in, 84
  cultural variations in, 11, 147
  dilemmas of free trade in, 35–36
  economic ties of, with Mexico/
    U.S., 30–33, 40–45
  free trade opposition in, 149–151,
    155
  free trade support in, 40–45

materialist/postmaterialist values
in, 53–59
national pride in, 91
parent-child ties in, 72–75, 130
political value changes in, 15
Quebec separatism in, 1, 11
religious norms in, 12, 77
sexual norms in, 65–66, 77
value changes in, 15
work authority attitudes in, 118–
119
Canada-U.S. Free Trade Agreement,
5, 6, 166
Capitalism, 107–115
Child-rearing attitudes, 67–70
Civil permissiveness, attitudes about,
75–77
Communism, collapse of, 36, 106–107
Comparable surveys, 18, 132–133
Comparative advantages, 42
Cosmopolitan/parochial outlooks,
158–162
Cultural identity scenario of political
integration, 146–148, 162–163
Cultural value changes (*See* Social
value changes)
Cultural variations
in Canada, 11, 147
in Mexico, 147
in religious norms, 17
in scarcity vs. postmodern values,
18–21
studies on, 48
in traditional vs. rational-legal authority, 18–21
in United States, 11, 147

Democracy beliefs, 11, 14

Economic beliefs, 11
Economic integration
cross-national transactions and, 6–
7
debates about, 135–136
economic growth and, 9
economic interests and, 3
immigration issues and, 1

independence vs., 36
institution building and, 6
NAFTA and, 1
opposition to, 162
outlook for, 170–171
political disintegration and, 10–11
political factors and, 3
political integration and, 9–10,
151–164
trend toward, 1–2
trust and, 6–9
value changes and, 23–25
value compatibility and, 11–14,
154
values and, 3–5, 152
Economic ties, North American, 30–
33, 40–45, 155–158
Economic value changes
business management attitudes,
107–115, 119
Communism's collapse, 36, 106–
107
contradictions in, 105–106
poverty explanations, 123–127
predictions in, 25, 128–133
pride in work attitudes, 127–128
state-society balance, trend toward,
107
support of Left policies, decline in,
119–120
work authority attitudes, 115–119
work ethic attitudes, 120–122
Economies of scale, 42
Electoral participation, 85–86, 95, 98,
168–169
Elite, economic, 38
Environmental issues, 150–151, 171
Equality beliefs, 16–17
European Common Market, 10
European Community, 9–10, 15, 162–
164
European Union
cross-national interactions generated by NAFTA and, 8
Danish rejection of Maastricht treaty and, 5
members in, 2

European Union (*cont.*)
    political boundaries and, elimination of, 170–171
    success of, 27–28

Family unit, breakdown of, 61, 75
Free trade (*See also specific trade agreements*)
    consequences of, 34
    corporations and, 34
    debate about, 33, 34–35, 166
    dilemmas of, 34–38, 47
    economic case for, 2, 13
    economic status and, 44
    economic ties in North America and, 34
    elite and, economic, 38
    images evoked by, 163
    macroeconomic perspective of, 33
    materialist/postmaterialist values and, 136
    nationalism and, 158
    opposition to, 47, 149–151, 155, 166, 171
    support for, 38–45, 150
    total, 39
    trend toward, 2, 23–24, 27–28
    values and, 166–167
Free Trade Agreement (1989), 47

GATT, 27
General Agreement on Tariffs and Trade (GATT), 27
Global changes, 166
Global economy, regionalization of, 28–29
Globalization
    noneconomic factors affecting, 137–138
    realities of, 2, 164
    trend toward, 23–24, 165–166
Government institutions, confidence in, 83–84, 87–94
Greed, individual, 105

Health care scenario of political integration, 146, 148–150

Immigration issues, 1
Individualism, 105
Individual rights, 106
Integration, regional, 10 (*See also* Economic integration; Political integration)
Intergenerational population replacement
    materialist/postmaterialist values and, 52, 57–58
    sexual norms and, 65–66
    value changes due to, 65–66, 69–70, 132, 167, 169
Intergenerational shifts in values, 25–26, 49–52 (*See also* Age-related differences)
International relations, 4–5

Large markets, 42
Left, economic policies of, 111, 119–120

Maastricht treaty, 5
Macroeconomic perspective, 33
Marxism, 106–115
Materialist values
    activism and, political, 96–97, 100
    age-related differences in, 50–51, 55, 63, 66–67
    business management attitudes and, 110–111
    in Canada, 53–59
    child-rearing attitudes and, 68–69
    described, 49–50
    free trade and, 136
    intergenerational population replacement and, 52, 57–58
    measuring, 51–52
    in Mexico, 53–59
    political integration support and, 140–141, 143
    poverty explanations and, 123–126
    pride in work attitudes and, 127–128
    religious norms and, 78
    respect for authority and, 70–71
    shift from, to postmaterialist, 25–26, 52–59, 167

in United States, 53–59
work authority attitudes and, 115–117
work ethic attitudes and, 122
Mexico
activism in, political, 87, 100–101
business management attitudes in, 107–111, 113–114, 119
confidence in government institutions in, 84
confidence in nongovernment institutions in, 91
cultural variations in, 147
democratization in, 101–104
dilemmas of free trade in, 35–36
economic development in, 101–104
economic ties of, with Canada/U.S., 30–33, 40–45
financial problems in, 1, 53
free trade opposition in, 47, 149–151, 155
free trade support in, 40–45, 150
Marxism in, 107–111, 113–114
materialist/postmaterialist values in, 53–59
national pride in, 91
political integration support in, 150
political value changes in, 101–104
religious norms in, 12, 77
sexual norms in, 65–66, 77
value changes in, 14–15, 152–153
work authority attitudes in, 118–119
Mixed values, 50
Multinational corporations, rise of, 29–30

NAFTA
continental perspective of, 2–3
cross-national interactions generated by, 8
economic case for, 36, 42
economic integration and, 1
economic ties in North America and, 33
effects of, 30
establishment of, 2

expectations about, 14
historic importance of, 135
Mexican financial crisis of 1994 and, 1
opposition to, 13
passage of, 5
Quebec separatism and, 1
as response to realities of globalization, 2, 164
values and, 37
vision for, 2
National borders, 136–138, 148
Nationalism, 37, 85, 158
National pride, 91–94, 140
Nongovernmental institutions, confidence in, 90–92, 153–154
Norms (*See specific types*)
North American Free Trade Agreement (*See* NAFTA)

Oil industry, 29, 102
Open trade (*See* Free trade)

Parent-child ties, 71–75, 130
Parochial/cosmopolitan outlooks, 158–162
Period effects, 64, 66, 131–132, 169–170
Political authority, 83–84, 91
Political boundaries, 170–171
Political disintegration, 10–11
Political institutions, trend toward democratic, 23–24 (*See also* Government institutions)
Political integration
advantages of, 141–143
age-related differences in support of, 140–141
disadvantages of, 141–143
economic integration and, 9–10, 151–164
economic ties and, 155–158
environmental issues and, 150–151
in European Community, 15, 163–164
factors affecting attitudes about, 158

Political integration (*cont.*)
  materialist/postmaterialist values
    and, 140–141, 143
  nationalism and, 158
  opposition to, 149–150
  outlook for, 170–171
  parochial/cosmopolitan outlooks
    and, 158–162
  regional variations and, 139
  scenarios of, 144–150
  support for, 138–141, 148, 149–150
  value compatibility and, 154
  values and, 152, 154
Political participation (*See* Activism,
    political)
Political union (*See* Political
    integration)
Political value changes
  authority attitudes, 83–84, 91
  in Canada, 15
  Communism's collapse, 36, 106–
    107
  conventional activism, 83–87, 94–
    99
  government institutions, confi-
    dence in, 83–84, 87–94
  improved skill/knowledge of citi-
    zens, 36, 86
  in Mexico, 101–104
  national pride, 91–94
  nongovernmental institutions, con-
    fidence in, 90–92, 153–154
  predictions in, 25, 128–133
  unconventional activism, 99–101
  in United States, 15
  voting, 85–86, 95, 98, 168–169
Pollution problems, 150–151
Postmaterialist values
  activism and, political, 96–97, 100
  age-related differences in, 50–51,
    55, 63, 66–67
  business management attitudes
    and, 110–111
  in Canada, 53–59
  child-rearing attitudes and, 68–69
  described, 50
  environmental issues and, 151

free trade and, 136
intergenerational population re-
    placement and, 52, 57–58
measuring, 51–52
in Mexico, 53–59
political integration support and,
    140–141, 143
poverty explanations and, 123–126
pride in work attitudes and, 127–
    128
religious norms and, 78
respect for authority and, 70–71
shift to, from materialist, 25–26,
    52–59, 167
in United States, 53–59
work authority attitudes and, 115–
    117
work ethic attitudes and, 122
Postmodern values, 18–21
Poverty explanations, 123–127
Pride in work attitudes, 127–128
Private ownership (*See* Business
    management attitudes;
    Capitalism)
Protectionism
  benefits of, 34
  harm caused by, 34
  resurgence of, 28
  total, 39
  U.S. trend toward, 30
Public policies, 171

Rational-legal authority, 18–21
Reciprocity norms, 40
Regional variations, 139
Religious norms
  age-related differences in, 77–81
  in Canada, 12, 77
  cultural variations in, 17
  decline in, long-term, 77–78
  materialist/postmaterialist values
    and, 78
  in Mexico, 12, 77
  national pride and, 93–94
  social value changes in, 60–63, 77–
    81
  in United States, 12, 16–17, 77

Respect for authority, 70–71
Responsibility, abdication of, 105

Scarcity hypothesis, 48–49
Scarcity values, 18–21
Service sector, 43–44
Sexual norms, 60–66, 76–77
Short-term economic events, 64
Small markets, 43
Socialization hypothesis, 49
Social justice beliefs, 14
Social norms, 60–63, 66
Social value changes
  authority attitudes, 68, 70–71
  child-rearing attitudes, 67–70
  civil permissiveness, 75–77
  family unit, 61
  intergenerational population re-
    placement causing, 65–66, 69–70,
    132
  parent-child ties, 71–75, 130
  period effects causing, 66, 131–132
  predictions in, 25, 63–64, 66, 75,
    128–133
  religious norms, 60–63, 77–81
  sexual norms, 60–66, 76–77
  shift from materialist to post-
    materialist values, 25–26, 52–59,
    167
  social norms, 60–63, 66
Societal institutions. (*See* Nongovernment institutions)
Society's responsibility to individual,
  106
State ownership (*See* Business management attitudes; Marxism)
State-society balance, trend toward,
  119–120
Switzerland, 163

Trade agreements, 2 (*See also specific
  names*)
Trade patterns, 27–33
Trade policy, international, 166
Traditional authority, 18–21
Trust, 6–9, 154–155

United States
  activism in, political, 87, 100
  age-related differences in, 56
  bilateral trade agreement (1989)
    with Canada, 2
  business management attitudes in,
    107, 112, 114–115, 119
  confidence in government institu-
    tions in, 83–84
  cultural variations, 11, 147
  dilemmas of free trade in, 35–36
  economic ties of, with Canada/
    Mexico, 30–33, 40–45
  economic vulnerability of, 29–30
  free trade opposition in, 47
  free trade support in, 40–45
  GDP of, 29
  key characteristics emphasized in,
    15–17
  materialist/postmaterialist values
    in, 53–59
  NAFTA's effects on, 30
  national pride in, 91
  parent-child ties in, 72–75, 130
  political integration support in, 150
  political value changes in, 15
  post-World War II economy of, 28–
    29
  protectionism trend in, 30
  religious norms in, 12, 16–17, 77
  sexual norms in, 65–66, 77
  work authority attitudes in, 118–
    119
  world GNP and, 29

Value changes (*See also* Economic
  value changes; Political value
  changes; Social value changes)
  age-related differences in, 49–52,
    167
  in Canada, 15
  consequences of, 14–15
  economic integration and, 23–25
  intergenerational population re-
    placement causing, 65–66, 69–70,
    132, 167, 169
  in Mexico, 14–15, 152–153

Value changes (*cont.*)
  nationalistic feelings, decline in,
    37
  in North America, 52–59
  period effects causing, 66, 131–132,
    169–170
  responses to, 170
  sources of, 14
  of Western publics, 48–52
Value compatibility
  cultural, 167
  democracy beliefs, 11
  economic beliefs, 11
  economic integration and, 11–14,
    154
  economic realm of, 165, 168
  political integration and, 154
  political realm of, 165, 168–169
Values (*See also specific types*)
  convergence of, 152, 154, 165
  decline of traditional, 21–22
  differences in, 12–13, 15, 23
  economic forces and, 35
  economic growth and, 21–22
  economic integration and, 3–5,
    152

  elite, 6
  elite and, economic, 38
  free trade and, 166–167
  importance of, 4
  intergenerational shifts in, 25–26,
    49–52
  international relations and, 4–5
  main, 6, 138, 154
  NAFTA and, 37
  national, 138
  political integration and, 152, 154
  political significance of, 4
  postmodern, 18–21
  scarcity, 18–21
Value system
  in comparative perspectives, 18,
    173–183
  debate of common North Ameri-
    can, 17–21
  economic correlates of, 21–23
  political correlates of, 21–23
Voting, 85–86, 95, 98, 168–169

Welfare state, 61, 107
Work authority attitudes, 115–119
Work ethic attitudes, 120–122